COBOL DEBUGGING DIAGNOSTIC MANUAL

Eric Garrigue Vesely
The Analyst Workbench Consulting

 PRENTICE HALL

New York   London   Toronto   Sydney   Tokyo   Singapore

For information about our audio products, write us at:
Newbridge Book Clubs, 3000 Cindel Drive, Delran, NJ 08370

1 2 3 4 5 94 93 92 91 90

Typeset by Keyboard Wizards, Harbord, NSW.

Printed and bound in Australia by Impact Printing, Brunswick, Vic.

Cover design by Norman Baptista.

ISBN: 0 13 140187 4

**National Library of Australia
Cataloguing-in-Publication Data**

Vesely, Eric Garrigue.
   COBOL debugging diagnostic manual.

   Includes index.
   ISBN 0 13 140187 4.

   1. COBOL (Computer program language) - Handbooks,
   manuals, etc. 2. Debugging in computer science. I. Title.

005.133

**Library of Congress
Cataloguing-in-Publication Data**

Vesely, Eric Garrigue.
   COBOL debugging diagnostic manual / by Eric Garrigue Vesely.
   p.   cm.
Includes index.
ISBN 0-13-140187-4

   1. COBOL (Computer program language) 2. Debugging in
   computer science. I. Title.

QA76.73.C25V48   1990   90-43978
005.13'3--dc20   CIP

Prentice Hall, Inc., *Englewood Cliffs, New Jersey*
Prentice Hall Canada, Inc., *Toronto*
Prentice Hall Hispanoamericana, SA, *Mexico*
Prentice Hall of India Private Ltd, *New Delhi*
Prentice Hall International, Inc., *London*
Prentice Hall of Japan, Inc., *Tokyo*
Prentice Hall of Southeast Asia Pty Ltd, *Singapore*
Editora Prentice Hall do Brasil Ltda, *Rio de Janeiro*

 PRENTICE HALL

A division of Simon & Schuster

Contents

Acknowledgments

COBOL is an industry language and is not the property of any company or group of companies, or of any organization or group of organizations.

No warranty, expressed or implied, is made by any contributor or by the CODASYL Programming Language Committee as to the accuracy and functioning of the programming system and language. Moreover, no responsibility is assumed by any contributor, or by the committee, in correction therewith.

The authors and copyright holders of the copyrighted material used herein:

FLOW-MATIC (trademark of the Sperry-Rand Corporation, Programming for the Univac I and II, Data Automation Systems copyrighted 1958, 1959, Sperry-Rand Corporation; IBM Commercial Translator Form No. #28-8013, copyrighted 1958 by IBM; FACT, DSI 27A5260-2760, copyrighted by Minneapolis-Honeywell

have specifically authorized the use of this material in whole or in part, in the COBOL specification. Such authorization extends to the reproduction and use of COBOL specifications in programming manuals or similar publications.

My thanks to Andrew Binnie for commissioning my first book published through Prentice Hall Australia.

My thanks to Fiona Marcar who had to cope with an author traveling around Australasia when she was overseeing production and to Daphne Rawling for copy editing.

My special thanks to my wife Amy both for her superb support and for her clerical assistance in preparing this manual for publication.

A very special thankyou to you, the reader, for reading this manual. I hope that it assists you in maintaining your programs more easily and in reducing your maintenance workload. Maybe its use will allow you to do some new application programming!

Introduction

WHY YOU SHOULD READ THIS BOOK

This is almost certainly the first book that you will ever read on specific techniques for DEBUGGING **production** COBOL PROGRAMs. I have researched COBOL books for this and my other COBOL books (*COBOL: A Guide to Structured, Portable, Maintainable, and Efficient Program Design*, Prentice Hall, 1989; *Software Maintenance Life Cycle*, Cutter Information, 1989) and have found no serious discussion on DEBUGGING. Some hardware vendors do provide DEBUGGING aids or manuals such as IBM's *VS COBOL II Application Programming Debugging* (SC26-4049) but their discussion is normally limited to describing the syntax of their debugging tools (COBTEST) or to DEBUGGING **new** PROGRAMs.

Debugging new PROGRAMs is important but most **working** programmers do not have the luxury of writing new PROGRAMs. At present software maintenance takes 95 percent of the time spent so that only one out of 20 employed programmers writes new code. The rest are maintaining!

The accepted definition of maintenance is **any** change made to a production PROGRAM. A PROGRAM becomes production when it is first used for real work. It usually requires maintenance on the first day. The three types of PROGRAM maintenance are corrective, perfective, and enhancive.

Corrective maintenance

Corrective maintenance is fixing bugs. Bugs can be catastrophic, major, or minor. A catastrophic bug abends (abnormal end) the PROGRAM causing immediate panic. A major bug does not abend but creates significant information ERRORs or fails to produce important information. A minor bug does not abend nor cause information problems. It is something like a report header spelled incorrectly.

Perfective maintenance

Perfective maintenance is repairing, rejuvenating, and re engineering.

Repair activities

1. Inserting defensive traps to catch unusual but predictable processing anomalies. For instance, many COBOL PROGRAMs do not test for all I-O FILE STATUS thereby ensuring problems when the unusual FILE STATUS occurs. The defensive trap is to COPY an installation standard FILE STATUS routine after every I-O that checks for all FILE STATUS with appropriate processing.
2. Inserting eye-catchers to simplify memory dump reading. Appendix A contains ANSI COBOL 74 PROGRAMs that automatically insert defensive traps and the ANSI DEBUG Module into existing COBOL PROGRAMs. These are CARE (Computer Assisted Re Engineering) PROGRAMs because they assist programmers in doing maintenance. Some CARE PROGRAMs require a COBOL 85 compiler because they need explicit scope terminators.
3. Simplifying the PROGRAM by expanding IF statement abbreviated conditions, decomposing complex IF statements, eliminating ALTER statements, etc.

Rejuvenation

Rejuvenation includes data-name and alias (many names for the same data item) purification (also known as rationalization).

Re engineering

Re engineering includes code splitting and restructuring. Code splitting is breaking up large PROGRAMs into smaller manageable PROGRAMs. Restructuring is making unstructured code into structured code.

The complete subject of perfective maintenance is the subject of the forthcoming companion manual *COBOL REPAIR, REJUVENATION, and RE ENGINEERING MANUAL.*

Enhancive maintenance

Enhancive maintenance is the inclusion of new features, functions, or capabilities into existing PROGRAMs. Enhancive is defined as maintenance rather than new development because it works with existing PROGRAMs. New development starts from scratch and creates new PROGRAMs.

Defensive traps

This manual concentrates on catastrophic DEBUGGING although the techniques can also be adapted for major and minor bugs. It also discusses defensive traps and their use.

Appendix A takes the drudgery out of coding defensive traps by giving you pure ANSI COBOL 74 PROGRAMs that perform automatic insertion. Testing the newly trapped PROGRAMs is not necessary since only a previously untested for anomaly can cause an abend. However, Chapter V defines a testing and DEBUGGING environment for the skeptical.

This manual is also the first book to discuss fully the ANSI DEBUG module and IBM's VS COBOL II DEBUGGING module (COBTEST). Knowledge of COBTEST will be mandatory if your organization installs IBM's Software Analysis Test Tool (SATT). SATT is part of AD/Cycle and offers a comprehensive strategy for validating and verifying COBOL and PL/I PROGRAMs. SATT uses COBTEST for testing COBOL PROGRAMs.

Many programmers don't even know that ANSI DEBUG exists and almost none have used it. This is surprising since ANSI DEBUG and COBTEST permit you to do interactive PROGRAM flow and data tracing which greatly simplifies DEBUGGING. They are also free since they are included with the compiler! They cannot do everything that some of the commercial DEBUGGING products can but also they do not cost $50,000+. The discussed techniques can be adapted to the use of commercial DEBUGGING products improving their productivity and capabilities.

Finally, the use of these techniques will start reducing the swollen 95 percent maintenance workload. Maybe — just maybe — you might get to write some new code!

Appendix B contains a combined ANSI [ISO] 1974 and 1985 glossary of COBOL approved definitions. **Appendix C** contains an annotated list of COBOL 85 reserved WORDS. The annotation provides information as to which WORDS are new and which WORDS are obsolete. Obsolete means that the word will be eliminated in the next standard release of COBOL and therefore unsupported. There are also some obsolete word usages that are noted. ANSI and ISO have identified some verb usages that might incorrectly execute in COBOL 85 which are noted. Finally, both the COMMUNICATION module and the REPORT writer are now optional and do not need to be supported. Words associated with either are noted. **Appendix D** contains a CARE vendor address list.

Eric Garrigue Vesely

Syntax rules

This publication uses the following syntax rules:

1. MANUAL

WORDS

All UPPER-CASE WORDS are COBOL reserved WORDS. Key WORDS are <u>underlined</u> in statement formats. No distinction is made between key WORDS and optional WORDS in example statements. Optional WORDS are used to make reading easier where applicable.

UPPER-CASE WORDS in the text are WORDS used in their COBOL sense. Plurals where the plural itself is not a reserved word [the singular of WORDS is not reserved] use UPPER-CASE for the reserved word and a lower-case s. For example:

    CALLs   CANCELs   DISPLAYs   READs etc.

Other reserved word conjugations are lower-case such as copied (past tense of the reserved word COPY).

lowercase-words in example statements are used to represent entries that must be supplied by the programmer other than PARAGRAPH-NAMES which are capitalized for readability. The first letter of a lowercase-word in the text that starts a sentence is not capitalized as in the start of this paragraph.

Punctuation

Only required syntax punctuation is used in the examples. Commas (,) and semicolons (;) are not used. The sentence terminator of period/space (.) is used only where specifically required or in lieu of an explicit scope terminator.

Any required period/space is omitted in reserved WORDS used in the text to improve readability. The one exception is the alterable GO TO sentence (GO TO.) where the period/space is used to distinguish between the GO TO formats.

Slash (/) is used to separate alternate WORDS in statement formats.

2. APPENDIX A

UPPER-CASE WORDS are used in the CARE programs to conform to the requirement of some COBOL compilers for only UPPER-CASE WORDS.

1 Preparing an ANSI COBOL PROGRAM for DEBUGGING

Reading memory dumps and source code to debug COBOL PROGRAMs is painful, time consuming, and a dreadful waste of human resources. This manual minimizes memory dump reading to finding specific information and eliminates SOURCE code reading. The SOURCE code is only used to provide parameters for tracing which is the major technique used.

    This manual is based upon the ANSI COBOL DEBUG module since it is the world standard. IBM COBOL users can substitute TESTCOB commands if using OS COBOL and COBTEST commands if using VS COBOL II. COBTEST syntax is provided where appropriate. COBTEST is used because OS COBOL can be compiled with the TEST option by the COBOL II compiler. Also, most COBTEST commands are similar to TESTCOB commands.

    The ANSI COBOL DEBUG module requires the following PROGRAM entries:

ENVIRONMENT DIVISION

WITH DEBUGGING MODE clause in the SOURCE-COMPUTER paragraph:

```
      SOURCE-COMPUTER. [computer-name]
 [*]            WITH DEBUGGING MODE.
```

Note: The column positions used in this manual unless otherwise shown are:

column	7	D (DEBUGGING LINE)
		* (comment LINE)
		- (literal continuation LINE)
column	8	A area entries
column	12	Clauses and phrases
		PROCEDURE DIVISION verbs
column	28	verb objects
column	44	PIC clause
column	52	USAGE and VALUE clauses.

1

If the optional SOURCE-COMPUTER paragraph is missing then insert it. Appendix A contains an ANSI COBOL PROGRAM to insert, automatically, this modification and other defensive traps into fully COPY expanded ANSI subset COBOL SOURCE PROGRAMs.

WITH DEBUGGING MODE clause is a "compile time switch." If present then all DEBUG entries are compiled otherwise they are treated as comments.

WITH DEBUGGING MODE clause is placed on the next SOURCE line so that the * (comment) can be used as a "SOURCE time switch." If DEBUGGING is required then the * is deleted; when DEBUGGING is completed * is replaced in column 7.

The * SOURCE time switch permits placing the basic DEBUG capabilities into all COBOL PROGRAMs without affecting the generated object code or its performance efficiency. The SOURCE code is minimally affected since DEBUG entries are treated as comments if the WITH DEBUGGING MODE clause is a comment.

PROCEDURE DIVISION

The USE FOR DEBUGGING statement must be the first SECTION of the DECLARA-TIVES procedures:

```
PROCEDURE DIVISION.

DECLARATIVES.

DEBUG SECTION.

    USE FOR DEBUGGING ON ALL PROCEDURES.

DEBUG-PROGRAM-FLOW.

    DISPLAY     DEBUG-LINE
                DEBUG-NAME
                DEBUG-CONTENTS.

END DECLARATIVES.
```

If the PROGRAM does not contain DECLARATIVES then it and the END DE-CLARATIVES must also be inserted (Appendix A has PROGRAM).

Use For DEBUGGING STATEMENT syntax

```
USE FOR DEBUGGING ON   [cd-name-1/
                       [ALL REFERENCES OF] identifier-1/
                       file-name-1/

                       procedure-name-1/
```

ALL PROCEDURES]

Note: ANSI required reserved WORDS are underlined CAPITALIZED; ANSI optional reserved WORDS are CAPITALIZED but not underlined; lower-case WORDS are programmer entry; options are separated by a slash (/).

The data references are not available in Level 1 of the DEBUG module and are not supported by COBOL II [PROCEDURE traces are supported].

cd-name is a COMMUNICATION description entry name used in the COMMUNI-CATION SECTION. The COMMUNICATION SECTION is rarely used and is not discussed.

identifier-1 is any data-name; file-name-1 is any FD name. ALL REFERENCES invokes the DEBUG DECLARATIVES SECTION whenever there is any explicit reference to identifier-1 or to file-name-1.

procedure-name-1 is any paragraph or SECTION name; ALL PROCEDURES are all paragraph and/or SECTION names within a PROGRAM.

DEBUG-ITEM

Invoking the DEBUG DECLARATIVES SECTION creates a special DEBUG-ITEM register with the following implicit definition:

```
01 DEBUG-ITEM.
    02  DEBUG-LINE       PIC  X(6).
    02  FILLER           PIC  X       VALUE SPACE.
    02  DEBUG-NAME       PIC  X(30).
    02  FILLER           PIC  X       VALUE SPACE.
    02  DEBUG-SUB-1      PIC  S999    SIGN IS LEADING SEPARATE.
    02  FILLER           PIC  X       VALUE SPACE.
    02  DEBUG-SUB-2      PIC  S999    SIGN IS LEADING SEPARATE.
    02  FILLER           PIC  X       VALUE SPACE.
    02  DEBUG-SUB-3      PIC  S999    SIGN IS LEADING SEPARATE.
    02  FILLER           PIC  X       VALUE SPACE.
    02  DEBUG-CONTENTS PIC  X(n).
```

DEBUG-LINE identifies the specific SOURCE statement that caused the invocation of the USE FOR DEBUGGING statement. DEBUG-LINE is implementor defined. In IBM COBOL this is either the SOURCE sequence-number or the compiler-generated number depending on the chosen compiler options.

DEBUG-NAME contains the first 30 characters of the name that caused the invocation of the USE FOR DEBUGGING statement. IN or OF separate qualifiers if space is available.

DEBUG-SUB entries contain the subscript or INDEX VALUES for any subscripted or INDEXED data items.

DEBUG-CONTENTS depends on what caused the invocation. The entries are:

```
DEBUG-CONTENTS        MEANING

START PROGRAM         first execution of first
                      nondeclarative statement
TO procedure-name     ALTER statement procedure-name
                      reference
SPACES                GO TO or any reference of file-name
                      other than READ
PERFORM LOOP          control mechanism of a PERFORM
                      statement
USE PROCEDURE         USE PROCEDURE
FALL THROUGH          implicit transfer of control
entire RECORD         READ of file-name
identifier contents   any identifier reference
SORT INPUT            SORT INPUT
SORT/MERGE OUTPUT     SORT or MERGE OUTPUT
```

DEBUG-PROGRAM-FLOW DISPLAY

The DEBUG-PROGRAM-FLOW DISPLAY statement interactively shows the module invocation within the PROGRAM. PROGRAM flow is always used since many bugs are caused by inappropriate or unexpected flow [obscure path]. However, the DISPLAY is usually rapid and therefore difficult to analyze. The last few invoked module identifications leading up to the abend are shown on the terminal and that may be all the information you need.

Two ANSI solutions are: an additional DISPLAY statement, and/or an ACCEPT statement.

1.   Additional DISPLAY

COBOL usually sends the DISPLAY MESSAGE to the online TERMINAL that initiated the job if the UPON phrase is missing. It is possible to use multiple DISPLAY statements to direct the MESSAGE to multiple OUTPUT devices. The preferred device is a local printer. UPON requires an entry in the SPECIAL-NAMES paragraph of the ENVIRONMENT DIVISION:

```
SPECIAL-NAMES implementor-name IS mnemonic-name.
```

implementor-name is whatever the installation standard is; mnemonic-name is local-printer or whatever printer is being used.

The DISPLAY UPON is inserted after the first DISPLAY:

```
PROCEDURE DIVISION.

DECLARATIVES.
```

```
DEBUG SECTION.
    USE FOR DEBUGGING ON ALL PROCEDURES.

DEBUG-PROGRAM-FLOW.

    DISPLAY        DEBUG-LINE
                   DEBUG-NAME
                   DEBUG-CONTENTS.

    DISPLAY UPON   mnemonic-name'
                   DEBUG-LINE
                   DEBUG-NAME
                   DEBUG-CONTENTS.

    END DECLARATIVES.
```

The first DISPLAY OUTPUTs to the TERMINAL, giving you flow of modules being invoked; the DISPLAY UPON OUTPUTs the complete trace flow to a printer if in-depth analysis is required.

2. ACCEPT

The Format 1 ACCEPT statement allows low level INPUT from the console. However, most compilers allow the FROM phrase to specify any suitable INPUT device and the INPUT device desired is the programmer's TERMINAL.

The ACCEPT statement suspends execution of the PROGRAM until there is INPUT and therefore provides interactive DEBUGGING for most ANSI compilers (COBTEST and TESTCOB are not required just to provide interactive DEBUGGING).

The ACCEPT statement is placed in a separate DEBUG paragraph:

```
PROCEDURE DIVISION.

DECLARATIVES.

DEBUG SECTION.

    USE FOR DEBUGGING ON ALL PROCEDURES.

DEBUG-PROGRAM-FLOW.

    DISPLAY        DEBUG-LINE
                   DEBUG-NAME
                   DEBUG-CONTENTS.

    DISPLAY UPON   mnemonic-name
                   DEBUG-LINE
```

```
                    DEBUG-NAME
                    DEBUG-CONTENTS.
        DEBUG-BREAKPOINT.

        *    ACCEPT    breakpoint    FROM        mnemonic-name.

        END DECLARATIVES.
```

* is used to disable the ACCEPT even if the COBOL DEBUG module is active. * is deleted when interactive breakpoints are required.

breakpoint is a 77 level with a PIC of 80(X) [COBOL requirement] and should have a D in column 7.

mnemonic-name must also be defined in SPECIAL-NAMES.

Many compilers display "AWAITING INPUT" or some other similar message. Most compilers allow <return> with no other input to resume program execution.

The debug flow with the ACCEPT active is:

```
invoke module-1
    invoke USE FOR DEBUGGING
    DISPLAY
    DISPLAY UPON
    ACCEPT
        <wait for INPUT>
<execute instructions for module-1>
invoke module-2
    invoke USE FOR DEBUGGING
    DISPLAY
    DISPLAY UPON
    ACCEPT
        <wait for INPUT>
<execute instructions for module-2>
...
```

Normally you don't want to break after every invocation. You want to break only when you believe the bug is beginning. That means the ACCEPT is usually in some form of IF statement to suspend execution when a specific incorrect condition is detected. The proper use of ACCEPT is described within the appropriate DEBUGGING SECTIONs.

Note: Before you can code these entries, you must run a sample test PROGRAM (see Appendix A) to determine what your compiler does with ACCEPT and DISPLAY.

Defensive termination dump

It is possible for a previously abended PROGRAM to run to EOJ in the test environment when tracing. This is also wrong but there is no evidence unless a dump can be forced. Place a DIVIDE ZERO BY ZERO defensive trap before each EXIT PROGRAM, STOP RUN, and GOBACK to force a dump. Place a D in column 7 to deactivate except when in debug mode. Appendix A contains PROGRAM.

2 Preparing a COBOL PROGRAM for DEBUGGING

IBM OS COBOL

OS COBOL is based on the ANSI COBOL-74 standard and therefore supports the ANSI COBOL DEBUG module. If TESTCOB is not available then use the procedures described for ANSI COBOL DEBUG module.

TESTCOB requires that the PROGRAM be compiled with the TEST option. TESTCOB commands are similar to COBTEST and are not described separately.

WITH DEBUGGING MODE clause should remain since it allows the activation of specific active defense programming traps which are described later. Deactivating ANSI DEBUG requires inserting * in column 7 of the SOURCE LINE containing WITH DEBUGGING MODE (SOURCE-COMPUTER paragraph). The DEBUG parameter can also remain in the JCL since it has no effect unless the other switches are set.

IBM VS COBOL II

VS COBOL II is based on the ANSI COBOL-85 standard. However, it only supports Level 1 of the COBOL DEBUG module which means it does not support ANSI data tracing. COBTEST is supplied with COBOL II and therefore is always available. COBTEST requires that the PROGRAM be compiled with the TEST option.

WITH DEBUGGING MODE clause should remain since it allows the activation of specific active defense programming traps which are described later.

Invoking the COBOL DEBUG module requires that the SOURCE and compile time switches be set within the PROGRAM and that an object time switch be set. The object time switch is implementor defined. This requires the DEBUG parameter on the JCL EXEC statement (DEBUG overrides COBOL II compiler TEST option).

OTHER COBOL

You must determine from your COBOL compiler manual how to use the ANSI DEBUG module. What you need to know is how to set the object time switch. The object time switch is external to the COBOL PROGRAM and is usually a COBOL compiler option or part of the invoking language such as IBM's JCL (Job Control Language).

3 General COBOL considerations

WORKING-STORAGE SECTION

Insert the following 77 statements to help locate WORKING-STORAGE in a memory dump:

```
77 FILLER    PIC X(28) VALUE  "***working-storage
                                          begin***".
```

after the WORKING-STORAGE SECTION header, and

```
77 FILLER    PIC X(28) VALUE  "***working-storage
                                          end*****."
```

before the PROCEDURE DIVISION header

Note: 01 levels can be used instead of 77 levels. 77s are used for visual identification. Some compilers only allow 77 levels at the beginning and would reject the 77 "end" FILLER. In that case use 01.

SECTION

If the DEBUG DECLARATIVES SECTION is inserted into a PROGRAM without SEC-TIONs then compile ERRORs might occur since ANSI standards require that all paragraphs be part of a SECTION if any SECTION is used. However, most compilers ignore this requirement if the only SECTION is a DECLARATIVES SECTION. In any case, the compile ERRORs do not affect the object code and can be safely ignored.

DEAD CODE IDENTIFICATION

A significant time waster in DEBUGGING is analyzing code that cannot be invoked. This code is called dead code. Current estimates show that about one-third of all code is dead!

One reason that desk DEBUGGING is odious is that so much of it is wasted on code that can't do anything. The DEBUG module cannot isolate dead code so other maintenance software is required. The recommended software is LT Inspector or CA Optimizer or VIA INSIGHT (see Appendix D for addresses). COBOL II OPTIMIZE also eliminates dead code.

Identified dead code is usually "commented out" by placing an * in column 7. The dead code is left in the PROGRAM either as documentation or for the possibility that it may be needed sometime in the future. Two problems exist:

1.　It is easy for the human eye to miss the * and waste time analyzing dead code
2.　It is easy for the human eye to miss an active coding line in a sea of
　　　**

Dead code should be deleted. However, some installation standards require dead code to remain. In this case, insert the following entries before any dead code:

```
***DEAD*CODE***DEAD*CODE***DEAD*CODE***DEAD*CODE***DEAD*CODE*****
        DIVIDE ZERO BY ZERO GIVING infinity
```

The DIVIDE BY ZERO defensive trap is inserted to force an abend in the improbable case that the dead code is invoked. Many compilers prohibit the use of the figurative constant ZERO in the DIVIDE trap. This requires a ZERO literal in WORKING-STORAGE (see Appendix A):

```
77 zero-lit                    PIC S99V  VALUE ZERO.
```

Also insert:

```
77 infinity                    PIC S99V  VALUE ZERO.
```

infinity is inserted to prevent a compiler syntax ERROR.

IBM users can CALL a memory dump to abend the PROGRAM and print a memory dump. For instance, CALL 'ILBOABNO' USING data-name where data-name is a user abend code.

PASSIVE DEFENSIVE PROGRAMMING

Defensive programming is a technique where you imagine anything and everything that could go wrong with a PROGRAM and then put in a trap to catch that anomaly. Passive defensive programming does not affect PROGRAM performance because the trap is only invoked if the anomaly occurs.

Runaway code

Runaway code has five distinct definitions:

1.   Invoking an unaltered GO TO sentence which causes an abend.
2.   Fall through the last executable statement which causes an abend (COBOL 74; COBOL 85 inserts an implicit EXIT PROGRAM if the last executable statement is not a transfer of control).
3.   Unexpected fall through caused by the sequential operation of the compiler.
4.   Unexpected fall through caused by an invalid identifier in a GO TO DEPENDING ON.
5.   Unexpected branch caused by the incorrect invocation of an active transfer of control.

1 and 2 [COBOL 74] take care of themselves since they force an abend. Place a DIVIDE BY ZERO trap as the last physical statement in any COBOL 85 PROGRAM to force the abend (see Appendix A). 3, 4 and 5 do not necessarily cause abends but always cause problems. Passive defensive programming traps 3 and 4 and active defensive programming traps 5.

Unexpected fall through by sequential operation

Some fall throughs are planned. For instance, many mainline routines look like:

```
PROCEDURE DIVISION.

INITIALIZATION-PARAGRAPH.

    . . .
    <fall through>

MAINLINE-PARAGRAPH.

    . . .
    <fall through>

TERMINATION-PARAGRAPH.
```

Note: . . . represents statements within the paragraph.

Insert a dummy GO TO or a CONTINUE [COBOL 85] to document that fall through was intended.

Most fall throughs are not planned and cause runaway. They are usually caused by invoking a performable module by a GO TO or by another fall through. A PERFORM activates a transfer of control trigger to return control to the next executable statement following the PERFORM when the PERFORM span is completed. A GO TO or a fall through does **not** activate the transfer of control. For example:

```
PARAGRAPH-A.

    . . .
```

```
PARAGRAPH-A-EXIT.    EXIT.
   <transfer of control>


PARAGRAPH-B.
```

If PARAGRAPH-A is invoked by PERFORM PARAGRAPH-A THRU PARA-GRAPH-A-EXIT then the transfer of control is activated and returns control when invoked. If PARAGRAPH-A is invoked by a GO TO or by a fall through from the preceding paragraph then the transfer of control is **not** activated and is null with execution continuing with the first statement in PARAGRAPH-B. There is no telling what mischief the runaway causes but the worst scenario is the PROGRAM somehow running to a normal EOJ.

The simple defensive programming trap is the DIVIDE BY ZERO trap which is after the EXIT PARAGRAPH (see Appendix A):

```
PARAGRAPH-A.

   . . .

PARAGRAPH-A-EXIT.    EXIT.

   <transfer of control>

PABORT-Pnnn.
*runaway code abend; nnn is paragraph numeric prefix or an
*odometer

   DIVIDE ZERO BY ZERO GIVING infinity.

PARAGRAPH-B.
```

The scenario does not change if the invocation is PERFORM PARAGRAPH-A and PARAGRAPH-A-EXIT is eliminated. The compiler still places a transfer of control between PARAGRAPH-A and PARAGRAPH-B which the PERFORM activates. DIVIDE BY ZERO is again the defensive trap.

The other flow problem is the reverse of fall through. It is an unexpected branch when an active transfer of control is accidentally invoked. This problem is discussed later in "Active defensive programming."

GO TO DEPENDING ON incorrect identifier

A GO TO DEPENDING ON identifier must be an unsigned integer whose value < the number of entered procedures-names. Control is transferred to the next sequential statement if the identifier is incorrect. This next sequential statement should be a defensive trap to process incorrect identifiers. Failure to code the defensive trap initiates runaway code. The simple solution is to insert a DIVIDE BY ZERO defensive trap after the last identifier (see Appendix A):

```
      GO TO           procedure-name-1
                      procedure-name-2
                      . . .
      DEPENDING ON  identifier-1
                      identifier-2
                      . . .
      DIVIDE ZERO BY ZERO GIVING INFINITY
     *defensive trap to prevent runaway
```

Arithmetic SIZE ERROR

All arithmetic statements (ADD, COMPUTE, DIVIDE, MULTIPLY, SUBTRACT) should contain an ON SIZE ERROR phrase to trap high order digit truncation. Some compilers provide a compile warning that truncation may occur and some provide a run time ERROR message if truncation occurs but many do not abend the PROGRAM. These messages may be overlooked and it is too late anyway. Truncation should be trapped immediately and the PROGRAM abended to prevent data corruption. Therefore, insert an

```
      ON SIZE ERROR
          DIVIDE ZERO BY ZERO GIVING infinity
      END-ADD/COMPUTE/DIVIDE/MULTIPLY/SUBTRACT
```

in any arithmetic statement that does not contain it (see Appendix A).

END-x is a COBOL 85 explicit scope terminator which specifically delimits the x statement. END-x is optional but desirable in any sentence where it is syntactically available. END-x is required if the arithmetic statement is part of a conditional sentence since the compiler does not know where the arithmetic statement ends. For instance:

```
      IF            condition-true
         ADD        identifier-1
         TO         identifier-2
       ON SIZE ERROR DIVIDE ZERO BY ZERO GIVING infinity
      *the following statements should be executed as part of
      *the if statement and are not part of the on size error
      *phrase
                    statement-1
                    statement-2
                    . . .
      ELSE
```

statement-1, statement-2, and . . . should be executed if there is NOT ON SIZE ERROR but the compiler only has the ELSE as a delimiter. The compiler includes statement-1, statement-2, and . . . as part of ADD statement and they are never executed which is incorrect. Adding END-ADD solves the problem:

```
IF              condition-true
    ADD         identifier-1
    TO          identifier-2
    ON SIZE ERROR DIVIDE ZERO BY ZERO GIVING infinity
    END-ADD
*the following statements are executed as part of the if
*statement and are not part of the on size error phrase
                statement-1
                statement-2
            . . .
    ELSE
```

The compiler recognizes the END-ADD as the delimiter for the ADD statement and therefore **does** execute statement-1, statement-2, and . . . if there is NOT ON SIZE ERROR.

If your compiler does not support END explicit scope terminators you must substitute a PERFORM to a module that contains both the arithmetic statement and ON SIZE ERROR:

```
IF              condition-true
    PERFORM  ADD-STATEMENT
    THRU     ADD-STATEMENT-X
*the following statements should be executed as part of
*the if statement and are not part of the on size error
*phrase
                statement-1
                statement-2
            . . .
    ELSE
```

```
###
    ADD-STATEMENT

    ADD     identifier-1
    TO      identifier-2
    ON SIZE ERROR DIVIDE ZERO BY ZERO GIVING infinity.

    ADD-STATEMENT-X. EXIT.
```

Note: ### represents a break in physical SOURCE statement sequence.

The period/space(.) terminator delimits the ADD statement. The period/space cannot be used within the IF statement since it would prematurely terminate the IF. The use of a separate module solves the problem since the compiler returns control to statement-1 if NOT ON SIZE ERROR.

If the PERFORM causes an unacceptable performance degradation then use the following coding:

```
      IF                condition-true
   D       PERFORM    ADD-STATEMENT
   D       THRU       ADD-STATEMENT-X
   *truncation can occur;activate debugging mode to test
   *for size error
              ADD        identifier-1
              TO         identifier-2
                         statement-1
                         statement-2
                         . . .
      ELSE


### 

   DADD-STATEMENT

   D     ADD          identifier-1
   D     TO           identifier-2
   D     ON SIZE ERROR  DIVIDE ZERO BY ZERO GIVING infinity.

   D     SUBTRACT     identifier-2
   D     FROM         identifier-1.
   *restores the values so that the mainline add works
   *correctly

   DADD-STATEMENT. EXIT.
```

STRING and UNSTRING OVERFLOW

STRING and UNSTRING statements can also have truncation problems which are trapped by an ON OVERFLOW phrase. Insert (see Appendix A):

```
   ON OVERFLOW DIVIDE ZERO BY ZERO GIVING infinity
   END-STRING/UNSTRING
```

INPUT-OUTPUT statement trappable ERRORs

There are three ways to trap INPUT-OUTPUT ERROR and EXCEPTION conditions:

1.   AT END or INVALID KEY phrases
2.   USE AFTER STANDARD EXCEPTION/ERROR statement
3.   FILE STATUS clause

AT END or INVALID KEY trap only those specific conditions. The USE statement traps AT END and INVALID KEY and other EXCEPTIONs or ERRORs but **not all possible conditions**.

The operating system places a VALUE in the FILE STATUS data item which defines every possible EXCEPTION or ERROR condition. There should be an installation standard case IF that transfers control to the appropriate processing routine for each EXCEPTION or ERROR condition. That case IF should be in the COPY library and copied into each PROGRAM after each I/O statement.

The current ANSI FILE STATUS is a two byte field with the LEFT CHARACTER being STATUS KEY 1 [SK1] which defines the basic result and the RIGHT CHARACTER being STATUS KEY 2 [SK2] which provides more information if available. The VALUES and meanings are:

SK1	SK2	85	MEANING
0			successful completion[all]
	0		no further information available[all]
	2		duplicate KEY[ind]
	4	*	RECORD LENGTH is incorrect[r]
	5	*	OPTIONAL FILE is not present[o]
	7	*	magnetic TAPE clause specified for non-reel UNIT[o]
1			AT END condition with <u>un</u>successful completion[r]
	0		end-of-file (EOF)[r]
	0	*	OPTIONAL INPUT FILE is not present[r]
	4	*	RELATIVE RECORD NUMBER > RELATIVE KEY[r]
2			INVALID KEY condition with <u>un</u>successful completion[rel/ind]
	1		SEQUENCE ERROR[t(ind)]
	2		DUPLICATE KEY[w/t]
	3		RECORD does not exist[r(ind)]
	3	*	OPTIONAL INPUT FILE is not present[s/r]
	4		boundary violation[w]
	4	*	RELATIVE RECORD NUMBER > RELATIVE KEY[w]
3			permanent ERROR condition with <u>un</u>successful completion[all]
	0		no further information available[all]
	4		boundary violation[w]
	5	*	non-optional FILE not present[o]
	7	*	OPEN MODE incorrect for FILE[o]
	8	*	FILE is locked[o]
	9	*	conflict between FILE attributes[o]
4		*	logic ERROR condition with <u>un</u>successful completion[all]
	1	*	FILE already OPEN[o]
	2	*	FILE not OPEN[o]
	3	*	required READ not successfully executed[t/d]
	4	*	boundary violation[w/t]
	6	*	EOF or previous unsuccessful READ[t] or START[r]
	7	*	FILE not OPEN in INPUT or I-O MODE[r/s/t]

| 8 | * | FILE not OPEN in OUTPUT or EXTEND MODE$^{t/w}$ |
| 9 | * | FILE not OPEN in I-O MODE$^{t/d}$ |

| 9 | | implementor defined |
| | any | implementor defined |

Notes: A* in 85 means that this FILE STATUS is only available in COBOL 85; the superscripts in the MEANING column mean:

all	=	ALL INPUT-OUTPUT statements
rel	=	RELATIVE INPUT-OUTPUT statements
ind	=	INDEXED INPUT-OUTPUT statements
c	=	CLOSE
d	=	DELETE
o	=	OPEN
r	=	READ
s	=	START
t	=	REWRITE
w	=	WRITE

Values not shown are not used.

COBOL II has expanded FILE STATUS to provide more information to an ERROR recovery routine.

CALL OVERFLOW or EXCEPTION

A called PROGRAM may not be invocable because it cannot fit into available memory (OVERFLOW) or for many other reasons including OVERFLOW [EXCEPTION {COBOL 85}]. Insert OVERFLOW or EXCEPTION with DIVIDE BY ZERO where applicable (see Appendix A).

SEARCH

The SEARCH statement has two potential problems:

1. the VALUE in the controlling INDEX or subscript
2. NOT satisfying the SEARCH condition

The compiler controls the INDEX setting in a SEARCH ALL so only the serial SEARCH can have an INDEX or subscript problem. This problem is discussed in "Indices and subscripts".

SEARCH has an optional AT END phrase which is used to trap the occurrence when none of the SEARCH conditions is satisfied. Insert AT END with DIVIDE BY ZERO (see Appendix A).

Note: It is possible that fall through was the intended result if none of the conditions was satisfied. If DEBUGGING proves this true then insert an AT END CONTINUE to document the fall through.

EVALUATE WHEN OTHER

The EVALUATE potential problem is not satisfying the WHEN conditions. EVALUATE has an optional WHEN OTHER phrase which is used to trap the occurrence of none of the WHEN conditions being satisfied. Insert WHEN OTHER with DIVIDE BY ZERO (see Appendix A).

Note: It is possible that fall through was the intended result if none of the conditions was satisfied. If DEBUGGING proves this true then insert a WHEN OTHER CONTINUE to document the fall through.

Indices and subscripts

Most memory boundary violations and PROGRAM internal data corruption are caused by the incorrect setting of indices and subscripts that access TABLEs. SET and PERFORM VARYING are the major statements that place VALUES into indices and subscripts. The best way to check out of range VALUES is a compiler option such as SSRANGE in COBOL II.

SSRANGE inserts code to test each use of an INDEX or subscript to determine if its VALUE is within the TABLE range. It abends any out of range VALUE. If SSRANGE is not available then insert the following statement before any serial SEARCH or PERFORM VARYING:

```
D   DISPLAY      index-subscript-1, ...
D   UPON         mnemonic-name
```

The D in column 7 identifies this as a DEBUGGING statement which the compiler treats as a comment unless both the SOURCE time and compile time switches are SET.

index-subscript-1 is the index-name or subscript-name of the first INDEX or subscript being used. Insert as many index-subscript-names as there are TABLE dimensions. The DISPLAY statement prints each VALUE of the INDEX or subscript, permitting a manual comparison to determine when the INDEX or subscript went out of bounds.

Reference modification

A new feature in COBOL 85 is reference modification. The syntax is:

```
data-name (leftmost-character-position: [length])
```

The colon (:) informs the compiler that this is a reference modification and not a subscript. For example:

```
02  data-name           PIC S9(9)V    VALUE  123456789.

MOVE data-name(3: 5) TO receiving-item would MOVE the digits
                                                  34567.
MOVE data-name(2:)   TO receiving-item would MOVE the digits
                                                  23456789.
MOVE data-name(6: 4) TO receiving-item would MOVE the digits
                                                  6789.
```

leftmost-character-position must not be < 1 nor > the data-name LENGTH. leftmost-character-position plus LENGTH must not exceed the data-name LENGTH. Most compilers abend if reference modification is outside the data-name region. If your compiler does not abend then you need to perform a PROGRAM data trace. See "Reference modification" in Chapter 6.

ACTIVE DEFENSIVE PROGRAMMING

Active defensive programming is inserting trap code into a PROGRAM that is executed during the normal PROGRAM operation. This trap code **does** affect the PROGRAM's performance and may be unacceptable in production.

For instance, SSRANGE is active defensive programming. If it impairs efficiency then it is only activated by a SSRANGE compiler option when the PROGRAM is in debug mode. The following active trap code can be deactivated by using D in column 7 and the SOURCE and compile time switches.

Incorrect invocation of active transfer of control

Compiler inserted transfer of control code is only activated by a PERFORM statement. It is only deactivated by a fall through from the last statement of the preceding module or by a GO TO an activated EXIT paragraph. The compiler does **not** know if the resultant branch is correct and simply does the transfer.

The technique is to insert a perform-return-counter. ADD 1 for each invoked PERFORM and SUBTRACT 1 for each return. The counter must be ZERO when the final return of control returns to the PERFORM statement that initiated the PERFORM path.

A PERFORM path is the set of PERFORM statements starting with the first PERFORM invoked to the last PERFORM invoked. For instance:

```
PERFORM PARAGRAPH-1
    PERFORM PARAGRAPH-2
        PERFORM PARAGRAPH-3
            PERFORM PARAGRAPH-4
```

```
PERFORM PARAGRAPH-5
    PERFORM  PARAGRAPH-6
        PERFORM PARAGRAPH-7
            PERFORM PARAGRAPH-8
```

PERFORM PARAGRAPH-1 is the beginning of the path and PERFORM PARA-GRAPH-8 is the end of the path. PERFORM paragraphs 1 through 8 comprise this specific PERFORM set. A set may be only one PERFORM (PARAGRAPH-1 does not invoke any PERFORMs returning control immediately) or *n* PERFORMs. *n* should be a small number although I have seen a set of 169 PERFORMs!

The perform-return-counter in the displayed set would start at 1 and would be increased to 2 by PERFORM PARAGRAPH-2, and to 3 by PERFORM PARAGRAPH-3, and so forth. Each return would subtract 1 and must be at ZERO after the final return to PERFORM PARAGRAPH-1. If it is NOT ZERO then runaway code has occurred.

1.   Starting PERFORM path

The trick is knowing when a PERFORM path has started and when it has ended. Starting is simple. If the perform-return-counter is ZERO before a PERFORM has been executed, then a new PERFORM path has started.

The trap coding to increment the perform-return-counter before each PERFORM is:

```
ADD             1
TO              perform-return-counter
ON SIZE ERROR DIVIDE ZERO BY ZERO GIVING infinity
END-ADD

PERFORM         ...
```

A simple 88 IF determines if a PERFORM path has been started:

```
IF              start-of-perform-path
*start-of-perform-path is an 88 of perform-return-code with a
*value of zero
    THEN        ...
```

The THEN must contain statements that activate a test of valid return of control after the next PERFORM.

2.   Ending PERFORM path

The trap coding to decrement the perform-return-counter after each PERFORM is:

```
PERFORM         ...

SUBTRACT        1
FROM            perform-return-counter
ON SIZE ERROR DIVIDE ZERO BY ZERO GIVING infinity
```

```
     END-SUBTRACT
```
The trap coding to test for a valid-return-of-control is:

```
    IF               valid-return-of-control
*valid-return-of-control is an 88 of perform-return-code
*with a value of zero
      NEXT SENTENCE
*return was correct & there is no runaway code; program
*proceeds
      ELSE DIVIDE ZERO BY ZERO GIVING infinity
*return was incorrect & there is runaway code; abend
*program
```

The preceding coding would only work for single level PERFORM paths since the VALUE of perform-return-counter > ZERO on any intermediate PERFORM. The coding must only be executed when control is returned to the starting PERFORM.

This requires a run-time switch to be coded in the SOURCE PROGRAM. The only run-time switches available to an executing COBOL PROGRAM are ALTER and USE.

(a) USE FOR DEBUGGING ON

USE FOR DEBUGGING ON perform-return-counter would be a run-time switch invoking the ANSI DEBUG module whenever there was an explicit modification to perform-return-counter. The ANSI DEBUG module can contain any COBOL statement and it is possible to code a routine that would only invoke the valid-return-of-control IF when return had been made to the starting PERFORM. However, data tracing is only supported in the ANSI [ISO] High Level and therefore does not have to be supported in a valid COBOL compiler. Many compilers, including IBM's COBOL II, do not support data tracing and therefore its use would not be portable across multiple compilers.

Note 1:   An interesting exercise which enhances your knowledge of the ANSI DEBUG module is to program the data trace.

Note 2:   ANSI [ISO] have defined what modules constitute COBOL and levels within those modules. COBOL 74 has twelve modules with each containing two or three levels. The levels are null, low, and high. A valid subset COBOL 74 compiler only has to support the null (which means no support) if it exists or the low level if null does not exist. High is always optional.

COBOL 85 has eleven modules with three levels of minimum, intermediate, and high. Data tracing is in high and is optional.

For more information, see Vesely, E., *COBOL: A Guide to Structured, Portable, Maintainable, and Efficient Program Design*, Prentice Hall, Englewood Cliffs, NJ., 1989.

It would also be possible to USE FOR DEBUGGING ON perform-procedure as a RUN time switch. perform-procedure is the module name invoked by the PERFORM:

```
    PERFORM           perform-procedure
*module name
```

The portability problem still exists even though PROCEDURE tracing is in the Low [74] or Minimum [85] Level. COBOL 74 has a null level which means no support is legitimate. COBOL 85 has made the DEBUG Module optional which also means that no support is legitimate (COBOL II does support PROCEDURE tracing).

(b) ALTER

ALTER is an obsolete verb in COBOL 85 which means that it becomes unsupported in the next standard COBOL. ALTER is in the Low or Minimum Level in the Nucleus Module. The Nucleus Module has no Null Level [74] and is required [85]. Therefore, ALTER is supported by all current legitimate COBOL compilers and is portable until the next standard COBOL.

The ALTER is placed in the coding preceding the PERFORM:

```
    IF NOT          start-of-perform-path
*start-of-perform-path is an 88 of perform-return-code
*with a value of zero
        ALTER      runaway-goto
        TO PROCEED TO    no-runaway-test
    ELSE   NEXT SENTENCE
    END-IF

    ADD            1
    TO             perform-return-counter
    ON SIZE ERROR DIVIDE ZERO BY ZERO GIVING infinity
    END-ADD

    PERFORM          ...
```

The IF after the PERFORM is replaced by another PERFORM:

```
    PERFORM        RUNAWAY-TEST
    THRU           RUNAWAY-TEST-EXIT
    END-PERFORM
###
```

The coding of the RUNAWAY-TEST module is:

```
RUNAWAY-TEST.

    SUBTRACT       1
    FROM           perform-return-counter
```

```
          ON SIZE ERROR DIVIDE ZERO BY ZERO GIVING infinity
          END-ADD

          GO TO             NO-RUNAWAY-GOTO.

      RUNAWAY-GOTO.

          GO TO             NO-RUNAWAY-TEST.
      *alterable goto; altered to do test-runaway if return to
      *perform path start

       TEST-RUNAWAY.
      *only executed if runaway-goto altered to test-runaway

          IF                valid-return-of-control
      *valid-return-of-control is an 88 of perform-return-code
      *with a value of zero
              GO TO     RUNAWAY-EXIT
      *return was correct & there is no runaway code; continue
          ELSE DIVIDE ZERO BY ZERO GIVING infinity.
      *return was incorrect & there is runaway code; abend

       NO-RUNAWAY-TEST.

          ALTER           runaway-goto
          TO PROCEED TO test-runaway

          GOT TO            runaway-exit.

      RUNAWAY-TEST-EXIT.   EXIT.
```

Note: I humbly apologize to all the programmers who have worked for me, all the students I have taught, and all the readers of my COBOL manuals for using an ALTER. I am and continue to be a vociferous denouncer of ALTER. Unfortunately, COBOL does not provide any other portable run-time switch to use in this specific and unusual programming situation.

The following entries must be made in WORKING-STORAGE to complete the defensive trap coding:

```
77  perform-return-counter      PIC S9999V    USAGE  COMP
                                               VALUE  ZERO.
    88  start-perform-path                     VALUE  ZERO.
```

Appendix A contains a PROGRAM for inserting the above code.

3. In-line PERFORM

COBOL 85 PERFORM syntax allows the procedure-name to be omitted (in-line PER-
FORM):

```
PERFORM              <no procedure name>
```

There is no need for a defensive trap since a transfer is never made.

Involuntary multiplication by -1

An easy way to create data corruption is to MOVE a signed NUMERIC operand to an
unsigned NUMERIC operand. Presto, a NEGATIVE NUMBER becomes POSITIVE. The
defensive trap is to insert:

```
IF             move-from-data-name NEGATIVE
    DIVIDE ZERO BY ZERO GIVING infinity
ELSE   NEXT SENTENCE
END-IF
```

before any such MOVE (see Appendix A). Again D can be used in column 7 to disable
except during a DEBUGGING session.

   Another subtle way to cause an involuntary multiplication by -1 is to SUBTRACT an
item > the FROM item where the FROM item PIC clause does not contain a SIGN [S]
CHARACTER. The defensive trap is to insert:

```
IF             subtract-item
>              from-item
    DIVIDE ZERO BY ZERO GIVING infinity
ELSE   NEXT SENTENCE
END-IF
```

before any such SUBTRACT.

4 Catastrophic DEBUGGING

Catastrophic DEBUGGING begins with an abend and usually some form of memory dump. It is recommended that SYMDMP or FDUMP be always specified as an IBM compiler option to provide the appropriate dump.

The recommended FDUMP provides:

1. program-name in RUN UNIT that was executing at the abend
2. statement that was executing at the abend
3. completion code [a cryptic number explaining why the abend occurred]
4. register contents
5. data-name with its data TYPE and VALUE; ERROR messages such as "INVALID DATA FOR THIS DATA TYPE, UNPRINTABLE DATA FOR THIS DATA TYPE, SUBSCRIPT OR 0D0 OBJECT WAS INVALID, . . ." are also printed when applicable.

FDUMP is used as the example memory dump. Other types of memory dumps provide similar information although it may require more human deciphering.

DERIVING INITIAL INFORMATION FROM A FDUMP

The FDUMP header provides the following data:

1. PROGRAM   PROGRAM name containing abend statement
2. Completion code   INDEX to ERROR message explaining cause
3. PSW at ABEND   PROGRAM STATUS word
4. The ABEND line number   PROGRAM LINE NUMBER where abend occurred
5. The ABEND verb number which verb on abend LINE NUMBER that caused abend

Note: An offset from the beginning of the PROGRAM is given instead of the ABEND line and verb NUMBER if the PROGRAM was compiled with the IBM OPTIMIZE option.

The preceding is all you need to start DEBUGGING. You have the PROGRAM statement that caused the abend plus an INDEX to a set of ERROR messages that describes the abend cause. The first three steps are:

1. Find the abend statement in the SOURCE listing.
2. Use the statement type and/or the completion code to isolate the generic bug type.
3. Find the generic bug type in the Contents and perform the specified DEBUGGING steps.

5 Establishing a DEBUGGING environment

The best way to test an abended PROGRAM is to simulate the conditions that caused it to fail as closely as possible. This means that the PROGRAM should be processing the same RECORDS as when it abended. ANSI DEBUG has no way to SET VALUES; COBTEST does have a SET command that allows VALUE setting. However, setting many VALUES is cumbersome, time consuming, and error prone. The best way is to reread the RECORDS. The steps are:

1. Determine the offset of the KEY from the SOURCE listing (requires IBM DMAP or MAP compiler option).
2. Find the KEY VALUE in the FDUMP using the offset.
3. Extract the specific identified RECORDS and place them into test FILEs with the same FD names.

Note 1: It is assumed that your site has both a PRODUCTION and TEST environment. If this is not the case then you need to affix -TEST to all FD names using ISPF or some other editor.

Note 2: If any FILES are on magnetic tape then request Operations to load the appropriate TAPE; create a one RECORD TAPE containing only the specific identified RECORD.

Note 3: If any FILES are DBMS (Data Base Management System) "records" then see your DBA (Data Base Administrator) or equivalent to provide you with a test database containing the requisite RECORDS. They will normally be created from a DBMS logging facility.

4. Activate DEBUGGING MODE if required:

    (a) remove * from WITH DEBUGGING MODE;
    (b) active object time switch [insert DEBUG on JCL EXEC card] and/or,
    (c) set TEST compiler option.

5. Run your PROGRAM.

Note: If your PROGRAM does not abend or abends at a different place then your problem probably is that internal switches are incorrectly set. A likely cause is a switch that is not initialized on each PROGRAM entry leaving its operation to chance — sometimes it works and sometimes it doesn't. This is a difficult DEBUGGING problem. (See Chapter 7).

6 Generic bug statement type

The FDUMP abend LINE NUMBER and verb NUMBER pinpoint the actual statement and verb that caused the abend. The completion code coupled with its documentation tells you what type of abend. Use this information to find the DEBUGGING steps.

Each subdivision contains the procedures for analyzing the abend. ANSI DEBUG module coding and the COBOL II COBTEST coding are provided where required. The generic procedures and code are as follows.

ANSI DEBUG

1. Establish the required DEBUGGING environment as described in Chapter 5.
2. The generic ANSI DEBUG module is:

```
PROCEDURE DIVISION.

DECLARATIVES.

DEBUG SECTION.

    USE FOR DEBUGGING ON    target-data-name
                            ALL PROCEDURES.

DEBUG-PROGRAM-FLOW.

    DISPLAY        DEBUG-LINE
                   DEBUG-NAME
                   DEBUG-CONTENTS.

    DISPLAY UPON mnemonic-name-1
                   DEBUG-LINE
                   DEBUG-NAME
                   DEBUG-CONTENTS.

DEBUG-BREAKPOINT.
```

```
    IF              DEBUG-NAME       =   target-data-name
    AND             DEBUG-CONTENTS   =   abend-test
        ACCEPT      breakpoint
        FROM        mnemonic-name-2
        IF          dump
            DIVIDE ZERO BY ZERO GIVING infinity
        END-IF
    END-IF

END DECLARATIVES.
```

target-data-name is the data-name plus any qualification [IN/OF] of the item that contains the FDUMP offending VALUE.

ALL PROCEDURES is retained because many production abends are caused by obscure path execution. The trace provides the actual module invocation path.

DEBUG-LINE, DEBUG-NAME, and DEBUG-CONTENTS are entries in the DEBUG-ITEM special register.

mnemonic-name-1 is the system name of the local printer.

abend-test is the test for the condition or VALUE that caused the abend, for instance, IF ALPHABETIC for an abend caused by alpha in a NUMERIC item or IF ZERO if the abend was a DIVIDE BY ZERO.

breakpoint is a 77 level defined with a PIC 80(X) clause; dump is an 88 level with a VALUE OF "D".

mnemonic-name-2 is the system name of the DEBUGGING TERMINAL.

3.   Start the DEBUGGING session.

COBOL II COBTEST COMMANDS

The generic procedures for DEBUGGING using COBTEST are the same as for ANSI DEBUG. The difference is the syntax.

```
COBTEST program-name
```

Initiates interactive COBTEST session on the abended PROGRAM.

```
TRACE ENTRY NAME PRINT
```

TRACE   Displays PROGRAM execution flow
ENTRY   Displays program-name on each entry
NAME   Displays module-name and line-number on each entry
PRINT   prints same information to printer specified by PRINTDD

```
FLOW ON
```

FLOW ON places the actual verb (not module) sequence execution in a FLOW TABLE which can later be displayed or printed.

```
LIST target-data-name BOTH PRINT
```

LIST BOTH displays the VALUE in target-data-name in both EBCDIC and hex. * is displayed if CHARACTER is nondisplayable. PRINT prints the VALUE to PRINTDD.

```
WHEN brek (target-data-name = fdump-value) (FLOW PRINT)
```

WHEN suspends PROGRAM execution whenever target-data-name contains the FDUMP offending VALUE (fdump-value). FLOW displays and PRINT prints the flow TABLE. brek is a four CHARACTER string supplied by you to identify multiple WHEN commands.

```
GO
```

GO invokes the COBTEST program-name. Execution continues until suspended by the WHEN command. You have two options after suspension:

```
DUMP
```

DUMP ends the DEBUGGING session and provides a SNAP dump. If you want to continue with the DEBUGGING session:

```
GO
```

which resumes PROGRAM execution with the statement following the suspended statement.

TERMINATION INFORMATION

You will have the following information when the PROGRAM suspends execution:

1.   the line-number of the offending statement, and
2.   a module trace of how the PROGRAM got to the module that contains the offending statement.

ARITHMETIC

The arithmetic verbs are ADD, COMPUTE, DIVIDE, INSPECT [TALLYING], MULTIPLY, SUBTRACT. The abend types are alpha in a numeric item, SEPARATE SIGN is not a + or a −, DIVIDE by ZERO, truncation [OVERFLOW], and overlapping items. (Exponent overflow and underflow are not covered since exponential arithmetic rarely occurs in a business PROGRAM.)

Alpha in a NUMERIC item

An abend occurs whenever an arithmetic operation is attempted with alpha. Alpha can be moved to a NUMERIC item **without** causing an abend. The typical cause is a MOVE to a REDEFINE item whose PIC clause is ALPHABETIC. DEBUGGING steps:

1. ANSI DEBUG

```
PROCEDURE DIVISION.

DECLARATIVES.

DEBUG SECTION.

    USE FOR DEBUGGING ON    alpha-data-name
                            ALL PROCEDURES.

DEBUG-PROGRAM-FLOW.

    DISPLAY         DEBUG-LINE
                    DEBUG-NAME
                    DEBUG-CONTENTS.

    DISPLAY UPON  mnemonic-name-1
                    DEBUG-LINE
                    DEBUG-NAME
                    DEBUG-CONTENTS.

DEBUG-BREAKPOINT.

    IF          DEBUG-NAME      =   alpha-data-name
    AND         DEBUG-CONTENTS      IS ALPHABETIC
        ACCEPT    breakpoint
        FROM      mnemonic-name-2
        IF        dump
            DIVIDE ZERO BY ZERO GIVING infinity
        END-IF
    END-IF

END DECLARATIVES.
```

The verbs that can place alpha into the NUMERIC item are ACCEPT, INSPECT REPLACING, MOVE [CORRESPONDING], READ, STRING, and UNSTRING.

(a) ACCEPT

A format 1 ACCEPT should not normally be in a production PROGRAM. Cause is typing error. Rerun PROGRAM ensuring that a proper NUMERIC VALUE is entered.

(b) INSPECT REPLACING

The INSPECT REPLACING syntax is incorrect. Correct and rerun.

(c) MOVE

The MOVE verb is the likely culprit although normally the alpha is moved to a redefined data-name. However, if the ACCEPT breakpoint trapped the alpha then it was a direct MOVE. The question is why does the sending item contain alpha.

    Determine the sending item PIC type:

1.   If PIC is NUMERIC then it has the same problem further "upstream" (problem occurred before the abend; the abend statement was only a trigger). Redo DEBUGGING procedure using the MOVE sending item as the alpha-data-name.
2.   If PIC is ALPHABETIC then an obscure path has been taken. An obscure path is code that is only used when the PROGRAM detects an anomaly or an unusual condition. It has to be an obscure path because if it were a normal condition the **production** PROGRAM would be continually abending with this problem. Often obscure paths are unchanged when other modifications are made to the PROGRAM such as changing an item to NUMERIC. This results in an abend when the obscure path is invoked.

    Examine the module trace to determine how the PROGRAM got to the module containing the offending statement. This is usually sufficient to isolate the anomaly. Determine what the obscure path should be doing and make the corrections. Rerun to verify.

(d) MOVE CORRESPONDING

The CORRESPONDING [CORR] phrase allows multiple items to be moved with a single MOVE statement. You must determine which item in the sending items is the "twin" of the receiving item containing alpha. Use the CORRESPONDING sending twin data-name as the alpha-data-name. Use the MOVE DEBUGGING procedures.

(e) READ

The other probable culprit is the READ verb. This means that the FILE being used by the PROGRAM already contains the offending alpha and that the actual problem was caused by an upstream PROGRAM.

1.   Refer to a Job Step Diagram (a graphic portrayal of how PROGRAMs are invoked and what resources they require) to determine the last previous PROGRAM that wrote the offending FILE.
2.   Determine the data-name containing the offending alpha from the 01 data description in that previous PROGRAM.
3.   Redo the DEBUGGING procedure using the previous PROGRAM data-name as the

alpha-data-name. It is possible that you may have to go back many PROGRAMs to find the actual culprit.

(f) STRING

The STRING verb has moved alpha into the data-name. Use the MOVE DEBUGGING procedures.

(g) UNSTRING

The UNSTRING verb has moved alpha into the data-name. Use the MOVE DEBUGGING procedures.

(h) REDEFINES

The REDEFINES clause where the PIC clause is ALPHABETIC is often the cause of alpha being in its parent NUMERIC item. If the original ACCEPT breakpoint did not trap the alpha then this must be the cause.

1. Ascertain the first REDEFINES data-name in the DATA DIVISION. Redo DEBUGGING steps using this data-name as the alpha-data-name.
2. If alpha is still not trapped then repeat with remaining REDEFINES data-names until the offender is found.

Note: It is possible to debug all REDEFINES data-names simultaneously by listing each data-name in the USE statement and testing them in the IF statement with OR logical operators. However, I believe it is simpler and faster to test them singularly.

2. VS COBOL II COBTEST

The generic procedures for DEBUGGING using COBTEST are the same as for using ANSI DEBUG. The difference is the syntax.

```
COBTEST program-name

TRACE ENTRY NAME PRINT

FLOW ON

LIST alpha-data-name BOTH PRINT

ONABEND (FLOW)
```

COBTEST does not have an ALPHABETIC test and therefore you must allow it to execute the abending statement. However, COBTEST does permit you to gain control after an abend [ONABEND] which ANSI DEBUG does not.

```
GO
```

Starts PROGRAM.

Review the TRACE and FLOW displays or printouts to determine where the alpha came from. Substitute the appropriate COBTEST commands for the ANSI DEBUG procedures previously described.

3. Quick fix

Infrequently the initial DEBUGGING procedures do not reveal the problem thereby requiring more analysis. Operational considerations may necessitate that the PROGRAM be run with the offending transactions being written to an ERROR REPORT for later correction. The quick fix is:

1. Insert a REDEFINES with an equivalent PIC X clause for the data-name having the alpha problem.

    ```
    ?? numeric-data-name           PIC S9(6)V.
    ?? alpha-redefinition  REDEFINES
       numeric-data-name           PIC X(6).
    ```

2. Insert IF ALPHABETIC defensive trap before each arithmetic statement that uses numeric-data-name.

    ```
    IF              alpha-redefinition  ALPHABETIC
        [WRITE installation standard ERROR REPORT]
    END-IF
    ```

SEPARATE SIGN is not a + or -

An abend occurs whenever an operation is attempted on data defined with a SEPARATE SIGN and that SIGN does not contain + or -. SEPARATE SIGN is not directly accessible and must be tested with its parent item.

1. ANSI DEBUG

```
PROCEDURE DIVISION.

DECLARATIVES.

DEBUG SECTION.

    USE FOR DEBUGGING ON    separate-sign-data-name
                            ALL PROCEDURES.

DEBUG-PROGRAM-FLOW.
```

```
DISPLAY         DEBUG-LINE
                DEBUG-NAME
                DEBUG-CONTENTS.

DISPLAY UPON  mnemonic-name-1
                DEBUG-LINE
                DEBUG-NAME
                DEBUG-CONTENTS.

  DEBUG-BREAKPOINT.

    IF          DEBUG-NAME    =  separate-sign-data-name
    AND         DEBUG-CONTENTS   IS ALPHABETIC
*alphabetic is used since + and - are treated as numeric
       ACCEPT    breakpoint
       FROM      mnemonic-name-2
       IF        dump
          DIVIDE ZERO BY ZERO GIVING infinity
       END-IF
    END-IF

  END DECLARATIVES.
```

The verbs that can place incorrect data into the SEPARATE SIGN are ACCEPT, INSPECT REPLACING, MOVE [CORRESPONDING], READ, STRING, and UNSTRING.

(a) ACCEPT
A format 1 ACCEPT should not normally be in a production PROGRAM. Cause is typing error. Rerun PROGRAM ensuring that a proper NUMERIC VALUE is entered.

(b) INSPECT REPLACING
The INSPECT REPLACING syntax is incorrect. Correct and rerun.

(c) MOVE
The MOVE verb is the likely culprit although normally the incorrect data is moved to a redefined data-name. However, if the ACCEPT breakpoint trapped the incorrect data then it was a direct MOVE. The question is why does the sending item contain incorrect data.
   Determine the sending item PIC type.

1. If PIC is NUMERIC then it has the same problem further "upstream" (problem occurred before the abend; the abend statement was only a trigger). Redo DEBUGGING procedure using the MOVE sending item as the separate-sign-dataname.
2. If PIC is ALPHABETIC then an obscure path has been taken. An obscure path is code that is only used when the PROGRAM detects an anomaly or an unusual condition. It

has to be an obscure path because, if it were a normal condition, the **production** PROGRAM would be continually abending with this problem. Often obscure paths are unchanged when other modifications are made to the PROGRAM such as changing an item to NUMERIC. This results in an abend when the obscure path is invoked.

Examine the module trace to determine how the PROGRAM got to the module containing the offending statement. This is usually sufficient to isolate the anomaly. Determine what the obscure path should be doing and make the corrections. Rerun to verify.

(d) MOVE CORRESPONDING

The CORRESPONDING [CORR] phrase allows multiple items to be moved with a single MOVE statement. You must determine which item in the sending items is the "twin" of the receiving item containing incorrect data. Use the CORRESPONDING sending twin data-name as the separate-sign-dataname. Use the MOVE DEBUGGING procedures.

(e) READ

The other probable culprit is a READ verb. This means that the FILE being used by the PROGRAM already contains the offending incorrect data and that the actual problem was caused by a PROGRAM upstream.

1.   Refer to a Job Step Diagram (a graphic portrayal of how PROGRAMs are invoked and what resources they require) to determine the last previous PROGRAM that wrote the offending FILE.
2.   Determine the data-name containing the offending incorrect data from the 01 data description in that previous PROGRAM.
3.   Redo the DEBUGGING procedure using the previous PROGRAM dataname as the separate-sign-data-name. It is possible that you may have to go back many PROGRAMs to find the actual culprit.

(f) STRING

The STRING verb has moved incorrect data into the data-name. Use the MOVE DEBUGGING procedures.

(g) UNSTRING

The UNSTRING verb has moved incorrect data into the data-name. Use the MOVE DEBUGGING procedures.

(h) REDEFINES

The REDEFINES clause where the PIC clause is ALPHABETIC is often the cause of incorrect data being in the SEPARATE SIGN. If the original ACCEPT breakpoint did not trap the incorrect data then this must be the cause.

1.   Ascertain the first REDEFINES data-name in the DATA DIVISION. Redo DEBUGGING steps using this data-name as the separate-sign-data-name.

2. If incorrect data is still not trapped then repeat with remaining REDEFINES data-names until the offender is found.

Note: It is possible to debug all REDEFINES data-names simultaneously by listing each data-name in the USE statement and testing them in the IF statement with OR logical operators. However, I believe it is simpler and faster to test them singularly.

2. VS COBOL II COBTEST

The generic procedures for DEBUGGING using COBTEST are the same as for using ANSI DEBUG. The difference is the syntax.

```
COBTEST program-name

TRACE ENTRY NAME PRINT

FLOW ON

LIST separate-sign-data-name BOTH PRINT

ONABEND (FLOW)
```

COBTEST does not have an ALPHABETIC test and therefore you must allow it to execute the abending statement. However, COBTEST does permit you to gain control after an abend [ONABEND] which ANSI DEBUG does not.

```
GO
```

Starts PROGRAM.

Review the TRACE and FLOW displays or printouts to determine where the incorrect data came from. Substitute the appropriate COBTEST commands for the ANSI DEBUG procedures previously described.

3. Quick fix

Infrequently the initial DEBUGGING procedures do not reveal the problem thereby requiring more analysis. Operational considerations may necessitate that the PROGRAM be run with the offending transactions being written to an ERROR REPORT for later correction. The quick fix is:

1. Insert a REDEFINES with an equivalent PIC X clause for the data-name having the incorrect data problem.

```
?? numeric-data-name          PIC S9(6)V
            SIGN IS LEADING/TRAILING SEPARATE CHARACTER.
?? incorrect data-redefinition   REDEFINES
   numeric-data-name             PIC X(6).
```

2. Insert IF ALPHABETIC defensive trap before each arithmetic statement that uses numeric-data-name.

```
IF            incorrect data-redefinition   ALPHABETIC
    [WRITE installation standard ERROR REPORT]
END-IF
```

DIVIDE BY ZERO

An abend occurs whenever the DIVIDE divisor is ZERO since the quotient would be infinity. If the abend was caused by a defensive trap such as the IF ALPHABETIC then use the defensive trap DEBUGGING procedures. Otherwise:

1. ANSI DEBUG

```
PROCEDURE DIVISION.

DECLARATIVES.

DEBUG SECTION.

    USE FOR DEBUGGING ON    zero-data-name
                            ALL PROCEDURES.

DEBUG-PROGRAM-FLOW.

    DISPLAY         DEBUG-LINE
                    DEBUG-NAME
                    DEBUG-CONTENTS.

    DISPLAY UPON mnemonic-name-1
                    DEBUG-LINE
                    DEBUG-NAME
                    DEBUG-CONTENTS.

DEBUG-BREAKPOINT.

    IF          DEBUG-NAME    =   zero-data-name
    AND         DEBUG-CONTENTS   IS ZERO
        ACCEPT  breakpoint
        FROM    mnemonic-name-2
        IF      dump
            DIVIDE ZERO BY ZERO GIVING infinity
        END-IF
    END-IF

END DECLARATIVES.
```

The verbs that can place zero into the numeric item are ACCEPT, INITIALIZE, INSPECT REPLACING, MOVE, MOVE CORRESPONDING, READ, SET, STRING, and UNSTRING.

(a) ACCEPT

A format 1 ACCEPT should not normally be in a production PROGRAM. Cause is typing ERROR. Rerun PROGRAM ensuring that a proper NUMERIC VALUE is entered.

(b) INITIALIZE

An INITIALIZE statement without the REPLACING phrase places ZERO into any receiving item with a NUMERIC or NUMERIC-EDITED PIC. The REPLACING phrase can also place ZERO into a NUMERIC or NUMERIC-EDITED item if the sending item or literal has a ZERO VALUE. If the receiving item is used without modification as a divisor then the DIVIDE BY ZERO abend occurs. An obscure path has been taken, otherwise the **production** PROGRAM would always abend with this anomaly.

Examine the module trace to determine how the PROGRAM got to the module containing the offending statement. This is usually sufficient to isolate the anomaly. Determine what the obscure path should be doing and make the corrections. Rerun to verify.

(c) INSPECT REPLACING

The INSPECT REPLACING syntax is incorrect. Correct and rerun.

(d) MOVE

The MOVE verb is the probable culprit. The question is why does the sending item contain ZERO. The probable answer is that an obscure path has been taken because the PROGRAM detected an anomaly or unusual condition.

Examine the module trace to determine how the PROGRAM got to the module containing the offending statement. This is usually sufficient to isolate the anomaly. Determine what the obscure path should be doing and make the corrections. Rerun to verify.

(e) MOVE CORRESPONDING

The CORRESPONDING [CORR] phrase allows multiple items to be moved with a single MOVE statement. You must determine which item in the sending items is the "twin" of the receiving item containing ZERO. Use the CORRESPONDING sending twin data-name as the zero-data-name. Use the MOVE DEBUGGING procedures.

(f) READ

The other probable culprit is a READ verb. This means that the FILE being used by the PROGRAM already contains the offending ZERO and that the actual problem was caused by a PROGRAM upstream.

1.   Refer to a Job Step Diagram (a graphic portrayal of how PROGRAMs are invoked and what resources they require) to determine the last previous PROGRAM that wrote the offending FILE.

2. Determine the data-name containing the offending ZERO from the 01 data description in that previous PROGRAM.
3. Redo the DEBUGGING procedure using the previous PROGRAM data-name as the zero-data-name. It is possible that you may have to go back many PROGRAMs to find the actual culprit.

(g) SET

The SET verb has placed ZERO into the data-name. Use the MOVE DEBUGGING procedures.

(h) STRING

The STRING verb has placed ZERO into the data-name. Use the MOVE DEBUGGING procedures.

(i) UNSTRING

The UNSTRING verb has placed ZERO into the data-name. Use the MOVE DEBUGGING procedures.

2. VS COBOL II COBTEST

The generic procedures for DEBUGGING using COBTEST are the same as for using ANSI DEBUG. The difference is the syntax.

```
COBTEST program-name

TRACE ENTRY NAME PRINT

FLOW ON

LIST zero-data-name BOTH PRINT

WHEN brek (zero-data-name = ZERO) (FLOW PRINT)

GO

DUMP or GO
```

3. Quick fix

Infrequently the initial DEBUGGING procedures do not reveal the problem thereby requiring more analysis. Operational considerations may necessitate that the PROGRAM be run with the offending transactions being written to an ERROR REPORT for later correction. The quick fix is:

Insert IF ZERO defensive trap before each arithmetic statement that uses zero-data-name.

```
IF              zero-data-name   ZERO
    [WRITE installation standard ERROR REPROT]
END-IF
```

truncation [OVERFLOW] defensive trap

A truncation abend occurs if the ON SIZE ERROR defensive trap has detected OVERFLOW. Truncation means that the receiving item PIC clause was insufficient to hold either the intermediate results or the final result of arithmetic operations. Failure to include the ON SIZE ERROR defensive trap leaves the receiving item undefined and permits the PROGRAM to continue executing with that **undefined** VALUE (some compilers do abend; use DEBUGGING steps described below). The offending VALUE is any VALUE > the maximum magnitude of the receiving item PIC clause. DEBUGGING is complicated because at least two items must be analyzed. For instance:

```
ADD        identifier-1 TO     identifier-2
```

is the simplest syntax possible. A truncation occurs if either the VALUE in identifier-1 is > identifier-2 magnitude or the result of adding identifier-1 TO identifier-2 is > identifier-2 magnitude. Assume that identifier-1 has a PIC of S999V and identifier-2 PIC is S99V. Truncation occurs if identifier-1 has any VALUE between 100 and 999; truncation also occurs if identifier-1 has a VALUE of 1 and identifier-2 has a VALUE of 99 since the result is 100 which exceeds identifier-2 PIC S99V. A GIVING item is inserted which becomes the trace and breakpoint item. Programming examples:

```
    ADD            identifier-1 TO     identifier-2
D   GIVING         identifier-3
*statement can overflow; activate debug to trace on
*identifier-3
    ON SIZE ERROR DIVIDE ZERO BY ZERO GIVING infinity
    END-ADD
```

The D marks this as a DEBUGGING statement and the comment explains its use. If the GIVING phrase already exists:

```
    ADD            identifier-1 TO     identifier-2
    GIVING         identifier-3
D                  identifier-4
*statement can overflow; activate debug to trace on
*identifier-4
    ON SIZE ERROR DIVIDE ZERO BY ZERO GIVING infinity
    END-ADD
```

COMPUTE syntax is an implicit GIVING since the arithmetic-expression is evaluated and the result placed in the item preceding the equal [=]. giving-data-name is the COMPUTE identifier-1 data-name.

The ACCEPT breakpoint STOPs execution when truncation occurs but that does not tell you what the offending VALUES are. You need to insert a DISPLAY statement in the breakpoint to show the identifier VALUES.

ADD and SUBTRACT can have CORRESPONDING phrases. The ON SIZE ERROR defensive trap is not executed until **after all** the arithmetic operations have been completed. The **DEBUGGING** technique is to decompose the CORRESPONDING into its component ADD or SUBTRACT statements and then trace each individual statement.

1. ANSI DEBUG

```
PROCEDURE DIVISION.

DECLARATIVES.

DEBUG SECTION.

    USE FOR DEBUGGING ON    giving-data-name
                            ALL PROCEDURES.

DEBUG-PROGRAM-FLOW.

    DISPLAY        DEBUG-LINE
                   DEBUG-NAME
                   DEBUG-CONTENTS.

    DISPLAY UPON mnemonic-name-1
                   DEBUG-LINE
                   DEBUG-NAME
                   DEBUG-CONTENTS.

DEBUG-BREAKPOINT.

    IF         DEBUG-NAME      = giving-data-name
    AND        DEBUG-CONTENTS > receiving-item-max-value
        DISPLAY    identifier-1
                   identifier-2
                   ...
*display the arithmetic identifiers that caused overflow
        ACCEPT     breakpoint
        FROM       mnemonic-name-2
        IF         dump
        DIVIDE ZERO BY ZERO GIVING infinity
        END-IF
    END-IF
```

```
END DECLARATIVES.
```

Determine which identifiers caused the truncation. Substitute their data-names for giving-data-name and modify the ANSI DEBUG module as follows:

```
PROCEDURE DIVISION.

DECLARATIVES.

DEBUG SECTION.

    USE FOR DEBUGGING ON    identifier-1-data-name
                            identifier-2-data-name
                            ...
                            ALL PROCEDURES.

DEBUG-PROGRAM-FLOW.

    DISPLAY         DEBUG-LINE
                    DEBUG-NAME
                    DEBUG-CONTENTS.

    DISPLAY UPON mnemonic-name-1
                    DEBUG-LINE
                    DEBUG-NAME
                    DEBUG-CONTENTS.

DEBUG-BREAKPOINT.

    IF              DEBUG-NAME      =  identifier-1-data-name
    OR              identifier-2-data-name
    OR              ...
    AND             DEBUG-CONTENTS =   identifier-1-value
    OR              identifier-2-value
    OR              ...
        DISPLAY     identifier-1
                    identifier-2
                    ...
*display the arithmetic identifiers that caused overflow
        ACCEPT      breakpoint
        FROM        mnemonic-name-2
        IF          dump
        DIVIDE ZERO BY ZERO GIVING infinity
        END-IF
    END-IF

END DECLARATIVES.
```

The truncation was caused by an obscure path otherwise the **production** PROGRAM would continually abend with this problem. Examine the module trace to determine how the PROGRAM got to the module containing the offending statement. This is usually sufficient to isolate the anomaly. Determine what the obscure path should be doing and make the corrections. Rerun to verify.

2. COBOL II COBTEST commands

The generic procedures for DEBUGGING using COBTEST are the same as for using ANSI DEBUG. The difference is the syntax.

```
COBTEST program-name

TRACE ENTRY NAME PRINT

FLOW ON

LIST truncation-data-name BOTH PRINT

WHEN brek (giving-data-name > receiving-item-maximum-
value)
(FLOW PRINT; LIST identifier-1, identifier-2, ...)
COMMENT list is COBTEST substitute for the additional ANSI
display

GO

DUMP or GO
```

3. Quick fix

Infrequently the initial DEBUGGING procedures do not reveal the problem thereby requiring more analysis. Operational considerations may necessitate that the PROGRAM be run with the offending transactions being written to an ERROR REPORT for later correction. There are two possible quick fixes.

(a) Increase PIC 9s

You can increase the number of 9s in the PIC clause if the receiving item is in WORKING-STORAGE or the LINKAGE SECTION whose storage is the calling PROGRAM's WORKING-STORAGE. You should notify the appropriate person of the truncation problem so that further analysis can be undertaken to determine if the item warrants expansion in other PROGRAMs.

You **cannot** increase the 9s if the item is in a 01 definition in the DATA DIVISION because that destroys the positional integrity of the FILE. That requires FILE reorganization to expand any FD item. FILE reorganization is not a quick fix.

(b) ON SIZE ERROR

Substitute a WRITE to standard ERROR REPORT for the DIVIDE BY ZERO defensive trap which forces an abend.

Overlapping items

ANSI standards require that any arithmetic operation between items that share the same storage are **undefined**. Most compilers adhere to the standard and do not abend, although many issue compile ERROR messages as a warning. If you suspect this problem then you must determine if there are overlapping items and what your compiler does with them.

You should write and compile a test PROGRAM (see Appendix A) that has overlapping items. Determine if the overlapping items cause a warning. If the object code is executable then run to determine if the overlapping items cause an abend or run time warning message. If your compiler does abend and that abend has occurred then the PROGRAM has executed an obscure path otherwise the **production** PROGRAM would continually abend with this problem. Examine the module trace to determine how the PROGRAM got to the module containing the offending statement. This is usually sufficient to isolate the anomaly. Determine what the obscure path should be doing and make the corrections. Rerun to verify.

If your compiler does not cause an abend — which is normal — then determine if either the compile or run-time messages warn about overlapping items. If so, check the trace REPORTs to see if the invalid statement was executed. If it has then you have found your problem. Again an obscure path must have been taken. Determine what the obscure path should be doing and make the corrections. Rerun to verify.

If you still suspect overlapping items and your compiler does not issue the appropriate warnings then you need to run an overlapping item analyzer to determine if the suspect PROGRAM has any. If so, check the trace REPORTs to see if the invalid statement was executed. If it has then you have found your problem. Again an obscure path must have been taken. Determine what the obscure path should be doing and make the corrections. Rerun to verify.

If overlapping items are not the culprit then you have to start over again. It is likely that you have a random switch anomaly and you should use the procedures detailed in Chapter 7.

1. Quick fix

Infrequently the initial DEBUGGING procedures do not reveal the problem thereby requiring more analysis. Operational considerations may necessitate that the PROGRAM be run with the offending transactions being written to an ERROR REPORT for later correction. The quick fix is to bypass the transaction by writing out the installation standard ERROR REPORT. You need to insert the following IF statement after each READ statement for the FILE containing the RECORD that caused the obscure path to be taken.

```
IF              record-key    =    record-key-bad-value
     [WRITE installation standard ERROR REPORT]
END-IF
```

record-key is the KEY item used to READ the RECORD. It is derivable from the READ statement or the file-control-entry in the ENVIRONMENT DIVISION. record-key-bad-value is the KEY VALUE that caused the PROGRAM to invoke the obscure path. It is derivable from the dump. If the FILE is SEQUENTIAL and the PROGRAM does not contain a KEY item then determine which item is used as the FILE SORT KEY.

DATA MOVEMENT

The data movement verbs are ACCEPT [DATE, DAY, DAY-OF-WEEK, TIME, MESSAGE [COUNT], INITIALIZE, INSPECT [REPLACING], MOVE, STRING, UNSTRING. The abend types are OVERFLOW, incompatible PIC clauses, and overlapping items.

OVERFLOW defensive trap

An OVERFLOW abend can only occur if the ON OVERFLOW defensive trap has detected OVERFLOW. Only the STRING and UNSTRING verbs have ON OVERFLOW phrases. OVERFLOW occurs when:

1.　The POINTER < 1
2.　The POINTER > STRING INTO identifier
3.　The POINTER > UNSTRING identifier
4.　All UNSTRING INTO identifiers have been used.

1.　POINTER < 1

(a) ANSI DEBUG

```
    PROCEDURE DIVISION.

    DECLARATIVES.

    DEBUG SECTION.

        USE FOR DEBUGGING ON    pointer-data-name
                                ALL PROCEDURES.

    DEBUG-PROGRAM-FLOW.

        DISPLAY     DEBUG-LINE
                    DEBUG-NAME
                    DEBUG-CONTENTS.

        DISPLAY UPON mnemonic-name-1
                    DEBUG-LINE
```

```
                    DEBUG-NAME
                    DEBUG-CONTENTS.

DEBUG-BREAKPOINT.

    IF          DEBUG-NAME       =    pointer-data-name
    AND         DEBUG-CONTENTS   <    one
        ACCEPT  breakpoint
        FROM    mnemonic-name-2
        IF      dump
            DIVIDE ZERO BY ZERO GIVING infinity
        END-IF
    END-IF

END DECLARATIVES.
```

The incorrect VALUE of < 1 was caused by an obscure path otherwise the **production** PROGRAM would continually abend with this problem. Examine the module trace to determine how the PROGRAM got to the module containing the offending statement. This is usually sufficient to isolate the anomaly. Determine what the obscure path should be doing and make the corrections. Rerun to verify.

(b) COBOL II COBTEST commands

The generic procedures for DEBUGGING using COBTEST are the same as for using ANSI DEBUG. The difference is the syntax.

```
COBTEST program-name

TRACE ENTRY NAME PRINT

FLOW ON

LIST pointer-data-name BOTH PRINT

WHEN brek (pointer-data-name < one)      (FLOW PRINT)

GO

DUMP OR GO
```

(c) Quick fix

Infrequently the initial DEBUGGING procedures do not reveal the problem thereby requiring more analysis. Operational considerations may necessitate that the PROGRAM be run with the offending transactions being written to an ERROR REPORT for later correction. The quick fix is:

Insert IF < one defensive trap before each STRING or UNSTRING statement that uses pointer-data-name.

```
IF              pointer-data-name   <   one
   [WRITE installation standard ERROR REPORT]
END-IF
```

2. POINTER > identifier-size

(a) ANSI DEBUG

```
PROCEDURE DIVISION.

DECLARATIVES.

DEBUG SECTION.

    USE FOR DEBUGGING ON    pointer-data-name
                            ALL PROCEDURES.

DEBUG-PROGRAM-FLOW.

    DISPLAY       DEBUG-LINE
                  DEBUG-NAME
                  DEBUG-CONTENTS.

    DISPLAY UPON mnemonic-name-1
                  DEBUG-LINE
                  DEBUG-NAME
                  DEBUG-CONTENTS.

DEBUG-BREAKPOINT.

    IF            DEBUG-NAME       =   pointer-data-name
    AND           DEBUG-CONTENTS   >   identifier-size
        ACCEPT    breakpoint
        FROM      mnemonic-name-2
        IF        dump
            DIVIDE ZERO BY ZERO GIVING infinity
        END-IF
    END-IF

END DECLARATIVES.
```

The incorrect VALUE was caused by an obscure path otherwise the **production** PROGRAM would continually abend with this problem. Examine the module trace to determine how the PROGRAM got to the module containing the offending statement. This is usually sufficient to isolate the anomaly. Determine what the obscure path should be doing and make the corrections. Rerun to verify.

(b) COBOL II COBTEST commands

The generic procedures for DEBUGGING using COBTEST are the same as for using ANSI DEBUG. The difference is the syntax.

```
COBTEST program-name

TRACE ENTRY NAME PRINT

FLOW ON

LIST pointer-data-name BOTH PRINT

WHEN brek (pointer-data-name > identifier-size) (FLOW
PRINT)

GO

DUMP or GO
```

(c) Quick fix

Infrequently the initial DEBUGGING procedures do not reveal the problem thereby requiring more analysis. Operational considerations may necessitate that the PROGRAM be run with the offending transactions being written to an ERROR REPORT for later correction. The quick fix is:

Insert IF > identifier-size defensive trap before each STRING or UNSTRING statement that uses pointer-data-name.

```
IF            pointer-data-name  >  identifier-size
   [WRITE installation standard ERROR REPORT]
END-IF
```

3. All UNSTRING INTO identifiers used

The UNSTRING identifier contains too many "fields" for the NUMBER of INTO identifiers. The cause is that are too many DELIMITERs in the identifier. The ANSI DEBUG module needs an INSPECT TALLYING statement to trap the offending identifier.

(a) ANSI DEBUG

```
PROCEDURE DIVISION.

DECLARATIVES.
```

```
DEBUG SECTION.

    USE FOR DEBUGGING ON     unstring-identifier-data-name
                             ALL PROCEDURES.

DEBUG-PROGRAM-FLOW.

    DISPLAY        DEBUG-LINE
                   DEBUG-NAME
                   DEBUG-CONTENTS.

    DISPLAY        UPON        mnemonic-name-1
                   DEBUG-LINE
                   DEBUG-NAME
                   DEBUG-CONTENTS.

 DEBUG-BREAKPOINT.

    IF             DEBUG-NAME    =    unstring-identifier-data-
-                             name
*debug-contents comparison not required
        INSPECT    unstring-identifier-data-name
        TALLYING   tally-counter
*tally-counter must be inserted into working-storage
        FOR        unstring-delimited-by-phrase
*use same clause as used in the unstring statement
        IF         tally-counter > number-of-into-
                   identifiers
*number of into phrases + 1
            ACCEPT breakpoint
            FROM   mnemonic-name-2
            IF     dump
                DIVIDE ZERO BY ZERO GIVING infinity
            END-IF
        END-IF
    END-IF

END DECLARATIVES.
```

The incorrect **NUMBER** of **DELIMITER**s was caused by an obscure path otherwise the **production** PROGRAM would continually abend with this problem. Examine the module trace to determine how the PROGRAM got to the module containing the offending statement. This is usually sufficient to isolate the anomaly. Determine what the obscure path should be doing and make the corrections. Rerun to verify.

(b) COBOL II COBTEST commands

The generic procedures for DEBUGGING using COBTEST are the same as for using ANSI DEBUG. The difference is the syntax.

```
COBTEST program-name

TRACE ENTRY NAME PRINT

FLOW ON

LIST unstring-identifier-data-name BOTH PRINT

ONABEND (FLOW)
```

COBTEST does not have an INSPECT command test and therefore you must allow it to execute the abending statement. However, COBTEST does permit you to gain control after an abend [ONABEND] which ANSI DEBUG does not.

```
GO
```

Starts PROGRAM.

Review the TRACE and FLOW displays or printouts to determine where the extra DELIMITERs came from. Substitute the appropriate COBTEST commands for the ANSI DEBUG procedures previously described.

(c) Quick fix

Infrequently the initial DEBUGGING procedures do not reveal the problem thereby requiring more analysis. Operational considerations may necessitate that the PROGRAM be run with the offending transactions being written to an ERROR REPORT for later correction. The quick fix is to insert an INSPECT defensive trap before each UNSTRING statement

```
      INSPECT         unstring-identifier-data-name
      TALLYING        tally-counter
 *tally-counter must be inserted into working-storage
    , FOR             unstring-delimited-by-phrase
 *use same clause as used in the unstring statement

      IF              tally-counter > number-of-into-
 -                    identifiers
 *number of into phrases + 1
          [WRITE installation ERROR REPORT]
      END-IF
```

Incompatible PIC clauses

ANSI standards require that any data movement between incompatible items leaves the receiving item undefined. Most compilers adhere to the standard and do not abend although many issue compile ERROR messages as a warning. If you suspect this problem then you must determine what is an invalid data movement and what your compiler does with it.

Your compiler manual usually contains a chart of valid and invalid MOVE statements. This chart can be used to determine the invalid data movements. For instance, the *IBM VS COBOL II Application Programming Language Reference* (GC26-4047) lists the following MOVEs as invalid:

1.   ALPHABETIC and SPACE TO NUMERIC and NUMERIC-EDITED
2.   ALPHABETIC edited TO NUMERIC and NUMERIC-EDITED
3.   NUMERIC integer including NUMERIC literals and ZERO TO ALPHABETIC
4.   Non-numeric noninteger TO ALPHABETIC, ALPHANUMERIC, and ALPHA-NUMERIC-EDITED
5.   NUMERIC-EDITED TO ALPHABETIC, NUMERIC, and NUMERIC-EDITED
6.   Figurative constants except SPACE and ZERO TO ALPHABETIC, NUMERIC, and NUMERIC-EDITED

You should write and compile a test PROGRAM that has a MOVE for each invalid data movement. Note which invalid MOVEs issue warnings and which do not. If the object code is executable then run to determine which invalid MOVEs cause an abend or run-time warning message. If your compiler does abend for any invalid data movement and that abend has occurred, then the PROGRAM has executed an obscure path otherwise the **production** PROGRAM would continually abend with this problem. Examine the module trace to determine how the PROGRAM got to the module containing the offending statement. This is usually sufficient to isolate the anomaly. Determine what the obscure path should be doing and make the corrections. Rerun to verify.

If your compiler does not cause an abend — which is normal — then determine if either the compile or run-time messages warn about invalid data movement. If so, check the trace REPORTs to see if the invalid statement was executed. If it has then you have found your problem. Again an obscure path must have been taken. Determine what the obscure path should be doing and make the corrections. Rerun to verify.

If you still suspect an invalid data movement and your compiler does not issue the appropriate warnings then you need to run an invalid data movement analyzer to determine if the suspect PROGRAM has any. If so, check the trace REPORTs to see if the invalid statement was executed. If it has then you have found your problem. Again an obscure path must have been taken. Determine what the obscure path should be doing and make the corrections. Rerun to verify.

If an invalid data movement is not the culprit then you have to start over again. It is likely that you have a random switch anomaly and you should use the procedures detailed in Chapter 7.

1. Quick fix

Infrequently the initial DEBUGGING procedures do not reveal the problem thereby requiring more analysis. Operational considerations may necessitate that the PROGRAM be run with the offending transactions being written to an ERROR REPORT for later correction. The quick fix is to bypass the transaction by writing out the installation standard ERROR REPORT. You need to insert the following IF statement after each READ statement for the FILE containing the RECORD that caused the obscure path to be taken.

```
IF              record-key  =  record-key-bad-value
    [WRITE installation standard ERROR REPORT]
END-IF
```

record-key is the KEY item used to READ the RECORD. It is derivable from the READ statement or the file-control-entry in the ENVIRONMENT DIVISION. record-key-bad-value is the KEY VALUE that caused the PROGRAM to invoke the obscure path. It is derivable from the dump. If the FILE is SEQUENTIAL and the PROGRAM does not contain a KEY item then determine which item is used as the FILE SORT KEY.

Overlapping items

ANSI standards require that any data movement between items that share the same storage is undefined. Most compilers adhere to the standard and do not abend although many issue compile ERROR messages as a warning. If you suspect this problem then you must determine if there are overlapping items and what your compiler does with them.

You should write and compile a test PROGRAM (see Appendix A) that has overlapping items. Determine if the overlapping items cause a warning. If the object code is executable then run to determine if the overlapping items cause an abend or run-time warning message. If your compiler does abend and that abend has occurred then the PROGRAM has executed an obscure path otherwise the **production** PROGRAM would continually abend with this problem. Examine the module trace to determine how the PROGRAM got to the module containing the offending statement. This is usually sufficient to isolate the anomaly. Determine what the obscure path should be doing and make the corrections. Rerun to verify.

If your compiler does not cause an abend — which is normal — then determine if either the compile or run-time messages warn about overlapping items. If so, check the trace REPORTs to see if the invalid statement was executed. If it has then you have found your problem. Again an obscure path must have been taken. Determine what the obscure path should be doing and make the corrections. Rerun to verify.

If you still suspect overlapping items and your compiler does not issue the appropriate warnings then you need to run an overlapping item analyzer to determine if the suspect PROGRAM has any. If so, check the trace REPORTs to see if the invalid statement was executed. If it has then you have found your problem. Again an obscure path must have been taken. Determine what the obscure path should be doing and make the corrections. Rerun to verify.

If overlapping items are not the culprit then you have to start over again. It is likely that you have a random switch anomaly and you should use the procedures detailed in Chapter 7.

1. Quick fix

Infrequently the initial DEBUGGING procedures do not reveal the problem thereby requiring more analysis. Operational considerations may necessitate that the PROGRAM be run with the offending transactions being written to an ERROR REPORT for later correction. The quick fix is to bypass the transaction by writing out the installation standard ERROR REPORT. You need to insert the following IF statement after each READ statement for the FILE containing the RECORD that caused the obscure path to be taken.

```
IF             record-key  =  record-key-bad-value
    [WRITE installation standard ERROR REPORT]
END-IF
```

record-key is the KEY item used to READ the RECORD. It is derivable from the READ statement or the file-control-entry in the ENVIRONMENT DIVISION. record-key-bad-value is the KEY VALUE that caused the PROGRAM to invoke the obscure path. It is derivable from the dump. If the FILE is SEQUENTIAL and the PROGRAM does not contain a KEY item then determine which item is the FILE SORT KEY.

ENDING

The ending verbs are STOP [RUN], EXIT PROGRAM, and GOBACK [IBM]. STOP [RUN] in any PROGRAM or a GOBACK in a main PROGRAM causes an abend if it is invoked in a SORT or MERGE INPUT or OUTPUT PROCEDURE and the SORT or MERGE is still active. Problems can occur if a called PROGRAM executes a STOP RUN which terminates the RUN UNIT instead of returning to the calling PROGRAM by an EXIT PROGRAM or GOBACK.

Note 1: A RUN UNIT is one or more object PROGRAMs interacting together to do specific processing.
Note 2: The RUN UNIT main PROGRAM is the first COBOL PROGRAM invoked.
Note 3: The GOBACK verb is treated as a STOP RUN in a main PROGRAM and an EXIT PROGRAM in a callable PROGRAM.

SORT or MERGE active

The STOP [RUN] or GOBACK must be in an obscure path otherwise the **production** PROGRAM would continually abend with this anomaly. Run a PROGRAM trace to see how the PROGRAM got to the offending statement:

1. ANSI DEBUG

```
PROCEDURE DIVISION.

DECLARATIVES.

DEBUG SECTION.

    USE FOR DEBUGGING ON    ALL PROCEDURES.

DEBUG-PROGRAM-FLOW.

    DISPLAY        DEBUG-LINE
                   DEBUG-NAME
                   DEBUG-CONTENTS.

    DISPLAY UPON  mnemonic-name-1
                   DEBUG-LINE
                   DEBUG-NAME
                   DEBUG-CONTENTS.

END DECLARATIVES.
```

The ANSI DEBUG module need only trace PROGRAM flow. COBTEST is not required since PROCEDURE tracing is supported in COBOL II.

2. Quick fix

Infrequently the initial DEBUGGING procedures do not reveal the problem thereby requiring more analysis. Operational considerations may necessitate that the PROGRAM be run with the offending transactions being written to an ERROR REPORT for later correction. The quick fix is to bypass the transaction by writing out the installation standard ERROR REPORT. You need to insert the following IF statement after each READ statement for the FILE containing the RECORD that caused the obscure path to be taken.

```
IF              record-key    =    record-key-bad-value
    [WRITE installation standard ERROR REPORT]
END-IF
```

record-key is the KEY item used to READ the RECORD. It is derivable from the READ statement or the file-control-entry in the ENVIRONMENT DIVISION. record-key-bad-value is the KEY VALUE that caused the PROGRAM to invoke the obscure path. It is derivable from the dump. If the FILE is SEQUENTIAL and the PROGRAM does not contain a KEY item then determine which item is the FILE SORT KEY.

STOP [RUN] in a callable PROGRAM

The easy way to determine if a PROGRAM is callable is to check the PROCEDURE DIVISION header. If it contains a USING phrase then it is a called PROGRAM. While it is possible to CALL a PROGRAM without USING, it is unlikely.

The operating system treats a STOP RUN as a normal EOJ and therefore there is no dump. It is impossible to know that this "abend" has happened unless the called PROGRAM issued some sort of message. If you suspect this problem then you must determine what PROGRAMs constitute the RUN UNIT and if any of the callable PROGRAMs can execute a STOP RUN.

A RUN UNIT is defined by JCL in the IBM world. The JCL run book contains the names of all PROGRAMs that are directly invoked by JCL; it does **not** contain any callable PROGRAMs.

JCL is text and can be searched by using text editors such as ISPF. A KWIC (Key Word In Context) search on the JCL PGM keyword identifies each PROGRAM name within the JCL RUN UNIT. The named PROGRAMs are then searched for any CALL statements. The called PROGRAMs are then searched for CALL statements and so forth until all callable PROGRAMs are identified. Each callable PROGRAM is searched for STOP RUN statements with a DIVIDE BY ZERO defensive trap inserted before each occurrence. All RUN UNIT PROGRAMs are prepared for DEBUGGING and run against the test FILES. The defensive trap traps the offending STOP RUN statement. Either the called PROGRAM was invoked by an obscure path within the calling PROGRAM or the STOP RUN was in an obscure path within the called PROGRAM. The trace information tells you which.

In either case, the STOP RUN is replaced by an EXIT PROGRAM with a return code specifying the CALL results including failure. The called PROGRAM must be modified to test for the return code and to abend if the failure was catastrophic. It is likely that more analysis is required to determine what the obscure path should be doing.

In summary:

1. Identify RUN UNIT PROGRAM names by KWIC SEARCH on JCL PGM.
2. Identify each CALL statement within the RUN UNIT PROGRAMs.
3. Identify each CALL statement within each callable PROGRAM.

Note: Software such as Adpac PM/SS can generate the PROGRAM list created by 1, 2, and 3 with a simple command.

4. Insert DIVIDE BY ZERO defensive trap before each STOP RUN in the callable PROGRAMs.
5. Prepare each RUN UNIT PROGRAM for DEBUGGING.
6. Run the RUN UNIT against the test FILES.

1. ANSI DEBUG

```
PROCEDURE DIVISION.

DECLARATIVES.
```

```
DEBUG SECTION.

    USE FOR DEBUGGING ON    ALL PROCEDURES.

DEBUG-PROGRAM-FLOW.

    DISPLAY        DEBUG-LINE
                   DEBUG-NAME
                   DEBUG-CONTENTS.

    DISPLAY UPON  mnemonic-name-1
                   DEBUG-LINE
                   DEBUG-NAME
                   DEBUG-CONTENTS.

END DECLARATIVES.
```

The ANSI DEBUG module need only trace PROGRAM flow. COBTEST is not required since PROCEDURE tracing is supported in COBOL II.

2. Quick fix

Infrequently the initial DEBUGGING procedures do not reveal the problem thereby requiring more analysis. Operational considerations may necessitate that the PROGRAM be run with the offending transactions being written to an ERROR REPORT for later correction. Substituting EXIT PROGRAM for STOP RUN is the quick fix. The calling PROGRAM WRITEs the installation standard ERROR REPORT for an invalid return code.

INPUT-OUTPUT

The INPUT-OUTPUT verbs are ACCEPT [IDENTIFIER], CLOSE, DELETE, DISABLE, DISPLAY, ENABLE, OPEN, PURGE, READ, RECEIVE, REWRITE, SEND, START, STOP [literal], and WRITE.

ACCEPT [IDENTIFIER] should not be a verb in production PROGRAMs since it requires human intervention for processing. ACCEPT [IDENTIFIER] is used by the ANSI DEBUGGING module in a DEBUGGING environment. The abends are equipment failure or incorrect device name. Equipment failure must be rectified by **hardware** maintenance. Incorrect device name must be corrected.

STOP [literal] is a form of ACCEPT [IDENTIFIER] in that the PROGRAM sends a message to the operator console requesting input. The RUN UNIT is suspended until the operator inputs the necessary data. The operator also has the option of canceling the RUN UNIT. The operator log must be analyzed to determine why the operator canceled the RUN UNIT. The RUN UNIT is restarted when the termination condition has been corrected. STOP [literal] should not be a verb in production PROGRAMs since it requires human intervention for processing. The STOP [literal] should be eliminated.

DISPLAY should not be a verb in production PROGRAMs since it is only suitable for low volume OUTPUT. DISPLAY is used by the ANSI DEBUGGING module in a DEBUGGING environment. The abends are equipment failure or incorrect device name. Equipment failure must be rectified by **hardware** maintenance. Incorrect device name must be corrected.

DISABLE, ENABLE, PURGE, RECEIVE, SEND are COBOL MESSAGE control system verbs within the COMMUNICATION module. The COMMUNICATION module is rarely used and its verbs are not discussed.

Thus, the INPUT-OUTPUT verbs discussed are CLOSE, DELETE, OPEN, READ, REWRITE, START, and WRITE. START is rarely used but it is included since its invocation causes a FILE STATUS return code.

An INPUT-OUTPUT abort occurs if the defensive traps of either AT END, INVALID KEY, USE AFTER STANDARD EXCEPTION/ERROR PROCEDURE ON, or a TEST of FILE STATUS has detected an operating system return code signaling a failure to execute the requested INPUT-OUTPUT statement and the PROGRAM has self-aborted. IBM compilers also have a USE AFTER STANDARD BEGINNING/ENDING [FILE/REEL/ UNIT] LABEL PROCEDURE ON for any LABELs specified in the LABEL RECORDS clause in the FILE description entry for additional LABEL checking.

LABELs are normally present on removable media such as TAPEs and disks. Specifying LABEL RECORD IS STANDARD informs the compiler to generate instructions to check the LABEL as instructed by the implementor rules. The implementor also specifies how to do additional LABEL checking such as verifying a DATE on the LABEL record. In IBM's case, it is coding the USE . . . LABEL DECLARATIVE. You need to check your COBOL compiler manual to determine what your implementor procedures are.

ANSI specifies that at least one of the defensive traps be specified for each INPUT-OUTPUT verb. However, it leaves to the implementor what to do if **no** defensive trap is specified. Many compilers do **nothing**, assuming that the programmer has done **something**. For instance the IBM VS COBOL II manual states:

> The most important thing to remember about input/output errors is that you choose whether or not your program will continue executing after a less-than-severe input/output error occurs. VS COBOL II does **not** perform corrective action. If you choose to have your program continue (by incorporating error-handling in your design), you must also code the appropriate error recovery. (VS COBOL II Application Programming Guide SC26-4045)

If you fail to code the appropriate ERROR recovery then your PROGRAM continues processing with undefined data and undefined KEY of reference. The FILE position indicator is SET to INVALID NEXT RECORD for READ statements. An uncompleted WRITE does not transfer the data to the external media as required. These are serious ERRORs that cause data corruption and they must be trapped (see Appendix A).

If your compiler does abend then the abend code should tell you what the problem is. Use the abend code as an INDEX into the INPUT-OUTPUT bug types. For instance, a COBOL II PROGRAM has an unsuccessful FILE OPEN or CLOSE abend. You would check **OPEN** or **CLOSE** for DEBUGGING steps.

Note 1: KEY of reference is either the current primary or ALTERNATE KEY VALUE used to access INDEXED RECORDS.

Note 2: FILE position indicator is a COBOL concept that contains the current KEY VALUE or a return code for the exception conditions of NO NEXT LOGICAL RECORD, INVALID KEY, AT END, OPTIONAL FILE not present, or that a valid NEXT RECORD has not been established. Each implementor must decide how to implement the FILE position indicator.

A subtle ERROR is to check FILE STATUS for some but not **all** possible return codes. The untested return code will happen sometime and will invariably cause a serious problem. An installation standard FILE STATUS verification routine should be copied into every PROGRAM after every INPUT-OUTPUT statement that TESTs for every possible return code with installation defined processing for each.

Similarly, an installation standard verification routine should be copied into every PROGRAM after every DBMS CALL that TESTs for every possible DBMS return code with installation defined processing for each.

ANSI specifies three INPUT-OUTPUT FILE structures: SEQUENTIAL, RELATIVE, and INDEXED. SEQUENTIAL is a structure in which a RECORD is identified by a predecessor/successor relationship established when the RECORD is placed into the FILE (this is FIFO [First In First Out]). RELATIVE is a SEQUENTIAL structure that also contains a RELATIVE KEY whose VALUE specifies the RECORD's logical ordinal POSITION within the FILE. INDEXED is a structure in which each RECORD is identified by the VALUE of one or more KEYs within the RECORD itself. Most INDEXED ACCESS methods such as IBM VSAM (Virtual Sequential Access Method) can also ACCESS INDEXED FILEs sequentially.

DUPLICATE KEY

ANSI FILE STATUS 02 [INDEXED READ, REWRITE, START]

The SELECT clause in the FILE-CONTROL entry in the ENVIRONMENT DIVISION for an INDEXED FILE allows the specification of an ALTERNATE RECORD KEY . . . WITH DUPLICATES. If WITH DUPLICATES is present then the operating system permits RECORDS to have DUPLICATE ALTERNATE KEYs (the primary KEY must always be unique). The first digit of 0 means successful completion which means that the operating system has detected an acceptable DUPLICATE ALTERNATE KEY. The second digit of 2 warns the PROGRAM that a DUPLICATE KEY has been detected. Normally a FILE STATUS of 02 is okay and is not an anomaly. It could be a problem if the PROGRAM did not expect DUPLICATE KEYs and processes the wrong RECORD. If you suspect this problem then your only course of action is to analyze the PROGRAM.

ANSI FILE STATUS 22 [RELATIVE or INDEXED REWRITE, WRITE]

22 means that the PROGRAM attempted to REWRITE or WRITE a RECORD that would create a DUPLICATE primary KEY or a DUPLICATE ALTERNATE KEY where the WITH DUPLICATES phrase was not specified for this FILE. The RECORD has **not** been written. Continuing processing causes data corruption.

1. REWRITE

REWRITE logically replaces an existing RECORD. This means that the PROGRAM must have READ the RECORD for modification and incorrectly modified a KEY item. The DEBUGGING steps are:

1.   Determine the KEY data-names from the SELECT clause in the ENVIRONMENT DIVISION.
2.   Determine the offset of each KEY data-name.
3.   Determine the ABEND VALUES of each KEY data-name from the FDUMP.

(a) ANSI DEBUG

```
PROCEDURE DIVISION.

DECLARATIVES.

DEBUG SECTION.

    USE FOR DEBUGGING ON    key-data-name-x
                            ALL PROCEDURES.

DEBUG-PROGRAM-FLOW.

    DISPLAY         DEBUG-LINE
                    DEBUG-NAME
                    DEBUG-CONTENTS.

    DISPLAY UPON mnemonic-name-1
                    DEBUG-LINE
                    DEBUG-NAME
                    DEBUG-CONTENTS.

DEBUG-BREAKPOINT.

    IF              DEBUG-NAME      =   key-data-name-x
    AND             DEBUG-CONTENTS  =   invalid-key-value
    THEN
        ACCEPT      breakpoint
        FROM        mnemonic-name-2
        IF          dump
            DIVIDE ZERO BY ZERO GIVING infinity
        END-IF
    END-IF

END DECLARATIVES.
```

Note: key-data-name-x where x = the key-data-name being tested. It is possible to debug all KEY data-names simultaneously by listing each KEY data-name in the USE statement and testing them in the IF statement with OR logical operators. However, I believe it is simpler and faster to TEST them singularly.

The contents of DEBUG-LINE tell you which LINE in the COBOL PROGRAM caused the incorrect modification. The probable verb is MOVE and it must be in an obscure path otherwise the **production** PROGRAM would continually abend with this problem. Examine the module trace to determine how the PROGRAM got to the module containing the offending statement. This is usually sufficient to isolate the anomaly. Determine what the obscure path should be doing and make the corrections. Rerun to verify.

(b) COBOL II COBTEST commands

The generic procedures for DEBUGGING using COBTEST are the same as for using ANSI DEBUG. The difference is the syntax.

```
COBTEST program-name

TRACE ENTRY NAME PRINT

FLOW ON

LIST pointer-data-name BOTH PRINT

WHEN brek (key-data-name-x = invalid-key-value)    (FLOW
PRINT)

GO

DUMP or GO
```

(c) Quick fix

Infrequently the initial DEBUGGING procedures do not reveal the problem thereby requiring more analysis. Operational considerations may necessitate that the PROGRAM be run with the offending transactions being written to an ERROR REPORT for later correction. The operating system has provided the quick fix by not allowing the PROGRAM to REWRITE an incorrect DUPLICATE KEY. The installation FILE STATUS 22 routine should contain a WRITE installation ERROR REPORT before continuing.

2. WRITE

The WRITE of a DUPLICATE KEY is normally a data entry problem where data entry has assigned an incorrect VALUE. The PROGRAM should skip this RECORD after writing an installation standard ERROR REPORT.

RECORD LENGTH incorrect

ANSI FILE STATUS 04 [any READ]

A READ statement has been successfully executed but the RECORD LENGTH does not conform to its fixed FILE attributes. The fixed FILE attributes are established when the FILE is created and cannot be subsequently changed. These attributes include FILE ORGANIZATION, RECORD KEYs, CODESET, RECORD LENGTH, RECORD TYPE [fixed or variable], KEY COLLATING SEQUENCE, PADDING CHARACTER [an ALPHANUMERIC CHARACTER used to fill the unused CHARACTER POSITIONs in a physical RECORD], and RECORD DELIMITER [how the LENGTH of a VARIABLE LENGTH RECORD is determined].

COBOL 85 prevents a REWRITE or WRITE of a RECORD with an incorrect LENGTH. COBOL 74 does not define what to do with incorrect RECORD LENGTH and this FILE STATUS VALUE has been added to warn a PROGRAM of the anomaly.

If you suspect this problem then you must determine what your compiler does with incorrect RECORD LENGTH. You must write a test COBOL PROGRAM whose RECORD LENGTH differs from the FILE RECORD LENGTH of a TEST FILE. Compile, execute, and check the results. If the READ abends then follow the DEBUGGING steps below. If the READ does not abend and you still suspect this problem then you should do three separate TEST PROGRAM invocations with dumps to provide a damage assessment. The first invocation uses the correct RECORD LENGTH, the second uses a shorter RECORD LENGTH, and the third uses a greater RECORD LENGTH. The memory dumps provide you with the information on what your compiler does. For instance, does it READ in the large RECORD and overwrite, or does it only READ up to the RECORD LENGTH specified by the fixed FILE attributes. Continue with the DEBUGGING procedures starting in the next paragraph.

The problem has probably happened upstream. It can happen in this PROGRAM if the PROGRAM also does WRITE or REWRITE and the FILE ORGANIZATION IS INDEXED or RELATIVE and ACCESS MODE IS RANDOM or DYNAMIC and the FILE is OPEN I-O. The DEBUGGING steps are:

1.   Check the PROGRAM to determine if the incorrect RECORD could have been written by the PROGRAM.

        (a)   If yes then GO TO 2.
        (b)   If no then:

                (i)   Refer to a Job Step Diagram to determine the last previous PROGRAM that wrote the offending FILE.
                (ii)   GO TO 1.

2.   Determine the data-name containing the offending VALUE from the 01 data description in the PROGRAM. Use that data-name and offending VALUE as the target in either the ANSI DEBUG or COBTEST coding.

1. ANSI DEBUG

```
PROCEDURE DIVISION.

DECLARATIVES.

DEBUG SECTION.

    USE FOR DEBUGGING ON    target-data-name
                            ALL PROCEDURES.

DEBUG-PROGRAM-FLOW.

    DISPLAY         DEBUG-LINE
                    DEBUG-NAME
                    DEBUG-CONTENTS.

    DISPLAY UPON  mnemonic-name-1
                    DEBUG-LINE
                    DEBUG-NAME
                    DEBUG-CONTENTS.

DEBUG-BREAKPOINT.

    IF              DEBUG-NAME      =   target-data-name
    AND             DEBUG-CONTENTS  =   invalid-value
    THEN
        ACCEPT      breakpoint
        FROM        mnemonic-name-2
        IF          dump
        DIVIDE ZERO BY ZERO GIVING infinity
        END-IF
    END-IF

END DECLARATIVES.
```

The contents of DEBUG-LINE tell you which LINE in the COBOL PROGRAM caused the incorrect modification. The probable verb is MOVE and it must be in an obscure path otherwise the **production** PROGRAM would continually abend with this problem. Examine the module trace to determine how the PROGRAM got to the module containing the offending statement. This is usually sufficient to isolate the anomaly. Determine what the obscure path should be doing and make the corrections. Rerun to verify.

2. COBOL II COBTEST commands

The generic procedures for DEBUGGING using COBTEST are the same as for using ANSI DEBUG. The difference is the syntax.

```
COBTEST program-name

TRACE ENTRY NAME PRINT

FLOW ON

LIST pointer-data-name BOTH PRINT

WHEN brek (target-data-name = invalid-value)    (FLOW
PRINT)

GO

DUMP or GO
```

3. Quick fix

Infrequently the initial DEBUGGING procedures do not reveal the problem thereby requiring more analysis. Operational considerations may necessitate that the PROGRAM be run with the offending transactions being written to an ERROR REPORT for later correction. The quick fix is to insert the following defensive trap before each REWRITE or WRITE of the target RECORD.

```
IF              record-key   =   record-key-bad-value
   [WRITE installation standard ERROR REPORT]
END-IF
```

record-key is the KEY item used to READ the RECORD. It is derivable from the READ statement or the file-control-entry in the ENVIRONMENT DIVISION. record-key-bad-value is the KEY VALUE that caused the PROGRAM to invoke the obscure path. It is derivable from the dump. If the FILE is SEQUENTIAL and the PROGRAM does not contain a KEY item then determine which item is the FILE SORT KEY.

OPTIONAL FILE NOT present

ANSI FILE STATUS 05 [any OPEN]

An OPEN for a FILE specified as OPTIONAL in the SELECT clause of the FILE-CONTROL entry in the ENVIRONMENT DIVISION is not present. The OPEN has been successfully executed as indicated by the 0 first digit. This FILE STATUS is an informational warning that there is no INPUT FILE or that a FILE has been created if the OPEN was for I-O or EXTEND. Normally a FILE STATUS of 05 is okay and is not an anomaly. It could be a problem if the PROGRAM expects the OPTIONAL FILE to be present. If you suspect this problem then your only course of action is to analyze the PROGRAM.

Magnetic TAPE clause specified for non-reel UNIT

ANSI FILE STATUS 07 [SEQUENTIAL OPEN or CLOSE]

The first digit of 0 means successful completion of the OPEN or CLOSE but provides a warning that a magnetic TAPE phrase was used with a non-reel UNIT such as DASD (Direct Access Storage Device). The offending phrases are:

```
OPEN   NO REWIND.
CLOSE  NO REWIND, REEL/UNIT, FOR REMOVAL.
```

FILE STATUS 07 is probably caused by a maintenance programmer overlooking the TAPE clauses when modifying the PROGRAM to use DASD instead of TAPE. The compiler ignores the offending phrases and their inclusion has no effect on the PROGRAM execution.
It is recommended that the offending phrases be deleted to avoid this FILE STATUS.

NO NEXT logical RECORD exists

ANSI FILE STATUS 10 [any SEQUENTIAL READ]

A sequential READ can be performed by either the ANSI SEQUENTIAL, RELATIVE, or INDEXED modules. This is an AT END condition caused by an EOF (End Of File) or an attempt to READ an OPTIONAL INPUT FILE that is NOT present (see below).
You must determine from the FDUMP whether it is a true EOF or a nonexistent OPTIONAL FILE since the FILE STATUS does not provide that information.

1. EOF

An EOF signals EOJ (End Of Job) and is not an anomaly. The PROGRAM should begin EOJ processing. If it does not then you must analyze the PROGRAM.

2. READ of a nonexistent OPTIONAL FILE

This is similar to FILE STATUS 05 except that STATUS 05 must have been ignored by the OPEN. Subsequent attempts to READ this FILE will continue to cause FILE STATUS 10. An obscure path has been taken. It has to be an obscure path otherwise the **production** PROGRAM would be continually having this problem if it were a normal condition. Only a PROGRAM flow trace is required.

(a) ANSI DEBUG

```
PROCEDURE DIVISION.

DECLARATIVES.

DEBUG SECTION.
```

```
            USE FOR DEBUGGING ON    ALL PROCEDURES.

     DEBUG-PROGRAM-FLOW.

         DISPLAY       DEBUG-LINE
                       DEBUG-NAME
                       DEBUG-CONTENTS.

         DISPLAY UPON mnemonic-name-1
                       DEBUG-LINE
                       DEBUG-NAME
                       DEBUG-CONTENTS.

     END DECLARATIVES.
```

COBTEST is not required since COBOL II supports PROCEDURE tracing.

Examine the module trace to determine how the PROGRAM got to the module containing the offending statement. This is usually sufficient to isolate the anomaly. Determine what the obscure path should be doing and make the corrections. Rerun to verify.

(b) Quick fix

The operating system has provided the quick fix by informing the PROGRAM that there is NO NEXT RECORD. The installation FILE STATUS 10 routine should contain a WRITE installation ERROR REPORT before continuing.

RELATIVE RECORD NUMBER > RELATIVE KEY

ANSI FILE STATUS 14 [RELATIVE SEQUENTIAL READ]

The NUMBER of significant digits in the RELATIVE RECORD NUMBER > the FILE RELATIVE KEY data item. This is similar to DUPLICATE KEY and the DEBUGGING steps are also similar:

1. Determine the RELATIVE KEY data-name from the SELECT clause in the FILE-CONTROL entry in the ENVIRONMENT DIVISION.
2. Determine the offset of the RELATIVE KEY data-name.
3. Determine the abend VALUE of the RELATIVE KEY data-name from the FDUMP.

1. ANSI DEBUG

```
     PROCEDURE DIVISION.

     DECLARATIVES.

     DEBUG SECTION.
```

```
        USE FOR DEBUGGING ON    relative-key-data-name
                                ALL PROCEDURES.

DEBUG-PROGRAM-FLOW.

    DISPLAY         DEBUG-LINE
                    DEBUG-NAME
                    DEBUG-CONTENTS.

    DISPLAY UPON mnemonic-name-1
                    DEBUG-LINE
                    DEBUG-NAME
                    DEBUG-CONTENTS.

DEBUG-BREAKPOINT.

    IF              DEBUG-NAME       =    relative-key-data-
                                         name
    AND             DEBUG-CONTENTS   =    invalid-relative-key-
                                         value
        ACCEPT      breakpoint
        FROM        mnemonic-name-2
        IF          dump
        DIVIDE  ZERO BY ZERO GIVING infinity
        END-IF
    END-IF

END DECLARATIVES.
```

The contents of DEBUG-LINE tell you which LINE in the COBOL PROGRAM caused the incorrect modification. The probable verb is MOVE and it must be in an obscure path otherwise the **production** PROGRAM would continually abend with this problem. Examine the module trace to determine how the PROGRAM got to the module containing the offending statement. This is usually sufficient to isolate the anomaly. Determine what the obscure path should be doing and make the corrections. Rerun to verify.

2. COBOL II COBTEST commands

The generic procedures for DEBUGGING using COBTEST are the same as for using ANSI DEBUG. The difference is the syntax.

```
COBTEST program-name

TRACE ENTRY NAME PRINT

FLOW ON
```

```
LIST pointer-data-name BOTH PRINT

WHEN brek (relative-key-data-name =
invalid-relative-key-value)   (FLOW PRINT)

GO

DUMP or GO
```

3. Quick fix

The operating system has provided the quick fix by not allowing the PROGRAM to READ. The installation FILE STATUS 14 routine should contain a WRITE installation ERROR REPORT before continuing.

SEQUENCE ERROR

ANSI FILE STATUS 21 [INDEXED REWRITE]

This is an INVALID KEY condition caused when the PROGRAM attempts to REWRITE the last READ RECORD with a different primary KEY VALUE. This is similar to FILE STATUS 22 where the REWRITE would create an unacceptable DUPLICATE KEY. The DEBUGGING steps are also similar:

1. Determine the primary KEY data-name from the SELECT clause in the FILE-CONTROL entry in the ENVIRONMENT DIVISION.
2. Determine the offset of the primary KEY data-name.
3. Determine the abend VALUE of the primary KEY data-name from the FDUMP.

1. ANSI DEBUG

```
PROCEDURE DIVISION.

DECLARATIVES.

DEBUG SECTION.

   USE FOR DEBUGGING ON   primary-key-data-name
                          ALL PROCEDURES.

DEBUG-PROGRAM-FLOW.

   DISPLAY      DEBUG-LINE
                DEBUG-NAME
                DEBUG-CONTENTS.
```

```
DISPLAY UPON  mnemonic-name-1
                  DEBUG-LINE
                  DEBUG-NAME
                  DEBUG-CONTENTS.

DEBUG-BREAKPOINT.

    IF          DEBUG-NAME      =   primary-key-data-name
    AND         DEBUG-CONTENTS  =   invalid-key-value
        ACCEPT  breakpoint
        FROM    mnemonic-name-2
        IF      dump
            DIVIDE ZERO BY ZERO GIVING infinity
        END-IF
    END-IF

END DECLARATIVES.
```

The contents of DEBUG-LINE tell you which LINE in the COBOL PROGRAM caused the incorrect modification. The probable verb is MOVE and it must be in an obscure path otherwise the **production** PROGRAM would continually have this problem. Examine the module trace to determine how the PROGRAM got to the module containing the offending statement. This is usually sufficient to isolate the anomaly. Determine what the obscure path should be doing and make the corrections. Rerun to verify.

2. COBOL II COBTEST commands

The generic procedures for DEBUGGING using COBTEST are the same as for using ANSI DEBUG. The difference is the syntax.

```
COBTEST program-name

TRACE ENTRY NAME PRINT

FLOW ON

LIST primary-key-data-name BOTH PRINT

WHEN brek (primary-key-data-name = invalid-key-value)
    (FLOW PRINT)

GO

DUMP or GO
```

3. Quick fix

The operating system has provided the quick fix by not allowing the PROGRAM to REWRITE an incorrect primary KEY. The installation FILE STATUS 21 routine should contain a WRITE installation ERROR REPORT before continuing.

RECORD does NOT exist

ANSI FILE STATUS 23 [RELATIVE or INDEXED START or RANDOM READ]

This is an INVALID KEY condition caused by either attempting to access a RECORD that does not exist or accessing a nonexistent OPTIONAL FILE. You must determine from the FDUMP which condition caused the 23 since the FILE STATUS does not provide this information.

1. FILE present

The START or READ of a nonexistent RECORD is normally a data entry problem where data entry has assigned an incorrect VALUE. The PROGRAM should skip this transaction after writing an installation standard ERROR REPORT.

2. Nonexistent OPTIONAL FILE

This is probably an Operation's problem where a required OPTIONAL FILE was not mounted. Analyze the Operations Log to determine if this is the problem. If so, mount the OPTIONAL FILE and rerun.

This problem can also be an obscure path. If you suspect this problem then run a PROGRAM flow trace.

(a) ANSI DEBUG

```
PROCEDURE DIVISION.

DECLARATIVES.

DEBUG SECTION.

    USE FOR DEBUGGING ON    ALL PROCEDURES.

DEBUG-PROGRAM-FLOW.

    DISPLAY        DEBUG-LINE
                   DEBUG-NAME
                   DEBUG-CONTENTS.

    DISPLAY UPON  mnemonic-name-1
                   DEBUG-LINE
```

```
DEBUG-NAME
DEBUG-CONTENTS.
```

```
END DECLARATIVES.
```

COBTEST is not required since COBOL II supports PROCEDURE tracing.

Examine the module trace to determine how the PROGRAM got to the module containing the offending statement. This is usually sufficient to isolate the anomaly. Determine what the obscure path should be doing and make the corrections. Rerun to verify.

Boundary violation

ANSI FILE STATUS 24 [RELATIVE or INDEXED WRITE or RELATIVE
    SEQUENTIAL WRITE]
ANSI FILE STATUS 34 [SEQUENTIAL WRITE]
ANSI FILE STATUS 44 [any WRITE or REWRITE]

This is caused by a WRITE beyond the implementor's externally defined FILE boundaries or the RELATIVE RECORD NUMBER > magnitude of the RELATIVE KEY data-item (see "RELATIVE RECORD NUMBER > RELATIVE KEY") or RECORD LENGTH is different from the fixed FILE attributes (see "RECORD LENGTH incorrect"). You must determine from the FDUMP which condition caused the 24 since the FILE STATUS does not provide this information.

1. Boundary violation

You must determine from your compiler manual how it defines FILE external boundaries and how they can be violated. This will provide the basis for DEBUGGING. Modify the ANSI DEBUG module or COBTEST generic routine accordingly.

2. RELATIVE RECORD NUMBER incorrect

The NUMBER of significant digits in the RELATIVE RECORD NUMBER > the FILE RELATIVE KEY data item. This is similar to DUPLICATE KEY and the DEBUGGING steps are also similar:

1. Determine the RELATIVE KEY data-name from the SELECT clause in the FILE-CONTROL entry in the ENVIRONMENT DIVISION.
2. Determine the offset of the RELATIVE KEY data-name.
3. Determine the abend VALUE of the RELATIVE KEY data-name from the FDUMP.

(a) ANSI DEBUG

```
PROCEDURE DIVISION.
```

```
DECLARATIVES.
```

```
DEBUG SECTION.

    USE FOR DEBUGGING ON    relative-key-data-name
                            ALL PROCEDURES.

DEBUG-PROGRAM-FLOW.

    DISPLAY       DEBUG-LINE
                  DEBUG-NAME
                  DEBUG-CONTENTS.

    DISPLAY UPON  mnemonic-name-1
                  DEBUG-LINE
                  DEBUG-NAME
                  DEBUG-CONTENTS.

DEBUG-BREAKPOINT.

    IF            DEBUG-NAME       =    relative-key-data-
                                        name
    AND           DEBUG-CONTENTS   =    invalid-relative-key-
                                        value
        ACCEPT    breakpoint
        FROM      mnemonic-name-2
        IF        dump
            DIVIDE ZERO BY ZERO GIVING infinity
        END-IF
    END-IF

END DECLARATIVES.
```

The contents of DEBUG-LINE tell you which LINE in the COBOL PROGRAM caused the incorrect modification. The probable verb is MOVE and it must be in an obscure path otherwise the **production** PROGRAM would continually abend with this problem. Examine the module trace to determine how the PROGRAM got to the module containing the offending statement. This is usually sufficient to isolate the anomaly. Determine what the obscure path should be doing and make the corrections. Rerun to verify.

(b) *COBOL II COBTEST commands*

The generic procedures for DEBUGGING using COBTEST are the same as for using ANSI DEBUG. The difference is the syntax.

```
COBTEST program-name

TRACE ENTRY NAME PRINT
```

```
FLOW ON

LIST pointer-data-name BOTH PRINT

WHEN brek (relative-key-data-name =
invalid-relative-key-value)   (FLOW PRINT)

GO

DUMP or GO
```

(c) Quick fix

The operating system has provided the quick fix by not allowing the PROGRAM to WRITE. The installation FILE STATUS 24 routine should contain a WRITE installation ERROR REPORT before continuing.

3. RECORD LENGTH incorrect

A WRITE or REWRITE statement has been attempted with an incorrect RECORD LENGTH which does not conform to its fixed FILE attributes. The fixed FILE attributes are established when the FILE is created and cannot subsequently be changed. These attributes include FILE ORGANIZATION, RECORD KEYs, CODE-SET, RECORD LENGTH, RECORD TYPE [fixed or variable], KEY COLLATING SEQUENCE, PADDING CHARACTER [an ALPHANUMERIC CHARACTER used to fill the unused CHARACTER POSITIONs in a physical RECORD], and RECORD DELIMITER [how the LENGTH of a VARIABLE LENGTH RECORD is determined].

Determine the data-name containing the offending VALUE from the 01 data description in the PROGRAM. Use that data-name and offending VALUE as the target in either the ANSI DEBUG or COBTEST coding.

(a) ANSI DEBUG

```
PROCEDURE DIVISION.

DECLARATIVES.

DEBUG SECTION.

    USE FOR DEBUGGING ON   target-data-name
                           ALL PROCEDURES.

DEBUG-PROGRAM-FLOW.

    DISPLAY      DEBUG-LINE
                 DEBUG-NAME
                 DEBUG-CONTENTS.
```

```
        DISPLAY  UPON  mnemonic-name-1
                       DEBUG-LINE
                       DEBUG-NAME
                       DEBUG-CONTENTS.

    DEBUG-BREAKPOINT.

        IF              DEBUG-NAME       =    target-data-name
        AND             DEBUG-CONTENTS   =    invalid-value
            ACCEPT      breakpoint
            FROM        mnemonic-name-2
            IF          dump
                DIVIDE  ZERO  BY  ZERO  GIVING infinity
            END-IF
        END-IF

    END DECLARATIVES.
```

The contents of DEBUG-LINE tell you which LINE in the COBOL PROGRAM caused the incorrect modification. The probable verb is MOVE and it must be in an obscure path otherwise the production PROGRAM would continually abend with this problem. Examine the module trace to determine how the PROGRAM got to the module containing the offending statement. This is usually sufficient to isolate the anomaly. Determine what the obscure path should be doing and make the corrections. Rerun to verify.

(b) COBOL II COBTEST commands

The generic procedures for DEBUGGING using COBTEST are the same as for using ANSI DEBUG. The difference is the syntax.

```
    COBTEST program-name

    TRACE ENTRY NAME PRINT

    FLOW ON

    LIST pointer-data-name BOTH PRINT

    WHEN brek (target-data-name = invalid-value) (FLOW PRINT)

    GO

    DUMP or GO
```

(c) Quick fix

Infrequently the initial DEBUGGING procedures do not reveal the problem thereby requiring more analysis. Operational considerations may necessitate that the PROGRAM be run with the offending transactions being written to an ERROR REPORT for later correction. The quick fix is to bypass the transaction by writing out the installation standard ERROR REPORT. You need to insert the following IF statement after each READ statement for the FILE containing the RECORD that caused the obscure path to be taken.

```
IF  record-key   =   record-key-bad-value
    [WRITE installation standard ERROR REPORT]
END-IF
```

record-key is the KEY item used to READ the RECORD. It is derivable from the READ statement or the file-control-entry in the ENVIRONMENT DIVISION. record-key-bad-value is the KEY VALUE that caused the PROGRAM to invoke the obscure path. It is derivable from the dump. If the FILE is SEQUENTIAL and the PROGRAM does not contain a KEY item then determine which item is the FILE SORT KEY.

Permanent ERROR

ANSI FILE STATUS 30 [any I-O statement]

A permanent ERROR exists and the operating system is unable to supply any information as to its cause. A permanent ERROR is an anomaly that cannot be corrected by retry.

This FILE STATUS was probably caused by either a hardware failure or a software failure in the operating system access routines. Notify Operations and await their reply to retry.

Required FILE NOT present

ANSI FILE STATUS 35 [any OPEN statement except OPEN OUTPUT]

A required FILE [OPTIONAL phrase not specified in the SELECT clause of the FILE-CONTROL entry in the ENVIRONMENT DIVISION] is unavailable. This FILE STATUS was probably caused by Operations failing to mount the required media. Notify Operations and await their reply to retry.

The COBOL compiler creates a FILE if it is an OPEN OUTPUT and the FILE is unavailable.

OPEN MODE incorrect for FILE

ANSI FILE STATUS 37 [any OPEN statement]

An OPEN is attempted on a FILE which is required to be a mass storage FILE. A mass storage FILE is a medium which supports both SEQUENTIAL and RANDOM ACCESS MODEs. This is an improbable anomaly in a **production** PROGRAM otherwise the PROGRAM wouldn't function. It is possible that an obscure path has been taken which uses DASD when the PROGRAM has been converted to magnetic TAPE (also improbable). If you suspect this problem then run a PROGRAM flow trace:

1. ANSI DEBUG

```
PROCEDURE DIVISION.

DECLARATIVES.

DEBUG SECTION.

    USE FOR DEBUGGING ON    ALL PROCEDURES.

DEBUG-PROGRAM-FLOW.

    DISPLAY       DEBUG-LINE
                  DEBUG-NAME
                  DEBUG-CONTENTS.

    DISPLAY UPON  mnemonic-name-1
                  DEBUG-LINE
                  DEBUG-NAME
                  DEBUG-CONTENTS.

END DECLARATIVES.
```

COBTEST is not required since COBOL II supports PROCEDURE tracing.

Examine the module trace to determine how the PROGRAM got to the module containing the offending statement. This is usually sufficient to isolate the anomaly. Determine what the obscure path should be doing and make the corrections. Rerun to verify.

2. Quick fix

There is no quick fix. You will have to change the PROGRAM to use magnetic TAPE.

FILE LOCK

ANSI FILE STATUS 38 [any OPEN statement]

An OPEN statement has been attempted on a FILE CLOSE WITH LOCK during execution of the RUN UNIT. It is improbable that this problem happens in this PROGRAM. Look at all CLOSE statements for the offending FILE to see if any CLOSE WITH LOCK. If so, run a PROGRAM flow trace to see how the OPEN statement was reached.

If there is no CLOSE WITH LOCK for the FILE within the PROGRAM then the problem happened upstream. Refer to a Job Step Diagram to determine the last previous

PROGRAM that used the offending FILE. Look at all CLOSE statements for the offending FILE in that PROGRAM to see if there are any CLOSE WITH LOCK. If so, run a PROGRAM flow trace to see how the OPEN statement was reached.

If this PROGRAM does not have a CLOSE WITH LOCK then keep going back within the RUN UNIT until you find the PROGRAM. Run a PROGRAM flow trace.

1. ANSI DEBUG

```
PROCEDURE DIVISION.

DECLARATIVES.

DEBUG SECTION.

    USE FOR DEBUGGING ON    ALL PROCEDURES.

DEBUG-PROGRAM-FLOW.

    DISPLAY        DEBUG-LINE
                   DEBUG-NAME
                   DEBUG-CONTENTS.

    DISPLAY UPON  mnemonic-name-1
                   DEBUG-LINE
                   DEBUG-NAME
                   DEBUG-CONTENTS.

END DECLARATIVES.
```

COBTEST is not required since COBOL II supports PROCEDURE tracing.

Examine the module trace to determine how the PROGRAM got to the module containing the offending statement. This is usually sufficient to isolate the anomaly. Determine what the obscure path should be doing and make the corrections. Rerun to verify.

2. Quick Fix

The abend has provided the quick fix because it has removed the LOCK. Restart the run unit with the abended PROGRAM.

Conflict between FILE attributes

ANSI FILE STATUS 39 [any OPEN statement]

This is similar to "RECORD LENGTH incorrect" in that the OPEN conflicts with the fixed FILE attributes of ORGANIZATION, CODE SET, minimum and maximum RECORD LENGTH, RECORD TYPE, BLOCK factor, PADDING CHARACTER, and RECORD

DELIMITER. A major difference is that the READ is successful whereas the OPEN fails. This is an improbable anomaly in a **production** PROGRAM otherwise the PROGRAM wouldn't function. It is possible that an obscure path has been taken. If you suspect this problem then run a PROGRAM flow trace:

1. ANSI DEBUG

```
PROCEDURE DIVISION.

DECLARATIVES.

DEBUG SECTION.

    USE FOR DEBUGGING ON   ALL PROCEDURES.

DEBUG-PROGRAM-FLOW.

    DISPLAY       DEBUG-LINE
                  DEBUG-NAME
                  DEBUG-CONTENTS.

    DISPLAY UPON  mnemonic-name-1
                  DEBUG-LINE
                  DEBUG-NAME
                  DEBUG-CONTENTS.

END DECLARATIVES.
```

COBTEST is not required since COBOL II supports PROCEDURE tracing.

Examine the module trace to determine how the PROGRAM got to the module containing the offending statement. This is usually sufficient to isolate the anomaly. Determine what the obscure path should be doing and make the corrections. Rerun to verify.

2. Quick fix

There is no quick fix. You will have to change the PROGRAM to use the correct fixed FILE attributes.

FILE already OPEN

ANSI FILE STATUS 41 [any OPEN statement]

An OPEN statement is attempted for a FILE that is already OPEN. This is an improbable anomaly in a **production** PROGRAM otherwise the PROGRAM would not function. It is possible that an obscure path has been taken. If you suspect this problem then run a PROGRAM flow trace:

1. ANSI DEBUG

```
PROCEDURE DIVISION.

DECLARATIVES.

DEBUG SECTION.

    USE FOR DEBUGGING ON    ALL PROCEDURES.

DEBUG-PROGRAM-FLOW.

    DISPLAY        DEBUG-LINE
                   DEBUG-NAME
                   DEBUG-CONTENTS.

    DISPLAY UPON  mnemonic-name-1
                   DEBUG-LINE
                   DEBUG-NAME
                   DEBUG-CONTENTS.

END DECLARATIVES.
```

COBTEST is not required since COBOL II supports PROCEDURE tracing.

Examine the module trace to determine how the PROGRAM got to the module containing the offending statement. This is usually sufficient to isolate the anomaly. Determine what the obscure path should be doing and make the corrections. Rerun to verify.

2. Quick fix

There is no quick fix. You will have to change the PROGRAM to eliminate the second OPEN.

FILE NOT OPEN

ANSI FILE STATUS 42 [any CLOSE statement]

A CLOSE statement is attempted for a FILE NOT OPEN. This is an improbable anomaly in a **production** PROGRAM otherwise the PROGRAM would not function. It is possible that an obscure path has been taken. If you suspect this problem then run a PROGRAM flow trace:

1. ANSI DEBUG

```
PROCEDURE DIVISION.

DECLARATIVES.

DEBUG SECTION.
```

```
      USE FOR DEBUGGING ON    ALL PROCEDURES.

DEBUG-PROGRAM-FLOW.

    DISPLAY          DEBUG-LINE
                     DEBUG-NAME
                     DEBUG-CONTENTS.

    DISPLAY UPON  mnemonic-name-1
                     DEBUG-LINE
                     DEBUG-NAME
                     DEBUG-CONTENTS.

 END DECLARATIVES.
```

COBTEST is not required since COBOL II supports PROCEDURE tracing.

Examine the module trace to determine how the PROGRAM got to the module containing the offending statement. This is usually sufficient to isolate the anomaly. Determine what the obscure path should be doing and make the corrections. Rerun to verify.

2. Quick fix

There is no quick fix. You will have to change the PROGRAM to eliminate the unnecessary CLOSE.

Required READ NOT successfully executed

ANSI FILE STATUS 43 [RELATIVE or INDEXED DELETE for a mass storage FILE or any REWRITE for a mass storage FILE]

A DELETE or REWRITE to a mass storage FILE is done "in place." The REWRITE replaces the RECORD in the same physical location; a DELETE either makes the same physical location available for new RECORDS or sets a flag making the deleted RECORD unavailable for normal access depending on the implementor's implementation. In all cases, a READ of that RECORD has to have been successfully executed prior to the DELETE or REWRITE. This was probably caused by failing to TEST the FILE STATUS for the required READ. Use a KWIC search to find the required READ (if you do not find a READ then an obscure path has been taken and you need to do a PROGRAM trace as illustrated below).

Determine if the required READ TESTs for all possible FILE STATUS. If so then the problem is an obscure path which requires a PROGRAM trace as illustrated below.

If the PROGRAM does not TEST for all possible FILE STATUS then correct and restart the RUN UNIT from the abended PROGRAM.

1. ANSI DEBUG

```
PROCEDURE DIVISION.
```

```
DECLARATIVES.

DEBUG SECTION.

    USE FOR DEBUGGING ON    ALL PROCEDURES.

DEBUG-PROGRAM-FLOW.

    DISPLAY        DEBUG-LINE
                   DEBUG-NAME
                   DEBUG-CONTENTS.

    DISPLAY UPON  mnemonic-name-1
                   DEBUG-LINE
                   DEBUG-NAME
                   DEBUG-CONTENTS.

    END DECLARATIVES.
```

COBTEST is not required since COBOL II supports PROCEDURE tracing.

Examine the module trace to determine how the PROGRAM got to the module containing the offending statement. This is usually sufficient to isolate the anomaly. Determine what the obscure path should be doing and make the corrections. Rerun to verify.

2. Quick fix

The operating system has provided the quick fix by not allowing the PROGRAM to DELETE or REWRITE. The installation FILE STATUS 43 routine should contain a WRITE installation REPORT before continuing.

NO valid NEXT RECORD established

ANSI FILE STATUS 46 [Any SEQUENTIAL READ]

A SEQUENTIAL READ has been attempted but the FILE POSITION indicator has not been established or contains NO NEXT RECORD or AT END. This was probably caused by failing to TEST the FILE STATUS for a previous READ or START. Use a KWIC search to find the required READ or START (if you do not find a READ or START then an obscure path has been taken and you need to do a PROGRAM trace as illustrated below).

Determine if the required READ or START TESTs for all possible FILE STATUS. If so then the problem is an obscure path which requires a PROGRAM trace as illustrated below.

If the PROGRAM does not TEST for all possible FILE STATUS then correct and restart the run unit from the abended PROGRAM.

1. ANSI DEBUG

```
PROCEDURE DIVISION.

DECLARATIVES.

DEBUG SECTION.

    USE FOR DEBUGGING ON    ALL PROCEDURES.

DEBUG-PROGRAM-FLOW.

    DISPLAY        DEBUG-LINE
                   DEBUG-NAME
                   DEBUG-CONTENTS.

    DISPLAY UPON  mnemonic-name-1
                   DEBUG-LINE
                   DEBUG-NAME
                   DEBUG-CONTENTS.

END DECLARATIVES.
```

COBTEST is not required since COBOL II supports PROCEDURE tracing.

Examine the module trace to determine how the PROGRAM got to the module containing the offending statement. This is usually sufficient to isolate the anomaly. Determine what the obscure path should be doing and make the corrections. Rerun to verify.

2. Quick fix

The operating system has provided the quick fix by not allowing the PROGRAM to READ. The installation FILE STATUS 44 routine should contain a WRITE installation REPORT before continuing.

FILE NOT OPEN in INPUT or I-O MODE

ANSI FILE STATUS 47 [any READ or START]

A READ or START is attempted on a FILE NOT OPEN in INPUT or I-O MODE. This is an improbable anomaly in a **production** PROGRAM otherwise the PROGRAM would not function. It is possible that an obscure path has been taken. If you suspect this problem then run a PROGRAM flow trace:

1. ANSI DEBUG

```
PROCEDURE DIVISION.
```

```
DECLARATIVES.

DEBUG SECTION.

    USE FOR DEBUGGING ON    ALL PROCEDURES.

DEBUG-PROGRAM-FLOW.

    DISPLAY        DEBUG-LINE
                   DEBUG-NAME
                   DEBUG-CONTENTS.

    DISPLAY UPON  mnemonic-name-1
                   DEBUG-LINE
                   DEBUG-NAME
                   DEBUG-CONTENTS.

    END DECLARATIVES.
```

COBTEST is not required since COBOL II supports PROCEDURE tracing.

Examine the module trace to determine how the PROGRAM got to the module containing the offending statement. This is usually sufficient to isolate the anomaly. Determine what the obscure path should be doing and make the corrections. Rerun to verify.

2. Quick fix

There is no quick fix. You must insert the appropriate OPEN statement.

FILE NOT OPEN in OUTPUT or EXTEND MODE

ANSI FILE STATUS 48 [any WRITE]

A WRITE is attempted on a FILE NOT OPEN in OUTPUT or I-O MODE. This is an improbable anomaly in a **production** PROGRAM otherwise the PROGRAM would not function. It is possible that an obscure path has been taken. If you suspect this problem then run a PROGRAM flow trace:

1. ANSI DEBUG

```
    PROCEDURE DIVISION.

    DECLARATIVES.

    DEBUG SECTION.

        USE FOR DEBUGGING ON    ALL PROCEDURES.
```

```
DEBUG-PROGRAM-FLOW.

    DISPLAY         DEBUG-LINE
                    DEBUG-NAME
                    DEBUG-CONTENTS.

    DISPLAY UPON  mnemonic-name-1
                    DEBUG-LINE
                    DEBUG-NAME
                    DEBUG-CONTENTS.

END DECLARATIVES.
```

COBTEST is not required since COBOL II supports PROCEDURE tracing.

Examine the module trace to determine how the PROGRAM got to the module containing the offending statement. This is usually sufficient to isolate the anomaly. Determine what the obscure path should be doing and make the corrections. Rerun to verify.

2. Quick fix

There is no quick fix. You must insert the appropriate OPEN statement.

FILE NOT OPEN in I-O MODE

ANSI FILE STATUS 49 [RELATIVE or INDEXED DELETE or any REWRITE]

A RELATIVE or INDEXED DELETE or any REWRITE is attempted on a FILE NOT OPEN in I-O M0DE. This is an improbable anomaly in a **production** PROGRAM otherwise the PROGRAM wouldn't function. It is possible that an obscure path has been taken. If you suspect this problem then run a PROGRAM flow trace:

1. ANSI DEBUG

```
    PROCEDURE DIVISION.

    DECLARATIVES.

    DEBUG SECTION.

        USE FOR DEBUGGING ON    ALL PROCEDURES.

    DEBUG-PROGRAM-FLOW.

        DISPLAY         DEBUG-LINE
                        DEBUG-NAME
                        DEBUG-CONTENTS.
```

```
DISPLAY UPON  mnemonic-name-1
              DEBUG-LINE
              DEBUG-NAME
              DEBUG-CONTENTS.

END DECLARATIVES.
```

COBTEST is not required since COBOL II supports PROCEDURE tracing.

Examine the module trace to determine how the PROGRAM got to the module containing the offending statement. This is usually sufficient to isolate the anomaly. Determine what the obscure path should be doing and make the corrections. Rerun to verify.

2. Quick fix

There is no quick fix. You must insert the appropriate OPEN statement.

Implementor defined

ANSI FILE STATUS 9x

FILE STATUS VALUES of 90 through 99 are reserved for implementor defined anomalies. If you received this FILE STATUS then you must determine from your compiler manual what it means and modify the ANSI DEBUG or COBTEST routine accordingly.

INTER-PROGRAM

The inter-program verbs are CALL and CANCEL. A recursive CALL (PROGRAM A CALLs PROGRAM B which then attempts to CALL PROGRAM A) causes an abend. ON OVERFLOW or ON EXCEPTION defensive trap causes an abend. CANCEL causes an abend if it attempts to CANCEL an active PROGRAM (PROGRAM A CALLs PROGRAM B which CALLS PROGRAM C which tries to CANCEL PROGRAM B).

CALL

CALL is used by a PROGRAM [the calling PROGRAM] to invoke a subroutine (the called PROGRAM) to do a specific task such as checking if a DATE is valid. A CALL can be static or dynamic. A static CALL is compiled as part of the PROGRAM load module (executable object code created by the compiler). A dynamic CALL is compiled in its own separate load module and is connected to the RUN UNIT (see "Ending" for description of RUN UNIT) when invoked.

A CALL statement containing a variable program-name identifier is always dynamic. A CALL statement containing a literal program-name is static unless a compiler option makes it dynamic. For instance, COBOL II has a DYNAM option which makes all CALL statements within the PROGRAM being compiled dynamic.

1. Recursive CALL

You must establish the RUN UNIT CALL hierarchy. A RUN UNIT is one or more object PROGRAMs interacting together to do specific processing. A RUN UNIT is defined by JCL (Job Control Language) in the IBM world. The JCL runbook contains the names of all PROGRAMs directly invoked by JCL; it does not contain any callable PROGRAMs.

JCL is text and can be searched by using text editors such as ISPF. A KWIC (Key Word In Context) search on the JCL PGM keyword identifies each PROGRAM name within the JCL run unit. The named PROGRAMs are then searched for any CALL statements. The called PROGRAMs are then searched for CALL statements and so forth until all callable PROGRAMs are identified. All RUN UNIT PROGRAMs are prepared for DEBUGGING and run against the TEST FILES. The called PROGRAM was invoked by an obscure path otherwise this **production** RUN UNIT would fail continually with this anomaly.

In summary:

1. Identify RUN UNIT PROGRAM names by KWIC search on JCL PGM.
2. Identify each CALL statement within the RUN UNIT PROGRAMs.
3. Identify each CALL statement within each callable PROGRAM.

Note: Software such as Adpac PM/SS can generate the PROGRAM list created by 1, 2, and 3 with a simple command.

4. Prepare each RUN UNIT PROGRAM for DEBUGGING.
5. Run the RUN UNIT against the TEST FILES with a PROGRAM flow trace.

2. ANSI DEBUG

```
PROCEDURE DIVISION.

DECLARATIVES.

DEBUG SECTION.

    USE FOR DEBUGGING ON    ALL PROCEDURES.

DEBUG-PROGRAM-FLOW.

    DISPLAY        DEBUG-LINE
                   DEBUG-NAME
                   DEBUG-CONTENTS.

    DISPLAY UPON  mnemonic-name-1
                   DEBUG-LINE
                   DEBUG-NAME
                   DEBUG-CONTENTS.

END DECLARATIVES.
```

Only the ANSI DEBUG module is needed for PROGRAM flow trace. COBTEST is not required since PROCEDURE tracing is supported in COBOL II.

3. Quick fix

Infrequently the initial DEBUGGING procedures do not reveal the problem thereby requiring more analysis. Operational considerations may necessitate that the PROGRAM be run with the offending transactions being written to an ERROR REPORT for later correction. The quick fix is to bypass the transaction by writing out the installation standard ERROR REPORT. You need to insert the following IF statement after each READ statement for the FILE containing the RECORD that caused the obscure path to be taken.

```
IF              record-key    =  record-key-bad-value
    [WRITE installation standard ERROR REPORT]

END-IF
```

record-key is the KEY item used to READ the RECORD. It is derivable from the READ statement or the file-control-entry in the ENVIRONMENT DIVISION. record-key-bad-value is the KEY VALUE that caused the PROGRAM to invoke the obscure path. It is derivable from the dump. If the FILE is SEQUENTIAL and the PROGRAM does not contain a KEY item then determine which item is the FILE SORT KEY.

4. ON OVERFLOW or ON EXCEPTION

ANSI specifies that execution continues with the next statement if the called PROGRAM is not available and ON OVERFLOW or ON EXCEPTION phrase is not present. This ensures disaster since the called PROGRAM's function has not been done. The defensive trap of ON OVERFLOW or ON EXCEPTION must be included in all CALL statements (see Appendix A).

ON OVERFLOW TESTs only for the condition that there is insufficient memory to load a called PROGRAM. This is obsolescent since most mainframe computers have virtual storage (using DASD to extend the real memory) and there is always "enough memory." Burroughs and Hewlett Packard still have some computers that use "stack" architecture of a specific SIZE to hold PROGRAMs and a memory OVERFLOW is possible.

ON EXCEPTION TESTs for any condition including insufficient memory that makes the called PROGRAM unavailable.

Either OVERFLOW or EXCEPTION are operating system problems that must be resolved by system programmers. Inform them and await their reply to rerun.

CANCEL

CANCEL disconnects a dynamic called PROGRAM from the RUN UNIT.

1. CANCEL of an active PROGRAM

You must establish the RUN UNIT CALL hierarchy. A RUN UNIT is one or more object

PROGRAMs interacting together to do specific processing. A RUN UNIT is defined by JCL (Job Control Language) in the IBM world. The JCL runbook contains the names of all PROGRAMs directly invoked by JCL; it does not contain any callable PROGRAMs.

JCL is text and can be searched by using text editors such as ISPF. A KWIC (Key Word In Context) search on the JCL PGM keyword identifies each PROGRAM name within the JCL RUN UNIT. The named PROGRAMs are then searched for any CALL statements. The called PROGRAMs are then searched for CALL statements and so forth until all callable PROGRAMs are identified. All RUN UNIT PROGRAMs are prepared for DEBUGGING and run against the TEST FILES. The called PROGRAM was invoked by an obscure path otherwise this **production** RUN UNIT would fail continually with this anomaly.

In summary:

1. Identify RUN UNIT PROGRAM names by KWIC search on JCL PGM.
2. Identify each CALL statement within the RUN UNIT PROGRAMs.
3. Identify each CALL statement within each callable PROGRAM.

Note: Software such as Adpac PM/SS can generate the PROGRAM list created by 1, 2, and 3 with a simple command.

4. Prepare each RUN UNIT PROGRAM for DEBUGGING.
5. Run the RUN UNIT against the TEST FILEs with a PROGRAM flow trace.

(a) ANSI DEBUG

```
    PROCEDURE DIVISION.

    DECLARATIVES.

    DEBUG SECTION.

        USE FOR DEBUGGING ON   ALL PROCEDURES.

    DEBUG-PROGRAM-FLOW.

        DISPLAY        DEBUG-LINE
                       DEBUG-NAME
                       DEBUG-CONTENTS.

        DISPLAY UPON mnemonic-name-1
                       DEBUG-LINE
                       DEBUG-NAME
                       DEBUG-CONTENTS.

    END DECLARATIVES.
```

Only the ANSI DEBUG module is needed for PROGRAM flow trace. COBTEST is not required since PROCEDURE tracing is supported in COBOL II.

(b) Quick fix

Infrequently the initial DEBUGGING procedures do not reveal the problem thereby requiring more analysis. Operational considerations may necessitate that the PROGRAM be run with the offending transactions being written to an ERROR REPORT for later correction. The quick fix is to bypass the transaction by writing out the installation standard ERROR REPORT. You need to insert the following IF statement after each READ statement for the FILE containing the RECORD that caused the obscure path to be taken.

```
IF              record-key   =   record-key-bad-value
    [WRITE installation standard ERROR REPORT]
END-IF
```

record-key is the KEY item used to READ the RECORD. It is derivable from the READ statement or the file-control-entry in the ENVIRONMENT DIVISION. record-key-bad-value is the KEY VALUE that caused the PROGRAM to invoke the obscure path. It is derivable from the dump. If the FILE is SEQUENTIAL and the PROGRAM does not contain a KEY item then determine which item is the FILE SORT KEY.

2. CANCEL of an unconnected PROGRAM

ANSI specifies that a CANCEL of an unconnected called PROGRAM is a null instruction with execution continuing with the next statement. The unexecuted CANCEL statement has no effect on the PROGRAM flow but should raise a warning. Why did the programmer code a CANCEL if there is no called PROGRAM to disconnect? The probable answer is that the CANCEL is in an obscure path which was left unmodified when a PROGRAM change eliminated the need for the called PROGRAM. If you suspect this problem then run a PROGRAM flow trace:

(a) ANSI DEBUG

```
    PROCEDURE DIVISION.

    DECLARATIVES.

    DEBUG SECTION.

        USE FOR DEBUGGING ON    ALL PROCEDURES.

    DEBUG-PROGRAM-FLOW.

        DISPLAY         DEBUG-LINE
                        DEBUG-NAME
                        DEBUG-CONTENTS.
```

```
         DISPLAY UPON mnemonic-name-1
                     DEBUG-LINE
                     DEBUG-NAME
                     DEBUG-CONTENTS.

     END DECLARATIVES.
```

COBTEST is not required since COBOL II supports PROCEDURE tracing.

Examine the module trace to determine how the PROGRAM got to the module containing the offending statement. This is usually sufficient to isolate the anomaly. Determine what the obscure path should be doing and make the corrections. Rerun to verify.

(b) Quick fix

The compiler has provided the quick fix by treating the unconnected CANCEL as a NOP (No OPeration).

USING

The USING phrase permits items in the calling PROGRAM to be used by the called PROGRAM via the LINKAGE SECTION. Data is aligned positionally from the CALL USING phrase to the called PROGRAM PROCEDURE DIVISION phrase. If the CALL USING is a, b, c and the PROCEDURE DIVISION phrase is x, y, z then the VALUE of a is available in the called PROGRAM as x, b as y, and c as z. Three problems exist:

1.   the NUMBER of USING identifiers differ
2.   one or more PIC clauses differ
3.   the total storage LENGTH between the USING phrases differ.

1. NUMBER of USING identifiers differ

An abend occurs if the NUMBER of USING identifiers differ. This must be an obscure path otherwise the **production** PROGRAM would continually abend with this problem. Run a PROGRAM flow trace:

(a) ANSI DEBUG

```
     PROCEDURE DIVISION.

     DECLARATIVES.

     DEBUG SECTION.

         USE FOR DEBUGGING ON   ALL PROCEDURES.

     DEBUG-PROGRAM-FLOW.

         DISPLAY       DEBUG-LINE
```

```
                    DEBUG-NAME
                    DEBUG-CONTENTS.

    DISPLAY UPON  mnemonic-name-1
                    DEBUG-LINE
                    DEBUG-NAME
                    DEBUG-CONTENTS.
```

```
END DECLARATIVES.
```

COBTEST is not required since COBOL II supports PROCEDURE tracing.

Examine the module trace to determine how the PROGRAM got to the module containing the offending statement. This is usually sufficient to isolate the anomaly. Determine what the obscure path should be doing and make the corrections. Rerun to verify.

(b) Quick fix

Infrequently the initial DEBUGGING procedures do not reveal the problem thereby requiring more analysis. Operational considerations may necessitate that the PROGRAM be run with the offending transactions being written to an ERROR REPORT for later correction. The quick fix is to bypass the transaction by writing out the installation standard ERROR REPORT. You need to insert the following IF statement after each READ statement for the FILE containing the RECORD that caused the obscure path to be taken.

```
    IF            record-key    =   record-key-bad-value
        [WRITE installation standard ERROR REPORT]
    END-IF
```

record-key is the KEY item used to READ the RECORD. It is derivable from the READ statement or the file-control-entry in the ENVIRONMENT DIVISION. record-key-bad-value is the KEY VALUE that caused the PROGRAM to invoke the obscure path. It is derivable from the dump. If the FILE is SEQUENTIAL and the PROGRAM does not contain a KEY item then determine which item is the FILE SORT KEY.

2. · PIC clauses differ

ANSI does **not** require the PIC clauses to be the same, thereby allowing compiler conversions between different PIC formats. If an **Incompatible PIC clause** or an overlapping item is discovered then the calling PROGRAM must have executed an obscure path otherwise the **production** PROGRAM would continually have this problem. The obscure path was probably not modified when the called PROGRAM PIC clause was changed. Use a PROGRAM flow trace to isolate the obscure path:

(a) ANSI DEBUG

```
    PROCEDURE DIVISION.
```

```
DECLARATIVES.

DEBUG SECTION.

    USE FOR DEBUGGING ON    ALL PROCEDURES.

DEBUG-PROGRAM-FLOW.

    DISPLAY        DEBUG-LINE
                   DEBUG-NAME
                   DEBUG-CONTENTS.

    DISPLAY UPON  mnemonic-name-1
                   DEBUG-LINE
                   DEBUG-NAME
                   DEBUG-CONTENTS.

END DECLARATIVES.
```

COBTEST is not required since COBOL II supports PROCEDURE tracing.

Examine the module trace to determine how the PROGRAM got to the module containing the offending statement. This is usually sufficient to isolate the anomaly. Determine what the obscure path should be doing and make the corrections. Rerun to verify.

(b) Quick fix

Infrequently the initial DEBUGGING procedures do not reveal the problem thereby requiring more analysis. Operational considerations may necessitate that the PROGRAM be run with the offending transactions being written to an ERROR REPORT for later correction. The quick fix is to bypass the transaction by writing out the installation standard ERROR REPORT. You need to insert the following IF statement after each READ statement for the FILE containing the RECORD that caused the obscure path to be taken.

```
IF             record-key    =   record-key-bad-value
    [WRITE installation standard ERROR REPORT]
END-IF
```

record-key is the KEY item used to READ the RECORD. It is derivable from the READ statement or the file-control-entry in the ENVIRONMENT DIVISION. record-key-bad-value is the KEY VALUE that caused the PROGRAM to invoke the obscure path. It is derivable from the dump. If the FILE is SEQUENTIAL and the PROGRAM does not contain a KEY item then determine which item is the FILE SORT KEY.

3. Storage LENGTH differs

ANSI does **not** require that the actual storage LENGTH be the same. If the LENGTH is different then the called PROGRAM can cause data corruption in the calling PROGRAM if the USING was BY REFERENCE (BY REFERENCE passes the calling PROGRAM memory address for use by the called PROGRAM; BY CONTENT only passes the VALUE thereby protecting the calling PROGRAM memory). If you suspect this problem then do the following:

1. Calculate the actual storage LENGTH of each PIC clause including slack bytes [bytes inserted by the compiler to align items on word or half word boundaries] as noted in your compiler rules.
2. Determine where the discrepancy begins.
3. Prepare the called PROGRAM for a data trace on the USING identifiers that can be corrupted.

(a) ANSI DEBUG

```
WORKING-STORAGE SECTION.

D      ?? using-identifier-a-ws      PIC ??
D      ?? using-identifier-?-ws      PIC ??
D      ?? using-identifier-z-ws      PIC ??
*this called program may corrupt data in the calling program
*by modifying the above items in the using clause; activate
*debugging mode to test
```

Note: The level numbers and the PIC clauses as represented by the ?? must be the same as their counterpart in the LINKAGE SECTION.

```
PROCEDURE DIVISION  USING  ...

DECLARATIVES.

DEBUG SECTION.

    USE FOR DEBUGGING ON    using-identifier-a
                            using-identifier-?
                            using-idnetifier-z
                            ALL PROCEDURES.

DEBUG-PROGRAM-FLOW.

    DISPLAY        DEBUG-LINE
                   DEBUG-NAME
                   DEBUG-CONTENTS.

    DISPLAY UPON mnemonic-name-1
                   DEBUG-LINE
```

```
                              DEBUG-NAME
                              DEBUG-CONTENTS.

      DEBUG-BREAKPOINT.

          IF              DEBUG-NAME    =    using-identifier-a
          OR              DEBUG-NAME    =    using-identifier-?
          OR              DEBUG-NAME    =    using-identifier-z
              DISPLAY     using-identifier-a-ws
                          using-identifier-?-ws
                          using-identifier-z-ws
    *the ansi debug display shows the new values; the displays
    *above show the calling program value upon entry; analyze to
    *determine if the modification has caused data corruption
              ACCEPT      breakpoint
              FROM        mnemonic-name-2
              IF          dump
                  DIVIDE ZERO BY ZERO GIVING infinity
              END-IF
          END-IF

      END DECLARATIVES.
```

Note: In this specific case it is better to test all using-identifiers concurrently rather than singularly since the offending PROGRAM is a subprogram called by another PROGRAM. Singular testing requires multiple invocations of both PROGRAMs which can be tedious.

first paragraph or SECTION in the PROGRAM

```
    D MOVE               using-identifier-a
    D TO                 using-identifier-a-ws

    D MOVE               using-identifier-?
    D TO                 using-identifier-?-ws

    D MOVE               using-identifier-z
    D TO                 using-identifier-z-ws

    *the preceding moves preserve the calling program values
    *for future analysis
```

Note: If the called PROGRAM has multiple ENTRY points (IBM compiler verb that is not ANSI) then you must insert the preceding MOVE statements after every ENTRY point. If this is an odious task then use the HIGH VALUE equivalent coding used in COBTEST.

The contents of DEBUG-LINE tell you which LINE in the COBOL called PROGRAM caused the data corruption. The probable verb is MOVE and it must be in an obscure path otherwise the **production** PROGRAM would continually have this problem. Examine the module trace to determine how the PROGRAM got to the module containing the offending statement. This is usually sufficient to isolate the anomaly. Determine what the obscure path should be doing and make the corrections. Rerun to verify.

(b) *COBOL II COBTEST commands*

The generic procedures for DEBUGGING using COBTEST are the same as for using ANSI DEBUG. The difference is the syntax.

```
COBTEST program-name

TRACE ENTRY NAME PRINT

FLOW ON

LIST using-identifier-a:using-identifier-z BOTH PRINT
     *the : lists a range of identifiers

WHEN brek (using-identifier-a <> HIGH-VALUE)    (FLOW
PRINT)
WHEN brek (using-identifier-? <> HIGH-VALUE)    (FLOW
PRINT)
WHEN brek (using-identifier-z <> HIGH-VALUE)    (FLOW
PRINT)
*high-value is used to force a break

GO

DUMP or GO
```

(c) *Quick fix*

Infrequently the initial DEBUGGING procedures do not reveal the problem thereby requiring more analysis. Operational considerations may necessitate that the PROGRAM be run with the offending transactions being written to an ERROR REPORT for later correction. The quick fix is to bypass the transaction by writing out the installation standard ERROR REPORT. You need to insert the following IF statement after each READ statement for the FILE containing the RECORD that caused the obscure path to be taken.

```
IF              record-key   =   record-key-bad-value
     [WRITE installation standard ERROR REPORT]
END-IF
```

record-key is the KEY item used to READ the RECORD. It is derivable from the READ statement or the file-control-entry in the ENVIRONMENT DIVISION. record-key-bad-value is the KEY VALUE that caused the PROGRAM to invoke the obscure path. It is derivable from the dump. If the FILE is SEQUENTIAL and the PROGRAM does not contain a KEY item then determine which item is the FILE SORT KEY.

ORDERING

The ordering verbs are MERGE, RELEASE, RETURN, and SORT. The SORT-MERGE Module is rarely used and is not discussed in detail. Some old COBOL PROGRAMs do use SORT and MERGE. It is recommended that these PROGRAMs be replaced by more efficient external SORTs and MERGEs. COBOL II Release 3 does have a fast SURT.

MERGE, RELEASE, and SORT do not have any defensive traps. Any abends on these verbs are usually equivalent to INPUT-OUTPUT abends and should be processed accordingly.

RETURN does have an AT END defensive trap which is equivalent to the READ AT END and signifies EOJ. EOJ should not be an anomaly in a **production** PROGRAM.

PROCEDURE BRANCHING

The PROCEDURE branching verbs are ALTER, CONTINUE, EXIT, GO TO, and PERFORM. There are also the COBOL concepts of fall through and transfer of control. The abends are unaltered GO TO., fall through from the last physical PROGRAM statement, and memory boundary violation. Runaway code is abended by defensive traps (see "Passive defensive programming and Active defensive programming").

ALTER

The execution of an ALTER statement does not cause a branch but changes the target GO TO statement to PROCEED TO a different procedure-name at run time. The GO TO statement must exist otherwise the compiler issues an unrecoverable ERROR warning and does not compile the object code.

1. unaltered GO TO.
GO TO. is a syntactically correct COBOL sentence. The compiler assumes that an ALTER will modify the GO TO. during execution. Some compilers issue an unrecoverable ERROR warning if there is no ALTER for the GO TO.. The PROGRAM abends if it attempts to execute an unaltered GO TO.. Either the ALTER or the GO TO. or both are in obscure paths otherwise the **production** PROGRAM would continually abend with this anomaly. The two questions are:

1.   How did the PROGRAM get to the unaltered GO TO. sentence?
2.   Which ALTER statements can ALTER that GO TO.?

(a) Unaltered GO TO sentence

The answer to question 1 is a **PROGRAM** flow trace:

```
PROCEDURE DIVISION.

DECLARATIVES.

DEBUG SECTION.

    USE FOR DEBUGGING ON    ALL PROCEDURES.

DEBUG-PROGRAM-FLOW.

    DISPLAY         DEBUG-LINE
                    DEBUG-NAME
                    DEBUG-CONTENTS.

    DISPLAY UPON mnemonic-name-1
                    DEBUG-LINE
                    DEBUG-NAME
                    DEBUG-CONTENTS.

END DECLARATIVES.
```

COBTEST is not required since COBOL II supports PROCEDURE tracing.

(b) No modifying ALTER statements

The compiler xref [cross-reference] REPORT should supply the answer to question 2. If there are no ALTER statements for the target GO TO. then you have identified your problem — the GO TO. is in an obscure path and the ALTER was in code that was eliminated. Use your editor to do a KWIC search on ALTER to determine if the target ALTER is in deadcode that has been "commented out."

(c) Quick fix

If the KWIC succeeds then your quick fix is to modify the abended GO TO. to GO TO the procedure-name specified by the "dead" ALTER.

If the KWIC fails then you are stuck. The quick fix is to bypass the transaction by writing out the installation standard ERROR REPORT. You need to insert the following IF statement after each READ statement for the FILE containing the RECORD that caused the obscure path to be taken.

```
IF              record-key   =   record-key-bad-value
    [WRITE installation standard ERROR REPORT]
END-IF
```

record-key is the KEY item used to READ the RECORD. It is derivable from the READ statement or the file-control-entry in the ENVIRONMENT DIVISION. record-key-bad-value is the KEY VALUE that caused the PROGRAM to invoke the obscure path. It is derivable from the dump. If the FILE is SEQUENTIAL and the PROGRAM does not contain a KEY item then determine which item is the FILE SORT KEY.

Analysis must be done to determine what should be happening. A possible information source is previous source listings if they are still available.

(d) One modifying ALTER statement

The xref REPORT shows only one ALTER that can modify the abended GO TO sentence. This ALTER is probably in deadcode that can no longer be invoked by the PROGRAM. You should run a deadcode analyzer (Inspector, Via Insight, etc.) if your organization has such tools to verify.

(e) Quick fix

Modify the GO TO. to GO TO the procedure-name specified by the ALTER statement.

(f) Multiple modifying ALTER statements

The normal case is multiple ALTERs. It is difficult to determine manually how any specific ALTER can be reached. Inspector and other analyzers can provide you with the pathways for analysis. However, this does not solve the abend. The only possibility is to use the techniques described in Chapter 8.

(g) Quick fix

Infrequently the initial DEBUGGING procedures do not reveal the problem thereby requiring more analysis. Operational considerations may necessitate that the PROGRAM be run with the offending transactions being written to an ERROR REPORT for later correction. The quick fix is to bypass the transaction by writing out the installation standard ERROR REPORT. You need to insert the following IF statement after each READ statement for the FILE containing the RECORD that caused the obscure path to be taken.

```
IF              record-key    =    record-key-bad-value
    [WRITE installation standard ERROR REPORT]
END-IF
```

record-key is the KEY item used to READ the RECORD. It is derivable from the READ statement or the file-control-entry in the ENVIRONMENT DIVISION. record-key-bad-value is the KEY VALUE that caused the PROGRAM to invoke the obscure path. It is derivable from the dump. If the FILE is SEQUENTIAL and the PROGRAM does not contain a KEY item then determine which item the FILE SORT KEY.

CONTINUE

CONTINUE should not cause an abend since it is a NOP [No OPeration] which falls through to the next executable statement. It is usually used as a substitute for a dummy GO TO:

```
PARAGRAPH-A.

    . . .

    GO  TO          PARAGRAPH-B
*go to is a dummy and can be replaced by continue

PARAGRAPH-B.
```

Either the dummy GO TO or CONTINUE is used to eliminate fall through which is treated as unstructured coding by many software metric rating PROGRAMs. The metric PROGRAMs usually severely demerit unstructured coding.

CONTINUE can cause an abend if it is the last physical PROGRAM statement **and** the compiler does not insert an EXIT PROGRAM as required by COBOL 85. See **fall through** next for DEBUGGING steps.

fall through

Fall through is the normal PROGRAM operation and is an implicit transfer of control from the previous sequential statement to the next sequential statement. It can only cause an abend if there is no next explicit or implicit sequential statement. Run a PROGRAM flow trace if this is the problem:

1. ANSI DEBUG

```
PROCEDURE DIVISION.

DECLARATIVES.

DEBUG SECTION.

    USE FOR DEBUGGING ON    ALL PROCEDURES.

DEBUG-PROGRAM-FLOW.

    DISPLAY       DEBUG-LINE
                  DEBUG-NAME
                  DEBUG-CONTENTS.

    DISPLAY UPON  mnemonic-name-1
                  DEBUG-LINE
                  DEBUG-NAME
                  DEBUG-CONTENTS.

END DECLARATIVES.
```

COBTEST is not required since COBOL II supports PROCEDURE tracing.

Examine the module trace to determine how the PROGRAM got to the module containing the last physical statement. This is usually sufficient to isolate the anomaly. Determine what the obscure path should be doing and make the corrections. Rerun to verify.

2. Quick fix

An EXIT PROGRAM does not help since that causes a normal EOJ which also "abends" the PROGRAM. The quick fix is to bypass the transaction by writing out the installation standard ERROR REPORT. You need to insert the following IF statement after each READ statement for the FILE containing the RECORD that caused the obscure path to be taken.

```
IF             record-key   =   record-key-bad-value
    [WRITE installation standard ERROR REPORT]
END-IF
```

record-key is the KEY item used to READ the RECORD. It is derivable from the READ statement or the file-control-entry in the ENVIRONMENT DIVISION. record-key-bad-value is the KEY VALUE that caused the PROGRAM to invoke the obscure path. It is derivable from the dump. If the FILE is SEQUENTIAL and the PROGRAM does not contain a KEY item then determine which item is the FILE SORT KEY.

EXIT

EXIT is a NOP which provides a common endpoint for a series of PROCEDURES. It falls through to a compiler inserted transfer of control which if set returns control to the next executable statement following the invoking PERFORM. EXIT is discussed under "transfer of control".

GO TO

GO TO can cause two abends — being unaltered and timeout caused by an infinite program loop. Unaltered is discussed under ALTER. GO TO can also cause a runaway code defensive trap to be invoked which is discussed under "transfer of control". GO TO DEPENDING ON can cause runaway code if the identifier is out of bounds, or signed, or a fraction and there is no defensive trap (see "Active defensive programming").

1. Timeout

Network GO TOs [GO TO invokes a different physical module] can sometimes cause an infinite loop. Most mainframes have a PROGRAM duration limit and abend any PROGRAM that exceeds this limit. If you receive a timeout abend then analyze your JCL [Job Control Language] or equivalent to determine that sufficient cpu time was provided. If insufficient time is provided then ask the appropriate person for an increase. If sufficient time was provided then you probably have an infinite loop caused by invoking an obscure path otherwise the **production** PROGRAM would always have a timeout abend. If you suspect this problem then run a PROGRAM trace:

(a) ANSI DEBUG

```
PROCEDURE DIVISION.

DECLARATIVES.

DEBUG SECTION.

    USE FOR DEBUGGING ON ALL PROCEDURES.

DEBUG-PROGRAM-FLOW.

    DISPLAY        DEBUG-LINE
                   DEBUG-NAME
                   DEBUG-CONTENTS.

    DISPLAY UPON mnemonic-name-1
                   DEBUG-LINE
                   DEBUG-NAME
                   DEBUG-CONTENTS.

END DECLARATIVES.
```

COBTEST is not required since COBOL II supports PROCEDURE tracing.

Examine the module trace to determine the start of the loop. This is usually sufficient to isolate the anomaly. Determine what the obscure path should be doing and make the corrections. Rerun to verify.

(b) Quick fix

Infrequently the initial DEBUGGING procedures do not reveal the problem thereby requiring more analysis. Operational considerations may necessitate that the PROGRAM be run with the offending transactions being written to an ERROR REPORT for later correction. The quick fix is to bypass the transaction by writing out the installation standard ERROR REPORT. You need to insert the following IF statement after each READ statement for the FILE containing the RECORD that caused the obscure path to be taken.

```
IF             record-key   =   record-key-bad-value
    [WRITE installation standard ERROR REPORT]
END-IF
```

record-key is the KEY item used to READ the RECORD. It is derivable from the READ statement or the file-control-entry in the ENVIRONMENT DIVISION. record-key-bad-value is the KEY VALUE that caused the PROGRAM to invoke the obscure path. It is derivable from the dump. If the FILE is SEQUENTIAL and the PROGRAM does not contain a KEY item then determine which item is the FILE SORT KEY.

GO TO DEPENDING ON

Control passes to the next sequential statement if the GO TO DEPENDING ON identifier is signed, or a fraction, or its VALUE exceeds the NUMBER of procedure-names. If that next statement is not a defensive trap (see Appendix A) then runaway code is initiated. If you suspect this problem then run the following PROGRAM trace:

1. ANSI DEBUG

```
PROCEDURE DIVISION.

DECLARATIVES.

DEBUG SECTION.

    USE FOR DEBUGGING ON     module-name-containing-goto
                             module-name-next

DEBUG-PROGRAM-FLOW.

    DISPLAY       DEBUG-LINE
                  DEBUG-NAME
                  DEBUG-CONTENTS.

    DISPLAY UPON  mnemonic-name-1
                  DEBUG-LINE
                  DEBUG-NAME
                  DEBUG-CONTENTS.

END DECLARATIVES.
```

module-name-containing-goto is the paragraph or SECTION name where the GO TO DEPENDING ON is located. module-name-next is the next sequential paragraph or SECTION that follows. If that module is included within the GO TO DEPENDING ON then you must insert a dummy paragraph name following the GO TO DEPENDING ON:

```
    GO TO         procedure-name-1
                  procedure-name-2
                  . . .
    DEPENDING ON
                  identifier-1
                  identifier-2
                  . . .

PARAGRAPH-RUNAWAY
    CONTINUE or dummy GO TO next module
```

COBTEST is not required since COBOL II supports PROCEDURE tracing.

Examine the module trace to determine if the next module has been invoked following the GO TO DEPENDING ON. If so then you have isolated the anomaly. Determine what the obscure path should be doing and make the corrections. Rerun to verify.

2. Quick fix

Infrequently the initial DEBUGGING procedures do not reveal the problem thereby requiring more analysis. Operational considerations may necessitate that the PROGRAM be run with the offending transactions being written to an ERROR REPORT for later correction. The quick fix is to bypass the transaction by writing out the installation standard ERROR REPORT. You need to insert the following IF statement after each READ statement for the FILE containing the RECORD that caused the obscure path to be taken.

```
IF            record-key   =   record-key-bad-value
     [WRITE installation standard ERROR REPORT]
END-IF
```

record-key is the KEY item used to READ the RECORD. It is derivable from the READ statement or the file-control-entry in the ENVIRONMENT DIVISION. record-key-bad-value is the KEY VALUE that caused the PROGRAM to invoke the obscure path. It is derivable from the dump. If the FILE is SEQUENTIAL and the PROGRAM does not contain a KEY item then determine which item is the FILE SORT KEY.

PERFORM

PERFORM VARYING can cause a memory boundary violation by a runaway INDEX or subscript. Some compilers, such as Univac COBOL, abend if the INDEX or subscript > TABLE SIZE. Some compilers (e.g. COBOL II) provide a compiler option to insert the defensive trap (SSRANGE). Incorrect PERFORM INDEX or subscript setting can also cause incorrect results and are discussed in this section.

1. PERFORM VARYING TABLE boundary violation

PERFORM VARYING is usually used to SEARCH a table — often a multidimensional table (COBOL 85 allows seven dimensions). PERFORM VARYING differs from SEARCH in that PERFORM VARYING is not terminated by the TABLE END but by satisfying the UNTIL condition. If the UNTIL condition is incorrectly SET then the PROGRAM may suffer corruption. If the UNTIL condition is SET to something like HIGH-VALUES then the PROGRAM will probably cause a memory boundary violation abend by trying to go past its assigned boundary.

The best way to defensively trap this anomaly is a compiler option such as SSRANGE. SSRANGE can be used in a DEBUGGING mode to minimize PROGRAM performance degradation of the trap always being tested while in production.

If a compiler option is not available or you wish to trace how the incorrect VALUE was inserted into the INDEX or subscript then do the following trace:

(a) ANSI DEBUG

```
PROCEDURE DIVISION

DECLARATIVES.

DEBUG SECTION.

    USE FOR DEBUGGING ON    until-identifier-a
                            until-identifier-?
                            until-identifier-z
                            ALL PROCEDURES.
*each until index or subscript in the perform varying must be
*traced

DEBUG-PROGRAM-FLOW.

    DISPLAY       DEBUG-LINE
                  DEBUG-NAME
                  DEBUG-CONTENTS.

    DISPLAY UPON  mnemonic-name-1
                  DEBUG-LINE
                  DEBUG-NAME
                  DEBUG-CONTENTS.

  DEBUG-BREAKPOINT.

    IF            DEBUG-CONTENTS   >   occurs-a
    OR            DEBUG-CONTENTS   >   occurs-?
    OR            DEBUG-CONTENTS   >   occurs-z
*the table occurs clause defines each table dimension
        DISPLAY   until-identifier-a
                  until-identifier-?
                  until-identifier-z
        ACCEPT    breakpoint
        FROM      mnemonic-name-2
        IF        dump
            DIVIDE ZERO BY ZERO GIVING infinity
        END-IF
    END-IF

END DECLARATIVES.
```

DEBUG-CONTENTS provide the incorrect VALUES for the indices or subscripts within the UNTIL conditions. The probable verb is MOVE or SET and it must be in an obscure path otherwise the **production** PROGRAM would continually have this problem.

Examine the module trace to determine how the PROGRAM got to the module containing the offending statement. This is usually sufficient to isolate the anomaly. Determine what the obscure path should be doing and make the corrections. Rerun to verify.

(b) COBOL II COBTEST commands

The generic procedures for DEBUGGING using COBTEST are the same as for using ANSI DEBUG. The difference is the syntax.

```
COBTEST program-name

TRACE ENTRY NAME PRINT

FLOW ON

LIST until-identifier-a:until-identifier-z BOTH PRINT
    *the : lists a range of identifiers

WHEN brek (until-identifier-a > occurs-a)    (FLOW PRINT)
WHEN brek (until-identifier-? > occurs-?)    (FLOW PRINT)
WHEN brek (until-identifier-z > occurs-z)    (FLOW PRINT)

GO

DUMP or GO
```

(c) Quick fix

Infrequently the initial DEBUGGING procedures do not reveal the problem thereby requiring more analysis. Operational considerations may necessitate that the PROGRAM be run with the offending transactions being written to an ERROR REPORT for later correction. The quick fix is to bypass the transaction by writing out the installation standard ERROR REPORT. You need to insert the following IF statement after each READ statement for the FILE containing the RECORD that caused the obscure path to be taken.

```
IF          record-key   =   record-key-bad-value
    [WRITE installation standard ERROR REPORT]
END-IF
```

record-key is the KEY item used to READ the RECORD. It is derivable from the READ statement or the file-control-entry in the ENVIRONMENT DIVISION. record-key-bad-value is the KEY VALUE that caused the PROGRAM to invoke the obscure path. It is derivable from the dump. If the FILE is SEQUENTIAL and the PROGRAM does not contain a KEY item then determine which item is the FILE SORT KEY.

2. PERFORM VARYING FROM

If the FROM item is not a literal such as 1 then the possibility exists that the INDEX or subscript has been incorrectly SET to start somewhere inside the TABLE rather than at the TABLE beginning. If you suspect this problem then run a data trace:

(a) ANSI DEBUG

```
PROCEDURE DIVISION

DECLARATIVES.

DEBUG SECTION.

    USE FOR DEBUGGING ON     until-identifier-a
                             until-identifier-?
                             until-identifier-z
                             ALL PROCEDURES.
*each until index or subscript in the perform varying must be
*traced

DEBUG-PROGRAM-FLOW.

    DISPLAY        DEBUG-LINE
                   DEBUG-NAME
                   DEBUG-CONTENTS.

    DISPLAY UPON mnemonic-name-1
                   DEBUG-LINE
                   DEBUG-NAME
                   DEBUG-CONTENTS.

DEBUG-BREAKPOINT.

    IF             DEBUG-CONTENTS   >   1
        DISPLAY    until-identifier-a
                   until-identifier-?
                   until-identifier-z
        ACCEPT     breakpoint
        FROM       mnemonic-name-2
        IF         dump
            DIVIDE ZERO BY ZERO GIVING infinity
        END-IF
    END-IF

END DECLARATIVES.
```

DEBUG-CONTENTS provide the incorrect VALUES for the indices or subscripts within the UNTIL conditions. The probable verb is MOVE or SET and it must be in an obscure path otherwise the **production** PROGRAM would continually have this problem.

Examine the module trace to determine how the PROGRAM got to the module containing the offending statement. This is usually sufficient to isolate the anomaly. Determine what the obscure path should be doing and make the corrections. Rerun to verify.

(b) COBOL II COBTEST commands

The generic procedures for DEBUGGING using COBTEST are the same as for using ANSI DEBUG. The difference is the syntax.

```
COBTEST program-name

TRACE ENTRY NAME PRINT

FLOW ON

LIST until-identifier-a:until-identifier-z BOTH PRINT
     *the : lists a range of identifiers

WHEN brek (until-identifier-a < 1)        (FLOW PRINT)
WHEN brek (until-identifier-? > table-length) (FLOW PRINT)
WHEN brek (until-identifier-z > table-length) (FLOW PRINT)

   GO

   DUMP or GO
```

(c) Quick fix

Infrequently the initial DEBUGGING procedures do not reveal the problem thereby requiring more analysis. Operational considerations may necessitate that the PROGRAM be run with the offending transactions being written to an ERROR REPORT for later correction. The quick fix is to bypass the transaction by writing out the installation standard ERROR REPORT. You need to insert the following IF statement after each READ statement for the FILE containing the RECORD that caused the obscure path to be taken.

```
IF            record-key   =   record-key-bad-value
     [WRITE installation standard ERROR REPORT]
END-IF
```

record-key is the KEY item used to READ the RECORD. It is derivable from the READ statement or the file-control-entry in the ENVIRONMENT DIVISION. record-key-bad-value is the KEY VALUE that caused the PROGRAM to invoke the obscure path. It is derivable from the dump. If the FILE is SEQUENTIAL and the PROGRAM does not contain a KEY item then determine which item is the FILE SORT KEY.

3. PERFORM n TIMES

If the *n* item is not a literal then the possibility exists that the *n* item has been incorrectly

SET thereby invoking the performable module an incorrect NUMBER of times. If you suspect this problem then run a data trace:

(a) ANSI DEBUG

```
    PROCEDURE DIVISION

    DECLARATIVES.

    DEBUG SECTION.

        USE FOR DEBUGGING ON    n-identifier
                                ALL PROCEDURES.

    DEBUG-PROGRAM-FLOW.

        DISPLAY        DEBUG-LINE
                       DEBUG-NAME
                       DEBUG-CONTENTS.

        DISPLAY UPON  mnemonic-name-1
                       DEBUG-LINE
                       DEBUG-NAME
                       DEBUG-CONTENTS.

    DEBUG-BREAKPOINT.

        IF             DEBUG-CONTENTS    NOT =  valid-n-times
            ACCEPT     breakpoint
            FROM       mnemonic-name-2
            IF         dump
                DIVIDE ZERO BY ZERO GIVING infinity
            END-IF
        END-IF

    END DECLARATIVES.
```

DEBUG-CONTENTS provides the incorrect VALUE for the *n* item. The probable verb is MOVE and it must be in an obscure path otherwise the **production** PROGRAM would continually have this problem. Examine the module trace to determine how the PROGRAM got to the module containing the offending statement. This is usually sufficient to isolate the anomaly. Determine what the obscure path should be doing and make the corrections. Rerun to verify.

(b) COBOL II COBTEST commands

The generic procedures for DEBUGGING using COBTEST are the same as for using ANSI DEBUG. The difference is the syntax.

```
COBTEST program-name

TRACE ENTRY NAME PRINT

FLOW ON

LIST n-identifier    BOTH PRINT

WHEN brek (n-identifier NE valid-n-times)    (FLOW PRINT)

GO

DUMP or GO
```

(c) Quick fix

Infrequently the initial DEBUGGING procedures do not reveal the problem thereby requiring more analysis. Operational considerations may necessitate that the PROGRAM be run with the offending transactions being written to an ERROR REPORT for later correction. The quick fix is to bypass the transaction by writing out the installation standard ERROR REPORT. You need to insert the following IF statement after each READ statement for the FILE containing the RECORD that caused the obscure path to be taken.

```
IF           record-key   =   record-key-bad-value
    [WRITE installation standard ERROR REPORT]
END-IF
```

record-key is the KEY item used to READ the RECORD. It is derivable from the READ statement or the file-control-entry in the ENVIRONMENT DIVISION. record-key-bad-value is the KEY VALUE that caused the PROGRAM to invoke the obscure path. It is derivable from the dump. If the FILE is SEQUENTIAL and the PROGRAM does not contain a KEY item then determine which item is the FILE SORT KEY.

Transfer of control

Transfer of control is a COBOL concept that permits the PROGRAM to return control to the next executable statement of a control mechanism. PERFORM is a control mechanism and the implementation of the transfer of control is left to the compiler. For a complete discussion of transfer of control see "Passive defensive programming" and "Active defensive programming."

The improper invocation of transfer of control causes runaway code where the PROGRAM inadvertently executes code. This inadvertent execution may cause an abend but the abend will be difficult to debug. Sometimes, the PROGRAM continues to a normal EOJ with discovery not happening until a user discovers an erroneous REPORT.

The defensive traps discussed under "defensive programming" have caused an abend. Run a PROGRAM flow trace to determine what invocation path caused the abend:

1. ANSI DEBUG

```
PROCEDURE DIVISION.

DECLARATIVES.

DEBUG SECTION.

    USE FOR DEBUGGING ON    ALL PROCEDURES.

DEBUG-PROGRAM-FLOW.

    DISPLAY        DEBUG-LINE
                   DEBUG-NAME
                   DEBUG-CONTENTS.

    DISPLAY UPON mnemonic-name-1
                   DEBUG-LINE
                   DEBUG-NAME
                   DEBUG-CONTENTS.

END DECLARATIVES.
```

COBTEST is not required since COBOL II supports PROCEDURE tracing.

2. Quick fix

You must unravel the spaghetti. The quick fix is to bypass the transaction by writing out the installation standard ERROR REPORT. You need to insert the following IF statement after each READ statement for the FILE containing the RECORD that caused the obscure path to be taken.

```
IF            record-key    =    record-key-bad-value
    [WRITE installation standard ERROR REPORT]
END-IF
```

record-key is the KEY item used to READ the RECORD. It is derivable from the READ statement or the file-control-entry in the ENVIRONMENT DIVISION. record-key-bad-value is the KEY VALUE that caused the PROGRAM to invoke the obscure path. It is derivable from the dump. If the FILE is SEQUENTIAL and the PROGRAM does not contain a KEY item then determine which item is the FILE SORT KEY.

REFERENCE MODIFICATION

Reference modification is not a verb category but a new data addressing feature in COBOL 85. The general format is:

```
data-name (leftmost-character-position: [length])
```

The colon [:] informs the compiler that this is a reference modification and not a subscript.
For example:

```
02 data-name                PIC S9(9)V   VALUE 123456789.

MOVE data-name(3: 5) TO receiving-item would MOVE the digits
                                                34567.
MOVE data-name(2:)   TO receiving-item would MOVE the digits
                                                23456789.
MOVE data-name(6: 4) TO receiving-item would MOVE the digits
                                                6789.
```

leftmost-character-position must not be < 1 nor > the data-name LENGTH. leftmost-character-position plus LENGTH minus 1 must not exceed the data-name LENGTH. Most compilers abend if the reference modification is outside the data-name region. The DEBUGGING technique is a trace on nonliteral leftmost-character-position and LENGTH:

ANSI DEBUG

```
PROCEDURE DIVISION

DECLARATIVES.

DEBUG SECTION.

    USE FOR DEBUGGING ON    leftmost-character-position
                            length
                            ALL PROCEDURES.

DEBUG-PROGRAM-FLOW.

    DISPLAY     DEBUG-LINE
                DEBUG-NAME
                DEBUG-CONTENTS.

    DISPLAY UPON mnemonic-name-1
                DEBUG-LINE
                DEBUG-NAME
                DEBUG-CONTENTS.

 DEBUG-BREAKPOINT.

*bypass if leftmost-character-position is a literal
```

```
        IF              DEBUG-NAME     =    leftmost-character-
-                                           position
        AND             DEBUG-CONTENTS    <   1
        OR               >   data-name-length
*data-name-length is the number of spaceholders symbols in
*the pic clause
        DISPLAY    data-name-length
                   leftmost-character-position
                   length
        ACCEPT     breakpoint
        FROM       mnemonic-name-2
        IF         dump
           DIVIDE ZERO BY ZERO GIVING infinity
        END-IF
     END-IF

*bypass if length is a literal
     IF              DEBUG-NAME     =    length
        AND          DEBUG-CONTENTS
                     + leftmost-character-position
                     - 1
                     > data-name-length
*data-name-length is the number of spaceholders symbols in
*the pic clause
        DISPLAY    data-name-length
                   leftmost-character-position
                   length
        ACCEPT     breakpoint
        FROM       mnemonic-name-2
        IF         dump
           DIVIDE ZERO BY ZERO GIVING infinity
        END-IF
     END-IF

   END DECLARATIVES.
```

Note 1: If both leftmost-character-position and LENGTH are literals then you have a coding problem.

Note 2: If either leftmost-character-position or LENGTH are an arithmetic expression then you will need to insert the following statement before the use of arithmetic expression:

```
D    temp = arithmetic expression.
```

Use temp as the target name for DEBUG-NAME.

COBOL II COBTEST commands

The generic procedures for DEBUGGING using COBTEST are the same as for using ANSI
DEBUG. The difference is the syntax.

```
COBTEST program-name

TRACE ENTRY NAME PRINT

FLOW ON

LIST leftmost-character-position, length    BOTH PRINT

*bypass if leftmost-character-position is a literal
WHEN brek (leftmost-character-position < 1)
    (FLOW PRINT)
WHEN brek (leftmost-character-position > data-name-length)
    (FLOW PRINT)
*data-name-length is the number of spaceholders symbols in
*the pic clause
*bypass if length is a literal
WHEN brek (leftmost-character-position + length - 1
    > data-name-length)     (FLOW PRINT)
*data-name-length is the number of spaceholders symbols in
*the pic clause

GO

DUMP or GO
```

Note 1: If both leftmost-character-position and length are literals then you have a coding
problem.

Note 2: If either leftmost-character-position or length are an arithmetic expression then
you will need to insert the following statement before the use of arithmetic
expression:

```
D   temp = arithmetic expression.
```

Use temp as the target name for WHEN condition.

Quick fix

Infrequently the initial DEBUGGING procedures do not reveal the problem thereby
requiring more analysis. Operational considerations may necessitate that the PROGRAM
be run with the offending transactions being written to an ERROR REPORT for later

correction. The quick fix is to bypass the transaction by writing out the installation standard ERROR REPORT. You need to insert the following IF statement after each READ statement for the FILE containing the RECORD that caused the obscure path to be taken.

```
IF              record-key   =   record-key-bad-value
    [WRITE installation standard ERROR REPORT]
END-IF
```

record-key is the KEY item used to READ the RECORD. It is derivable from the READ statement or the file-control-entry in the ENVIRONMENT DIVISION. record-key-bad-value is the KEY VALUE that caused the PROGRAM to invoke the obscure path. It is derivable from the dump. If the FILE is SEQUENTIAL and the PROGRAM does not contain a KEY item then determine which item is the FILE SORT KEY.

TABLE HANDLING

The TABLE handling verbs are SEARCH and SET. SET is used to SET the INDEX or subscript for a normal sequential SEARCH (SEARCH ALL is a binary SEARCH which SETs its own INDEX). SET does not have any abends or defensive trap abends.

SEARCH

SEARCH can abend with an AT END defensive trap.

1. AT END

SEARCH always ENDs when the INDEX or subscript VALUE exceeds the TABLE END. If the INDEX or subscript is SET to < 1 or > the TABLE END upon entry then the SEARCH is immediately ended. If the AT END phrase is not specified then control is transferred to the next executable statement. This is usually wrong although some program-mers use the fall through option to process the condition that no WHEN phrase was satisfied. If this is the case then the SEARCH should be modified to include an AT END CONTINUE or NEXT SENTENCE to document the fall through.

If the AT END defensive trap is triggered then the current transaction contains VALUES that do not fulfill any of the WHEN phrases **and** the PROGRAM is expecting such fulfillment. You must identify the items contained within the WHEN conditions and use them in a data trace:

(a) ANSI DEBUG

```
PROCEDURE DIVISION

DECLARATIVES.

DEBUG SECTION.
```

```
   USE FOR DEBUGGING ON      search-identifier-a
                             search-identifier-?
                             search-identifier-z
                             ALL PROCEDURES.


DEBUG-PROGRAM-FLOW.

   DISPLAY          DEBUG-LINE
                    DEBUG-NAME
                    DEBUG-CONTENTS.

   DISPLAY UPON  mnemonic-name-1
                    DEBUG-LINE
                    DEBUG-NAME
                    DEBUG-CONTENTS.


   END DECLARATIVES.
```

DEBUG-CONTENTS provide the offending transaction VALUES for the items within the WHEN conditions. It is probable that a data entry mistake has been made. Check with your user or user representative to determine which VALUE or VALUES are incorrect. Correct the transaction and rerun.

If the user states that all VALUES are correct then ask if any of the VALUES are unusual or rarely used. If the answer is yes then your problem is that the PROGRAM was not coded to process those unusual VALUES. You will need to work with the user to determine what to do and modify the PROGRAM accordingly.

If the user states that the VALUES are normal then the PROGRAM must have taken an obscure path otherwise the **production** PROGRAM would continually have this problem. Examine the module trace to determine how the PROGRAM got to the module containing the offending SEARCH. This is usually sufficient to isolate the anomaly. Determine what the obscure path should be doing and make the corrections. Rerun to verify.

(b) *COBOL II COBTEST commands*

The generic procedures for DEBUGGING using COBTEST are the same as for using ANSI DEBUG. The difference is the syntax.

```
COBTEST program-name

TRACE ENTRY NAME PRINT

FLOW ON

LIST search-identifier-a:search-identifier-z    BOTH PRINT
     *the : lists a range of identifiers

GO

DUMP or GO
```

(c) Quick fix

Substitute a WRITE to an installation standard ERROR REPORT for the defensive trap abend.

SET

SET cannot cause an abend by itself. However, it can place incorrect VALUES into an INDEX or subscript that causes either a PERFORM VARYING or a serial SEARCH to malfunction. See "PERFORM VARYING" and "PERFORM VARYING FROM" if you suspect this problem.

TESTING

The testing verbs are EVALUATE and IF. EVALUATE is a multibranch, multijoin verb that is used to EVALUATE multiple conditions. IF is the standard COBOL decision verb. IF has no abends.

EVALUATE

EVALUATE is similar to SEARCH in that if no evaluation is satisfied then PROGRAM execution continues with the next executable statement unless there is a WHEN OTHER phrase. As with SEARCH, the programmer may have selected the fall through option to process this condition. If this is the case, then the EVALUATE should be modified to include a WHEN OTHER CONTINUE to document the fall through.

If the WHEN OTHER defensive trap is triggered then the current transaction contains VALUES that do not fulfill any of the evaluations **and** the PROGRAM is expecting such fulfillment. You must identify the items contained within the EVALUATE and use them in a data trace:

1. ANSI DEBUG

```
PROCEDURE DIVISION

DECLARATIVES.

DEBUG SECTION.

    USE FOR DEBUGGING ON    evaluate-identifier-a
                            evaluate-identifier-?
                            evaluate-identifier-z
                            ALL PROCEDURES.
DEBUG-PROGRAM-FLOW.

    DISPLAY      DEBUG-LINE
```

```
                    DEBUG-NAME
                    DEBUG-CONTENTS.

        DISPLAY UPON  mnemonic-name-1
                    DEBUG-LINE
                    DEBUG-NAME
                    DEBUG-CONTENTS.
```

```
    END DECLARATIVES.
```

DEBUG-CONTENTS provide the offending transaction VALUES for the items within the EVALUATE. It is probable that a data entry mistake has been made. Check with your user or user representative to determine which VALUE or VALUES are incorrect. Correct the transaction and rerun.

If the user states that all VALUES are correct then ask if any of the VALUES are unusual or rarely used. If the answer is yes then your problem is that the PROGRAM was not coded to process those unusual VALUES. You will need to work with the user to determine what to do and modify the PROGRAM accordingly.

If the user states that the VALUES are normal then the PROGRAM must have taken an obscure path otherwise the **production** PROGRAM would continually have this problem. Examine the module trace to determine how the PROGRAM got to the module containing the offending EVALUATE. This is usually sufficient to isolate the anomaly. Determine what the obscure path should be doing and make the corrections. Rerun to verify.

2. COBOL II COBTEST commands

The generic procedures for DEBUGGING using COBTEST are the same as for using ANSI DEBUG. The difference is the syntax.

```
    COBTEST program-name

    TRACE ENTRY NAME PRINT

    FLOW ON

    LIST evaluate-identifier-a:evaluate-identifier-z   BOTH
    PRINT
        *the : lists a range of identifiers

    GO

    DUMP or GO
```

3. Quick fix

Substitute a WRITE to an installation standard ERROR REPORT for the defensive trap abend.

7 Random switch settings

RANDOM SWITCH SETTINGS

Many difficult abends are caused by random switch settings. A random switch is normally an item in WORKING-STORAGE used to control processing. It should be initialized or SET to a specific VALUE upon each PROGRAM iteration. The setting of a random switch is left to chance by not being initialized, thereby causing the PROGRAM to execute incorrect code **sometimes** and at random. The symptom is your PROGRAM running to EOJ or to a different abend location in DEBUGGING mode from the production PROGRAM abend location.

PROGRAM runs to EOJ in DEBUGGING mode

If your PROGRAM runs to EOJ then the anomaly is a random switch. All WORKING-STORAGE items with VALUE clauses are initialized to that VALUE upon PROGRAM entry in the DEBUGGING mode. Your PROGRAM running in production was using whatever VALUE was left in the random switch by the prior transaction processing. The DEBUGGING procedure is:

1. Insert a DIVIDE BY ZERO abort as the first statement in the PROGRAM, recompile, and rerun.
2. Identify any item in WORKING-STORAGE that has a VALUE clause from the compiler listing. Items with VALUE clauses are usually switches.
3. Use the offset to locate each item in both FDUMPs (the production FDUMP and the DEBUGGING FDUMP).
4. Highlight any items that have different VALUES. These are the random switches.
5. Determine if the previous DEBUGGING EOJ result is correct. If so, you have both identified and solved the anomaly.

1. EOJ result is correct

The anomaly is a random switch and the solution is to INITIALIZE all uninitialized VALUES. Most PROGRAMs have a mainline which controls processing.
The skeleton format is:

```
PROCEDURE DIVISION.
```

```
USE FOR DEBUGGING.

PERFORM INITIALIZE.

PERFORM PROCESS.

PERFORM TERMINATION.
```

The **PERFORM PROCESS** initiates transaction processing and the first statements should **INITIALIZE** all switches:

```
PROCESS.

    MOVE value-for-switch-a    TO  switch-a
    MOVE value-for-switch-?    TO  switch-?
    MOVE value-for-switch-z    TO  switch-z
```

Note: It is also possible to use the COBOL 85 INITIALIZE verb but I believe separate MOVEs are simpler to understand.

Make the changes, recompile, and rerun to verify.

2. EOJ result is incorrect

The anomaly is a random switch but initializing its VALUE would not solve the problem since the EOJ result was incorrect. Your PROGRAM is expecting some transitive VALUE to be in the random switch and it is not there. The DEBUGGING steps are:

1. Insert a DIVIDE BY ZERO abort as the first statement in the PROGRAM, recompile, and rerun.
2. Identify any item in WORKING-STORAGE that has a VALUE clause from the compiler listing. Items with VALUE clauses are usually switches.
3. Use the offset to locate each item in both FDUMPs (the production FDUMP and the DEBUGGING FDUMP).
4. Highlight any items that have different VALUES. These are the random switches.

Initiate a data trace:

(a) ANSI DEBUG
```
    PROCEDURE DIVISION.

    DECLARATIVES.

    DEBUG SECTION.

        USE FOR DEBUGGING ON    random-switch-a
                                random-switch-?
```

```
                            random-switch-z
                            ALL PROCEDURES.
        DEBUG-PROGRAM-FLOW.

            DISPLAY         DEBUG-LINE
                            DEBUG-NAME
                            DEBUG-CONTENTS.

            DISPLAY UPON    mnemonic-name-1
                            DEBUG-LINE
                            DEBUG-NAME
                            DEBUG-CONTENTS.

        DEBUG-BREAKPOINT.

            IF              DEBUG-NAME   =   random-switch-a
            OR              DEBUG-NAME   =   random-switch-?
            OR              DEBUG-NAME   =   random-switch-z
                DISPLAY     random-switch-a
                            random-switch-?
                            random-switch-z
                ACCEPT      breakpoint
                FROM        mnemonic-name-2
                IF          dump
                    DIVIDE  ZERO BY ZERO GIVING infinity
                END-IF
            END-IF

        END DECLARATIVES.
```

The contents of DEBUG-LINE tell you which LINE in the COBOL PROGRAM caused the data corruption. The probable verb is MOVE and it must be in an obscure path otherwise the **production** PROGRAM would continually have this problem. Examine the module trace to determine how the PROGRAM got to the module containing the offending statement. This is usually sufficient to isolate the anomaly. Determine what the obscure path should be doing and make the corrections. Rerun to verify.

(b) COBOL II COBTEST commands

The generic procedures for DEBUGGING using COBTEST are the same as for using ANSI DEBUG. The difference is the syntax.

```
COBTEST program-name

TRACE ENTRY NAME PRINT

FLOW ON
```

```
LIST random-switch-a:random-switch-z BOTH PRINT
     *the : lists a range of identifiers

WHEN brek (random-switch-a <> HIGH-VALUE)   (FLOW PRINT)
WHEN brek (random-switch-? <> HIGH-VALUE)   (FLOW PRINT)
WHEN brek (random-switch-z <> HIGH-VALUE)   (FLOW PRINT)
*high-value is used to force a break

GO

DUMP or GO
```

COBTEST provides you with the option of setting a VALUE into any random switch before resuming execution:

```
GO
```

COBTEST stops on breakpoint:

```
SET    random-switch-? =   VALUE
```

This permits you to place what you believe is the correct VALUE into any random switch before resuming execution. You can also bypass the breakpoints by invoking RUN. If your PROGRAM runs to normal EOJ with a correct result then you have identified the anomaly.

(c) Quick fix

A transitive random switch setting cannot be solved quickly. A thorough analysis must be done to determine what transitive VALUES are valid when. The approach is to run a megatrace (see Chapter 8).

The quick fix is to bypass the transaction by writing out the installation standard ERROR REPORT. You need to insert the following after each transaction READ:

```
IF          transaction-id  =   transaction-id-bad
     [WRITE installation standard ERROR REPORT]
END-IF
```

PROGRAM abends at a different location in DEBUGGING mode

PROGRAM abending at a different location to the production abend is another instance of a transitive random switch setting. Your PROGRAM is expecting some transitive VALUE to be in the random switch and it is not there. The DEBUGGING steps are:

1. Identify any item in WORKING-STORAGE that has a VALUE clause from the compiler listing. Items with VALUE clauses are usually switches.
2. Use the offset to locate each item in both FDUMPs [the production FDUMP and the DEBUGGING FDUMP].

3.   Highlight any items that have different VALUES. These are the random switches.

Initiate a data trace:

1. ANSI DEBUG

```
PROCEDURE DIVISION.

DECLARATIVES.

DEBUG SECTION.

    USE FOR DEBUGGING ON    random-switch-a
                            random-switch-?
                            random-switch-z
                            ALL PROCEDURES.

DEBUG-PROGRAM-FLOW.

    DISPLAY      DEBUG-LINE
                 DEBUG-NAME
                 DEBUG-CONTENTS.

    DISPLAY UPON mnemonic-name-1
                 DEBUG-LINE
                 DEBUG-NAME
                 DEBUG-CONTENTS.

DEBUG-BREAKPOINT.

    IF  DEBUG-NAME    =   random-switch-a
    OR  DEBUG-NAME    =   random-switch-?
    OR  DEBUG-NAME    =   random-switch-z
        DISPLAY           random-switch-a
                          random-switch-?
                          random-switch-z
        ACCEPT            breakpoint
        FROM              mnemonic-name-2
        IF                dump
            DIVIDE ZERO BY ZERO GIVING infinity
        END-IF
    END-IF

END DECLARATIVES.
```

The contents of DEBUG-LINE tell you which LINE in the COBOL PROGRAM caused the data corruption. The probable verb is MOVE and it must be in an obscure path otherwise the **production** PROGRAM would continually have this problem. Examine the module trace to determine how the PROGRAM got to the module containing the offending statement. This is usually sufficient to isolate the anom-aly. Determine what the obscure path should be doing and make the corrections. Rerun to verify.

2. COBOL II COBTEST commands

The generic procedures for DEBUGGING using COBTEST are the same as for using ANSI DEBUG. The difference is the syntax.

```
COBTEST program-name

TRACE ENTRY NAME PRINT

FLOW ON

LIST random-switch-a:random-switch-z BOTH PRINT
     *the : lists a range of identifiers

WHEN brek (random-switch-a <> HIGH-VALUE)    (FLOW PRINT)
WHEN brek (random-switch-? <> HIGH-VALUE)    (FLOW PRINT)
WHEN brek (random-switch-z <> HIGH-VALUE)    (FLOW PRINT)
     *high-value is used to force a break

GO

DUMP or GO
```

COBTEST provides you with the option of setting a VALUE into any random switch before resuming execution:

```
GO
```

COBTEST stops on breakpoint:

```
SET    random-switch-? =    VALUE
```

This permits you to place what you believe is the correct VALUE into any random switch before resuming execution. You can also bypass the breakpoints by invoking RUN. If your PROGRAM runs to normal EOJ with a correct result then you have identified the anomaly.

3. Quick fix

A transitive random switch setting cannot be solved quickly. A thorough analysis must be done to determine what transitive VALUES are valid when. The approach is to run a megatrace (see Chapter 8).

The quick fix is to bypass the transaction by writing out the installation standard ERROR REPORT. You need to insert the following after each transaction READ;

```
IF transaction-id   =   transaction-id-bad
   [WRITE installation standard ERROR REPORT]
END-IF
```

Megatrace

MEGATRACE

The most difficult debugging problem is caused by an unusual set of conditions or transactions which interact in an unanticipated fashion causing an "impossible" abend or data corruption discovered much later by users.

The only practical method to debug this problem is a megatrace. A megatrace reruns all the FILES completely using a normal module flow mask to print transactions that did not follow that normal module flow. Most transactions in production programs are standard and follow the same module flow. Run the first 100 transactions from a typical execution of your PROGRAM using only DEBUG-LINE with OUTPUT to your local printer. A quick scan should reveal the standard module flow.

Modified ANSI Debug DECLARATIVE

```
PROCEDURE DIVISION.

DECLARATIVES.

DEBUG SECTION.

    USE FOR DEBUGGING ON ALL PROCEDURES.

DEBUG-PROGRAM-FLOW.

    DISPLAY UPON    mnemonic-name
                    DEBUG LINE.

END DECLARATIVES.
```

Only DEBUG-LINE is used to minimize information transfer and to simplify analysis. A quick scan identifies the normal module flow. Insert the following items into the WORKING-STORAGE of the target program.

127

```
    WORKING-STORAGE SECTION.

    77  number-of-invoked-modules    PIC S999V  USAGE COMP
                                                VALUE number.
  *number = number of invoked modules; odometer count from
  *transaction-start to transaction-end

    01  module-sequence-numbers.
        02 FILLER                     PIC X(60)  USAGE DISPLAY
                                                VALUE
          seq1 seq2 seq3 seq4 seq5 seq6 seq7 seq8 seq9 seq10.
  *seq1 = first invoked module; seq2 = second invoked module;
  *etc.
  *filler is used since each sequence number is addressed via
  *an index
        02 FILLER                     PIC X(60)  USAGE DISPLAY
                                                VALUE
          seq11 seq12 seq13 seq14 seq15 seq16 seq17 seq18 seq19
  -       seq20.
  *repeat for as many invoked sequence numbers in normal module
  *flow
  *last pic must be exact and a multiple of 6

    01  sequence-number-table REDEFINES module-sequence-
  -                                         numbers
                                    PIC X(6)
        OCCURS 1 TO number DEPENDING ON number-of-invoked-
  -                                         modules
  *number = number of invoked modules
        INDEXED BY                          seqnum-index.
```

Warning: Megatrace assumes that the target program has individual unique sequence numbers of six characters (does **not** have to be numeric). Megatrace does not work without sequence numbers. If your sequence numbers have a different size then modify module-sequence-numbers table accordingly.

```
    01  megatrace-counter.
        02 transaction-odometer    PIC S9(6)V   USAGE COMP
                                                VALUE ZERO.
           88 first-read                        VALUE ZERO.
```

TRANSACTIONS

The normal module flow is usually associated with the reading of a specific FILE which starts the processing of a transaction. The transaction end is the reading of the next transaction.

Megatrace requires this type of program flow and **does not work** if your program uses some other type of flow.

The next step is to identify the transaction FILE which is then inserted into the megatrace DECLARATIVES module.

MEGATRACE DECLARATIVES MODULE

```
PROCEDURE DIVISION.

DECLARATIVES.
*two use for debugging statements are coded to separate
*transaction read from module invocation

DEBUG-READ SECTION.

    USE FOR DEBUGGING ON   transaction-file-name.
*transaction-file-name is the file whose read starts
*transaction processing

DEBUG-READ-PROCESSING.
*determine if invocation is by read; debug-contents will
*contain record contents; spaces means some other
*invocation such as open

    IF            DEBUG-CONTENTS
    NOT =         SPACES
        NEXT SENTENCE
    ELSE          GO TO     DEBUG-READ-EXIT.

*use invoked by read of transaction file
    IF NOT        first-read
          GO TO  DEBUG-TRANSACTION-START
    ELSE   NEXT SENTENCE.

*not first read; determine if module flow completely executed
    IF            sequence-number-sub
    =             number-of-invoked-modules
              GO TO     DEBUG-TRANSACTION-FINISH
    ELSE          GO TO     DEBUG-TRANSACTION-SHORT.

  DEBUG-TRANSACTION-SHORT.
*transaction flow was the same as the normal flow except
*that it stopped short; print on local printer
```

```
        DISPLAY UPON  mnemonic-name
                      "TRANSACTION "
                      transaction-odometer
                      " STOPPED SHORT; REMAINING NORMAL
                      MODULES".

    DEBUG-DISPLAY-NORMAL-FLOW.

        DISPLAY UPON  mnemonic-name
                      sequence-number-table (seqnum-index)

        SET           seqnum-index
        UP BY         1

*validate seqnum-index within range
        IF            seqnum-index
        >             number-of-invoked-modules
                      GO TO     DEBUG-TRANSACTION-FINISH
        ELSE          GO TO     DEBUG-DISPLAY-NORMAL-FLOW.
*simulates perform until

    DEBUG-TRANSACTION-FINISH.
*print finish on local printer

        DISPLAY UPON  mnemonic-name
                      "TRANSACTION "
                      transaction-odometer
                      " FINISHED"

        GO TO         DEBUG-READ-EXIT.

    DEBUG-TRANSACTION-START.
*set megatrend counters; display start on local printer

        ADD           1
        TO            transaction-odometer
        ON SIZE ERROR
                      DISPLAY UPON  mnemonic-name
                      "TRANSACTION OVERFLOW".

        SET           seqnum-index
        TO            1

        DISPLAY UPON  mnemonic-name
                      "TRANSACTION "
                      transaction-odometer
                      " STARTED"
```

```
    GO TO           DEBUG-READ-EXIT.

DEBUG-READ-EXIT. EXIT.

DEBUG-MODULE SECTION.

    USE FOR DEBUGGING ON        ALL PROCEDURES.

DEBUG-MODULE-PROCESSING.
*normal flow comparison begins only after first transaction
*read; bypass until transaction-odometer > 0

    IF NOT          first-read
          NEXT SENTENCE
    ELSE            GO TO       DEBUG-MODULE-EXIT.

*all procedures is generally invoked by invoking a new
*module; however, it can be invoked by an alter statement
*or the first invocation by the operating system; the if
*eliminates alter & operating system invocation by testing
*for module invocation
    IF              DEBUG-CONTENTS
    =               SPACES
*go to invocation
    OR              "SORT INPUT"
    OR              "SORT OUTPUT"
    OR              "MERGE OUTPUT"
    OR              "PERFORM LOOP"
    OR              "USE PROCEDURE"
*a use statement within the procedure division such as use
*after standard error procedure
    OR              "FALL THROUGH"
        NEXT SENTENCE
    ELSE            GO TO       DEBUG-MODULE-EXIT.
*invocation by alter or operating system

*determine if transaction has exceeded normal flow
    IF              seqnum-index
    >               number-of-invoked-modules
        NEXT SENTENCE
    ELSE            GO TO       DEBUG-MODULE-FLOW-TEST.

*transaction has overflowed; print on local printer
    DISPLAY UPON mnemonic-name
                "OVERFLOW "
                DEBUG-LINE
```

```
*contains overflow module sequence number

    GO TO           DEBUG-MODULE-EXIT.

DEBUG-MODULE-FLOW-TEST.
*determine if transaction is following normal flow

    IF              DEBUG-LINE
    =               sequence-number-table (seqnum-index)
        SET         seqnum-index
        UP BY       1
        GO TO       DEBUG-MODULE-EXIT
    ELSE    NEXT SENTENCE.

*normal flow sequence broken; print on local printer
    DISPLAY UPON mnemonic-name
                "SEQUENCE BROKEN AT "
                sequence-number-table (seqnum-index)
                " TRANSACTION SEQUENCE NUMBER IS "
                DEBUG LINE
                " SEQNUM-INDEX IS "
                seqnum-index

    SET             seqnum-index
    UP BY           1
*it is possible that transaction flow will resume normal
*pattern; setup by 1 accommodates this possibility

    GO TO           DEBUG-MODULE-EXIT.

DEBUG-MODULE-EXIT.   EXIT.

END DECLARATIVES.
```

Recommendation: Place the megatrace DECLARATIVES into a COPY library and COPY into target program.

MEGATRACE RESULTS

The megatrace printout shows those transactions that did **not** follow the normal program flow. One or more of these abnormal transactions caused the impossible abend or result. These problems include:

Unexpected fall through because of untested condition

Most old COBOL production PROGRAMs do **not** test for all possibilities and an abnormal transaction may fall through because something within the transaction was outside the testing domain.

1. EVALUATE [COBOL 85]

EVALUATE is a multibranch multijoin statement that can test multiple conditions. If the abnormal transaction fails to satisfy any of the conditions **and** the WHEN OTHER phrase is **not** present then fall through occurs. Check the module where the normal module flow was broken. If it contains an EVALUATE statement then you have probably found your problem. Desk debug the abnormal transaction conditions versus the EVALUATE conditions. This should reveal the untested condition. Discuss with the user what this condition should do and fix the PROGRAM accordingly.

(a) Quick fix

Insert a WHEN OTHER phrase that WRITEs the abnormal transaction to the site ERROR REPORT and bypasses it. INSSIZE (See Appendix A) inserts a WHEN OTHER phrase.

2. GO TO . . . DEPENDING ON

GO TO DEPENDING ON is used to invoke a specific module based on a specific VALUE. If the abnormal transaction VALUE is outside the domain, or signed, or a fraction then the GO TO DEPENDING ON is ignored and the unabended PROGRAM continues with the NEXT SOURCE statement. Check the module where the normal module flow was broken. If it contains a GO TO DEPENDING ON statement then you have probably found your problem. Desk debug the abnormal transaction VALUES versus the GO TO DEPENDING ON identifiers. This should reveal the invalid VALUE. Discuss with the user what this VALUE should do and fix the PROGRAM accordingly.

(a) Quick fix

Insert a PERFORM after the GO TO DEPENDING ON that WRITEs the abnormal transaction to the site error report and bypasses it. INSSIZE (see Appendix A) inserts a defensive trap.

3. IF

IF can test multiple conditions. If the abnormal transaction fails to satisfy any of these conditions then fall through occurs. Check the module where the normal module flow was broken. If it contains an IF statement then you have probably found your problem. Desk debug the abnormal transaction conditions versus the IF conditions. This should reveal the untested condition. Discuss with the user what this condition should do and fix the program accordingly.

(a) Quick fix

Insert a PERFORM after the IF that WRITEs the abnormal transaction to the site error report and bypasses it. INSSIZE (see Appendix A) inserts a defensive trap.

4. INPUT-OUTPUT verbs

CLOSE, DELETE, OPEN, READ, REWRITE, START, and WRITE verbs have some type of ERROR checking for determining if the requested operation was successfully completed.

A PROGRAM can have a USE AFTER STANDARD EXCEPTION/ERROR PROCE-DURE ON DECLARATIVES which is only invoked by the operating system after an EXCEPTION/ERROR has been detected.

All verbs can have a FILE STATUS data item that the operating system places a completion code into (see "INPUT-OUTPUT statement trappable error"). The FILE STATUS data item can be tested for the result of the requested operation.

DELETE, REWRITE, and START can have an INVALID KEY phrase. READ can have an AT END phrase. WRITE can have an AT END-OF-PAGE/EOP or INVALID KEY phrase.

ANSI requires the compiler to reject any INPUT-OUTPUT statement if none of the ERROR checking procedures are present. Some compilers ignore this restriction and process the INPUT-OUTPUT statement as valid. Many PROGRAMS include some ERROR checking but do not check for all ERRORs. The only foolproof ERROR checking procedure is to have an installation standard FILE STATUS checking routine that is copied into **every** PROGRAM that checks every completion code.

If the compiler does not reject or if the PROGRAM does not test for all ERRORs then the unabended PROGRAM continues with an "impossible" anomaly. The only way to trap this problem is to COPY the installation standard FILE STATUS routine into **every** program.

(a) Quick fix

The insertion of the installation standard FILE STATUS routine is the quick fix. SUBFILES (see Appendix A) inserts the COPY statement.

5. SEARCH [ALL]

SEARCH tests a TABLE for specific conditions. If the abnormal transaction fails to satisfy any of the conditions **and** the AT END phrase is **not** present then fall through occurs. Check the module where the normal module flow was broken. If it contains a SEARCH statement then you have probably found your problem. Desk debug the abnormal transaction conditions versus the SEARCH conditions. This should reveal the untested condition. Discuss with the user what this condition should do and fix the program accordingly.

(a) Quick fix

Insert an AT END phrase that WRITEs the abnormal transaction to the site ERROR REPORT and bypasses it. INSSIZE (See Appendix A) inserts an AT END phrase.

Unexpected result because ON missing

Many verbs contain an ON phrase to trap some form of overflow. The failure to code the ON phrase means that the unabended PROGRAM continues with unexpected results. The unexpected results cause the impossible abend or the impossible data VALUE. Most ON omission ERRORs should be trapped by the ANSI or COBTEST debugging techniques discussed in previous chapters. The megatrace was only initiated because single transaction debugging did not disclose the problem. It is therefore possible that an abnormal transaction triggered the problem.

1. Arithmetic verbs

All arithmetic verbs have an ON SIZE ERROR phrase. Failure to code an ON SIZE ERROR phrase means that if a SIZE ERROR condition exists then the VALUEs in the affected results identifiers are **undefined** in an unabended program Undefined VALUEs cause data corruption. Check the module where the normal module flow was broken. If it contains an arithmetic statement without an ON SIZE ERROR phrase then you probably have found you problem. Insert an ON SIZE ERROR DIVIDE ZERO defensive trap and rerun the PROGRAM with only that specific abnormal transaction. If the defensive trap is triggered then you have found your problem. Correct the offending item magnitude. This is usually a difficult process because you must correct it in all PROGRAMs that list the offending item in a xref listing.

(a) Quick fix

Insert an ON SIZE ERROR phrase that WRITEs the abnormal transaction to the site ERROR REPORT and bypasses it. INSSIZE (see Appendix A) inserts an ON SIZE ERROR phrase.

2. CALL

CALL can have an ON OVERFLOW or ON EXCEPTION [COBOL 85] phrase. Failure to code either means that if the called program is unavailable then the unabended program continues with the next source statement. Whatever the called PROGRAM was supposed to do has not been done. This has to cause problems. Check the module where the normal module flow was broken. If it contains a CALL statement without an ON OVERFLOW or ON EXCEPTION phrase then you probably have found your problem. Insert an ON OVERFLOW or ON EXCEPTION DIVIDE ZERO defensive trap and rerun the PROGRAM with only that specific abnormal transaction. If the defensive trap is triggered then you have found your problem.

(a) Quick fix

The insertion of the ON OVERFLOW or ON EXCEPTION phrase is the quick fix. The PROGRAM did not fail; the operating system did. INSSIZE (see Appendix A) inserts the ON OVERFLOW or ON EXCEPTION phrase.

3. STRING

STRING joins partial or complete contents of one or more data items into a single receiving data item. STRING has an optional POINTER phrase which is used to transfer partial contents. IF POINTER < 1 or > the maximum SIZE of the receiving item then OVERFLOW occurs. Control passes to the next executable statement if OVERFLOW occurs and there is no OVERFLOW phrase. Check the module where the normal module flow was broken. If it contains a STRING statement with a POINTER phrase without an OVERFLOW phrase then you have probably found your problem. Insert an ON OVERFLOW DIVIDE ZERO defensive trap and rerun the PROGRAM with only that specific abnormal transaction. If the defensive trap is triggered then you have found your problem.

(a) Quick fix

The insertion of the ON OVERFLOW phrase is the quick fix. INSSIZE (see Appendix A) inserts the ON OVERFLOW phrase.

4. UNSTRING

UNSTRING causes contiguous data in a sending data item to be separated and placed into multiple receiving data items. UNSTRING has an optional POINTER phrase which is used to transfer partial contents. IF POINTER < 1 or > the maximum size of the receiving item then OVERFLOW occurs. OVERFLOW also occurs if there is data left to transfer and there are no more receiving data items. Control passes to the next executable statement if OVERFLOW occurs and there is no OVERFLOW phrase. Check the module where the normal flow was broken. If it contains an UNSTRING statement without an ON OVER-FLOW phrase then you probably have found your problem. Insert an ON OVERFLOW DIVIDE ZERO defensive trap and rerun the PROGRAM with only that specific abnormal transaction. If the defensive trap is triggered then you have found your problem.

(a) Quick fix

The insertion of the ON OVERFLOW phrase is the quick fix. INSSIZE (see Appendix A) inserts the ON OVERFLOW phrase.

SUMMARY

The megatrace REPORT will have many transactions that did not take the normal module flow. You must process all abnormal transactions through the procedures stated in this chapter until you find all erroneous transactions. If none of the abnormal transactions is erroneous then you probably have **Random switch setting** combined with abnormal transactions. You need to modify the megatrace DECLARATIVES to include random switches as described in Chapter 7.

Appendix A
Care programs

CARE PROGRAMs

Appendix A contains nine CARE (Computer Assisted Re Engineering) PROGRAMs.

1. ACCPDISP
TEST PROGRAM to determine what a specific compiler does with ACCEPT and DISPLAY statements.

2. INSANSI
Inserts ANSI DEBUG module into COBOL PROGRAMs.

3. INSEXIT
Inserts DIVIDE BY ZERO defensive trap before each EXIT PROGRAM, STOP RUN, and GOBACK [IBM].

4. INSNEG
Inserts IF NEGATIVE defensive TEST on MOVE and IF ZERO defensive TEST on DIVIDE.

5. INSRUNAB
Inserts runaway abend paragraph after each EXIT paragraph.

6. INSSIZE
Inserts ON SIZE ERROR into arithmetic statements; ON EXCEPTION into CALL statements; ON OVERFLOW into STRING and UNSTRING statements; WHEN OTHER into EVALUATE statements; DIVIDE ZERO defensive trap into GO TO DEPENDING ON.

7. INSTOC
Inserts perform-return counters to trap runaway code.

8. OVERMOVE

TEST PROGRAM to see what host compilers do with overlapping MOVE.

9. SUBFILES

Substitutes installation standard FILE STATUS COPY for PROGRAM FILE STATUS; standard data-name is substituted or inserted into the FILE-CONTROL entry of the ENVIRONMENT DIVISION and WORKING-STORAGE.

ANSI COBOL 74

These PROGRAMs are written in ANSI COBOL 74 and therefore are portable to every valid subset COBOL 74 compiler that supports the High Level of the Nucleus Module (SEARCH, STRING, UNSTRING verbs and 66/88 levels are in the High Nucleus Module). If your compiler does not support these verbs then these CARE PROGRAMs will not work. The only other exceptions are:

1.   EJECT is used instead of the ANSI slash [/] to EJECT to TOP of PAGE since most compilers support EJECT and not /. If your compiler only supports / then use an editor to globally substitute / for EJECT.
2.   INSSIZE requires a valid ANSI COBOL 85 compiler since it requires the explicit scope terminators.

I have tried to keep the PROGRAMs as simple as possible but the need to manipulate CHARACTER strings in COBOL 74 has required some complex entries and sentences.

PC03-FIND-WORDS.

PC03 is a COMMON routine used by most of the CARE PROGRAMs to UNSTRING Area B into its separate WORDS. All the CARE PROGRAMs require formatted PROCEDURE DIVISIONs where a verb, if present, is the first word in the SOURCE LINE. The verb or any other word does not have to start in column 12. However, for the UNSTRING to work successfully the UNSTRING POINTER must be set to the column in Area B that contains the first alpha CHARACTER. This is accomplished by redefining Area B into separate CHARACTERS and using a SEARCH command to find the first alpha. SEARCH updates the UNSTRING POINTER and the UNSTRING does start with the first alpha character.

UNSTRING parses a maximum of eight WORDS. If your SOURCE LINEs contain more than eight WORDS then you need to modify B-WORDS in UNSTRING-ITEMS in WORKING-STORAGE and the UNSTRING sentence in PC03 accordingly.

1. UNSTRING-ITEMS.

The UNSTRING-ITEMS entry in WORKING-STORAGE looks formidable but its LENGTH is caused by the use of many 88 levels to simplify processing. Some of the CARE PROGRAMs need to know when the previous statement or sentence has been terminated and therefore WORD-1 contains a list of all COBOL verbs defined as 88s. Specific verb or verbs required by specific PROGRAMs are also defined by 88s.

PC01-READ-COBOLIN.

PC01 is a COMMON routine that READs the target SOURCE PROGRAM SOURCE LINEs. It REWRITEs any blank LINE or non-statement-line (*, D, /, or - in column 7) and then READs the NEXT SOURCE LINE. Return is only made when a non-blank statement LINE is READ.

PC01 also controls when the old (original) SOURCE LINE is written out. Many SOURCE LINEs do not require processing and therefore only need copying. PC01 uses the COPY-SWITCH to control reading and writing.

COPY-SWITCH is SET TO DO-COPY by a VALUE entry. DO-COPY means that PC01 immediately WRITEs (copies) the just READ SOURCE LINE. This means that no new SOURCE LINE can be inserted before the SOURCE LINE just READ.

If processing determines that insertion is possible then the COPY-SWITCH is SET TO DO-READ. DO-READ only READs the NEXT SOURCE LINE without writing it. PC01 then SETs COPY-SWITCH to DO-WRITE which means that the old SOURCE LINE will be written before the new SOURCE LINE is READ.

PCO2-WRITE-COBOLOUT.

PC02 WRITEs both old and new SOURCE LINEs. WRITE-SWITCH controls which. OLD-SOURCE-LINE WRITEs old and NEW-SOURCE-LINE WRITEs new.

PRACTICE WHAT YOU PREACH

These CARE programs deviate from three standards that I recommended in *COBOL: A Guide to Structured, Portable, Maintainable, and Efficient Program Design*, Prentice Hall, Englewood Cliffs, NJ, 1989 and I thought I should explain why.

1. Network GO TOs: The mainline PROCEDURE DIVISION consists of separate paragraphs to process specific subdivisions of a COBOL PROGRAM. A dummy network GO TO is used to transfer CONTROL to the next paragraph when the next subdivision is found. Spaghetti code is not created since there is only forward movement and a backward GO TO the previous subdivision processing paragraph is not possible.
2. literals: Literals were used because of readability and the lack of any requirement for impact analysis.
3. ALTER: I was forced to use ALTER in INSTOC because it is the only portable run-time switch available in COBOL 74. There is only one alterable GO TO that can only GO TO two different paragraphs. Both it and the two ALTER statements are well documented.

CAVEAT

The programs are only documentation of what the enclosed disk contains. There may be proofreading errors. The disk may also be more current since it is easier to produce disks than books.

This disk is in ASCII format. These CARE programs *only* work on COBOL programs that meet specified syntactical constraints. For more information, use MS-DOS to PRINT or TYPE the README.DOC on the enclosed disk.

COPYRIGHT

ACCPDISP

```
PROGRAM-ID        ACCPDISP.
*TEST PROGRAM TO DETERMINE WHAT A SPECIFIC COMPILER DOES
*WITH ACCEPT & DISPLAY STATEMENTS

AUTHOR.           ERIC GARRIGUE VESELY
                  THE ANALYST WORKBENCH CONSULTING SDN BHD

DATE-WRITTEN.    26 FEBRUARY 1990

DATE-COMPILED.

ENVIRONMENT DIVISION.

CONFIGURATION SECTION.

SOURCE COMPUTER.
*                      WITH DEBUGGING MODE.
*ABOVE * IS SOURCE TIME SWITCH

SPECIAL-NAMES. LOCAL-PRINTER IS PROGRAMMER-LOCAL-PRINTER.
*"PRINTER" IS THE PRINTER THAT A PROGRAMMER CAN DIRECT
*LOCAL OUTPUT TO

DATA DIVISION.

WORKING-STORAGE SECTION.
```

```
01  BREAKPOINT                PIC X(80)      USAGE DISPLAY.
    88 DUMP                                  VALUE "D".
*BREAKPOINT PROVIDES PROGRAMMER WITH INTERACTIVE DEBUGGING

EJECT
```

```
PROCEDURE DIVISION.

DECLARATIVES.

DEBUG SECTION.

    USE FOR DEBUGGING ON ALL PROCEDURES.

DEBUG-PROGRAM-FLOW.

    DISPLAY       DEBUG-LINE
                  DEBUG-NAME
                  DEBUG-CONTENTS.

DEBUG-BREAKPOINT.

*    ACCEPT       breakpoint   FROM mnemonic-name.
* *  USED TO DISABLE ACCEPT EVEN IF DEBUG MODULE IS ACTIVE
* *  IS DELETED WHEN INTERACTIVE BREAKPOINTS ARE REQUIRED

END DECLARATIVES.

P101-INITIATION.

    DISPLAY       "ACCPDISP PROGRAM START - SHOULD BE
-                 "DISPLAYED ON PROGRAMMER'S TERMINAL."

    DISPLAY       "PROGRAMMER TERMINAL SHOULD BE WAITING
-                 "FOR A <CR> OR "D" FOR DUMP - HIT <CR>."

    GO TO         P102-BREAKPOINT.

P102-BREAKPOINT.

    ACCEPT        BREAKPOINT

    IF            DUMP
                  DISPLAY    "D INCORRECT - HIT <CR>."
                  GO TO P102-BREAKPOINT
```

```
      ELSE          GO TO P103-DUMP.

  P103-DUMP.

      DISPLAY UPON LOCAL-PRINTER
                   "SHOULD PRINT UPON LOCAL PRINTER."

      DISPLAY      "PROGRAMMER TERMINAL SHOULD BE WAITING
  -                "FOR A <CR> OR D FOR DUMP - HIT D."

      IF NOT       DUMP
                   DISPLAY   "INCORRECT ENTRY - HIT D."
                   GO TO  P103-DUMP
      ELSE NEXT SENTENCE.

      DISPLAY      "SUCCESSFUL EXECUTION - ACCPDISP EOJ."

      STOP RUN.

      EJECT
```

INSANSI.

```
  IDENTIFICATION DIVISION.

  PROGRAM-ID.       INSANSI.
  *INSERTS ANSI DEBUG MODULE INTO COBOL PROGRAM

  AUTHOR.           ERIC GARRIGUE VESELY
                    THE ANALYST WORKBENCH CONSULTING SDN BHD

  DATE-WRITTEN.    26 FEBRUARY 1990

  DATE-COMPILED.


  ENVIRONMENT DIVISION.

  CONFIGURATION SECTION.

  SOURCE COMPUTER.
  *                             WITH DEBUGGING MODE.
  *ABOVE * IS SOURCE TIME SWITCH

  INPUT-OUTPUT SECTION.
```

```
 FILE CONTROL.
*SIMPLE SEQUENTIAL IO USED TO REDUCE COMPLEXITY
 SELECT              COBOLIN
*COBOLIN IS NAME OF FILE CONTAINING COBOL PROGRAM
     ASSIGN TO        SEQINPUT
*SEQINPUT IS NAME THAT COBOLIN IS ASSIGNED TO
     ORGANIZATION IS SEQUENTIAL
     ACCESS MODE  IS SEQUENTIAL
     FILE STATUS  IS    COBLPROG-FILE-STATUS.

 SELECT              COBOLOUT
*COBOLOUT IS NAME OF NEW FILE THAT CONTAINS TRAPPED COBOL
*PROGRAM
     ASSIGN TO        SEQOUTPT
*SEQOUTPT IS NAME THAT COBOLOUT IS ASSIGNED TO
     ORGANIZATION IS SEQUENTIAL
     ACCESS MODE  IS SEQUENTIAL
     FILE STATUS  IS    COBLPROG-FILE-STATUS.

     EJECT
```

```
 DATA DIVISION.

 FILE SECTION.

 FD          COBOLIN          LABEL RECORD STANDARD.

 01 COBOL-LINE-IN             PIC X(80) USAGE DISPLAY.
*ASSUMES 80 COLUMN [BYTE] RECORDS

 FD          COBOLOUT         LABEL RECORD STANDARD.

 01 COBOL-LINE-OUT            PIC X(80) USAGE DISPLAY.


 WORKING-STORAGE SECTION.

 01 COBOL-LINE-WS.
    02 SEQUENCE-NUMBER        PIC X(6)  USAGE DISPLAY.
    02 INDICATOR-A-B.
       03 INDICATOR           PIC X     USAGE DISPLAY.
          88 NON-STATEMENT-LINE         VALUE  "*"
                                               "D"
                                               "/"
                                               "-".

       03 AREA-AB.
```

```
          88  BLANK-SOURCE-LINE                 VALUE SPACES.
          04  AREA-A                 PIC X(4)   USAGE DISPLAY.
              88  IDENTIFICATION-DIVISION       VALUE "IDEN"
                                                      "ID D".
*IBM ABBREVIATION
              88  ENVIRONMENT-DIVISION          VALUE "ENVI".
              88  SELECT-CLAUSE                 VALUE "SELE".
              88  CONFIGURATION-SECTION         VALUE "CONF".
              88  SOURCE-COMP                   VALUE "SOUR".
              88  DATA-DIVISION                 VALUE "DATA".
              88  WS-SECTION                    VALUE "WORK".
              88  LEVEL-77                      VALUE "77  ".
              88  PROCEDURE-DIVISION            VALUE "PROC".
              88  DECLARE                       VALUE "DECL".
              88  BLANK-AREA-A                  VALUE SPACES.
          04  AREA-B                 PIC X(61) USAGE DISPLAY.
          04  AREA-B-BYTES REDEFINES AREA-B
                                     PIC X     OCCURS 61 TIMES
                                               INDEXED BY
                                               AREA-B-INDEX.
              88  ALPHA                         VALUE "A" THRU
                                                      "Z".
      02  IDEN-AREA                  PIC X(8)  USAGE DISPLAY.


01  COBLPROG-FILE-STATUS.
    02  SK1                          PIC X     USAGE DISPLAY.
        88  FILE-STATUS-OK                     VALUE "0".
    02  SK2                          PIC X     USAGE DISPLAY.


01  NEW-SOURCE-LINE                            VALUE SPACES.
    02  FILLER                       PIC X(6)  USAGE DISPLAY.
    02  NEW-INDICATOR-A-B.
        03  NEW-INDICATOR            PIC X     USAGE DISPLAY.
        03  NEW-AREA-AB.
            04  NEW-AREA-A           PIC X(4)  USAGE DISPLAY.
            04  NEW-AREA-B           PIC X(61) USAGE DISPLAY.
    02  FILLER                       PIC X(8)  USAGE DISPLAY.


01  DIVISION-PARAGRAPH-SWITCHES.
    02  ID-SWITCH                    PIC X(5)  USAGE DISPLAY
                                               VALUE SPACES.
        88  ID-NOT-FOUND                       VALUE SPACES.
        88  ID-FOUND                           VALUE "FOUND".
    02  ENVIRONMENT-SWITCH           PIC X(5)  USAGE DISPLAY
                                               VALUE SPACES.
        88  ENVIRONMENT-NOT-FOUND              VALUE SPACES.
```

```
        88  ENVIRONMENT-FOUND                    VALUE "FOUND".
    02  CONFIGURATION-SWITCH        PIC X(5)  USAGE DISPLAY
                                              VALUE SPACES.
        88  CONFIGURATION-NOT-FOUND            VALUE SPACES.
        88  CONFIGURATION-FOUND                VALUE "FOUND".
    02  SOURCE-SWITCH               PIC X(5)  USAGE DISPLAY
                                              VALUE SPACES.
        88  SOURCE-NOT-FOUND                   VALUE SPACES.
        88  SOURCE-FOUND                       VALUE "FOUND".
    02  SELECT-SWITCH               PIC X(5)  USAGE DISPLAY
                                              VALUE SPACES.
        88  SELECT-NOT-FOUND                   VALUE SPACES.
        88  SELECT-FOUND                       VALUE "FOUND".
    02  DATA-SWITCH                 PIC X(5)  USAGE DISPLAY
                                              VALUE SPACES.
        88  DATA-NOT-FOUND                     VALUE SPACES.
        88  DATA-FOUND                         VALUE "FOUND".
    02  WS-SWITCH                   PIC X(5)  USAGE DISPLAY
                                              VALUE SPACES.
        88  WS-NOT-FOUND                       VALUE SPACES.
        88  WS-FOUND                           VALUE "FOUND".
    02  PROCEDURE-SWITCH            PIC X(5)  USAGE DISPLAY
                                              VALUE SPACES.
        88  PROCEDURE-NOT-FOUND                VALUE SPACES.
        88  PROCEDURE-FOUND                    VALUE "FOUND".
    02  DECLARATIVES-SWITCH         PIC X(5)  USAGE DISPLAY
                                              VALUE SPACES.
        88  DECLARATIVES-NOT-FOUND             VALUE SPACES.
        88  DECLARATIVES-FOUND                 VALUE "FOUND".

 01  COPY-SWITCH                    PIC X(4)  USAGE DISPLAY
                                              VALUE "COPY".
        88  DO-COPY                            VALUE "COPY".
*READ & DO IMMEDIATE WRITE; INSERTION OF NEW SOURCE LINE
*NOT ON
        88  DO-READ                           VALUE "READ".
*READ ONLY; USED IMMEDIATELY AFTER AUTO COPY TURNED OFF
        88  DO-WRITE                          VALUE "WRIT".
*AUTO COPY TURNED OFF; WRITE PREVIOUS SOURCE LINE BEFORE
*READ

 01  WRITE-SWITCH                   PIC X(3)  USAGE DISPLAY
                                              VALUE "OLD".
        88  OLD-SOURCE-LINE                    VALUE "OLD".
            NEW-SOURCE-LINE                    VALUE "NEW".
 01  BREAKPOINT                     PIC X(80) USAGE DISPLAY.
```

```
        88  DUMP                                VALUE "D".

   01  TALLY-COUNTER              PIC S9V    USAGE COMP
                                             VALUE ZERO.
        88  DEBUG                            VALUE 1.
        88  DEFENSIVE-TRAP-FOUND             VALUE 1.
        88  END-DELIMITER                    VALUE 1.
        88  FULLSTOP                         VALUE 1.
        88  STATUS-FOUND                     VALUE 1.


   01  END-SCOPE-DELIMITER.
        02  FILLER                PIC X(4)   USAGE DISPLAY
                                             VALUE "END-".
        02  END-VERB              PIC X(26)  USAGE DISPLAY
                                             VALUE SPACES.


   01  NUMBER-OF-NUMERIC-ITEMS   PIC S999V  VALUE 999.
  *OCCURS DEPENDING ON DATA-NAME FOR NUMERIC-ITEM-TABLE; IF
  *TOO SMALL THEN CHANGE IT TO REQUIRED NUMBER


   01  NUMERIC-ITEM-TABLE.
        02  NUMERIC-ITEM          PIC X(30)
                                  OCCURS 1 TO 999 TIMES
  *SECOND INTEGER MUST BE THE SAME VALUE AS NUMBER-OF-
  *NUMERIC-ITEMS
                                  DEPENDING ON
                                  NUMBER-OF-NUMERIC-ITEMS
                                  INDEXED BY
                                  NUMERIC-ITEM-INDEX.


   01  UNSTRING-ITEMS.
        02  UNSTRING-POINTER      PIC S99V   USAGE COMP
                                             VALUE ZERO.
        02  B-WORDS.
            03  WORD-1            PIC X(30)  USAGE DISPLAY.
                88  ARITHMETIC-VERB          VALUE "ADD"
                                                   "COMPUTE"
                                                   "DIVIDE"
                                                   "MULTIPLY"
                                                   "SUBTRACT".
                88  CALL-VERB                VALUE "CALL".
                88  DIVIDE-VERB              VALUE "DIVIDE".
                88  END-PERFORM-VERB         VALUE
                                             "END-PERFORM."

                88  EVALUATE-VERB            VALUE
```

```
                                        "EVALUATE".
          88  EXIT-VERB                 VALUE "EXIT".
          88  GO-VERB                   VALUE "GO".
          88  GOBACK-VERB               VALUE "GOBACK".
*IBM
          88  IF-VERB                   VALUE "IF".
          88  IO-VERB                   VALUE "CLOSE"
                                            "DELETE"
                                            "OPEN"
                                            "READ"
                                            "REWRITE"
                                            "SEEK"
*IBM
                                            "WRITE".
*PLACE ANY NON-ANSI I-O VERBS OF YOUR COMPILER IN THIS LIST
          88  MOVE-VERB                 VALUE "MOVE".
          88  PERFORM-VERB              VALUE "PERFORM".
          88  SEARCH-VERB               VALUE "SEARCH".
          88  STOP-VERB                 VALUE "STOP".
          88  STRING-UNSTRING-VERB      VALUE "STRING"
                                            "UNSTRING".
          88  TARGET-VERB               VALUE "ADD"
                                            "CALL"
                                            "COMPUTE"
                                            "DIVIDE"
                                            "EVALUATE"
                                            "GO"
                                            "MULTIPLY"
                                            "SEARCH"
                                            "STRING"
                                            "SUBTRACT"
                                            "UNSTRING".
          88  VERB                      VALUE "ACCEPT"
                                            "ADD"
                                            "ALTER"
*OBSOLETE
                                            "CALL"
                                            "CANCEL"
                                            "CLOSE"
                                            "COMPUTE"
                                            "CONTINUE"
*COBOL-85
                                            "COPY"
*TREATED LIKE A VERB
                                            "DELETE"
                                            "DISABLE"
```

"DISPLAY"
"DIVIDE"
"ELSE"

*TREATED LIKE A VERB

"ENABLE"
"ENTER"

*OBSOLETE

"EVALUATE"

*COBOL-85

"EXAMINE"

*COBOL-68

"EXIT"
"GENERATE"
"GO"
"GOBACK"

*IBM

"IF"

"INITIALIZE"

*COBOL-85

"INITIATE"
"INSPECT"
"MERGE"
"MOVE"
"MULTIPLY"
"OPEN"
"PERFORM"
"PURGE"
"READ"
"RECEIVE"
"RELEASE"
"REPLACE"

*COBOL-85; TREATED LIKE A VERB

"RETURN"
"REWRITE"
"SEARCH"
"SEEK"

*IBM

"SEND"
"SET"
"SORT"
"START"
"STOP"
"STRING"
"SUBTRACT"
"SUPPRESS"

```
                                              "TERMINATE"
                                              "TRANSFORM"
*IBM
                                              "UNSTRING"
                                              "USE"
                                              "WRITE".
        03  WORD-2               PIC X(30)  USAGE DISPLAY.
*MUST CONTAIN PROGRAM-NAME FOR PROGRAM-ID PARAGRAPH
*ITEM DATA-NAME IF DATA DIVISION  BEING UNSTRING
*DIVISOR IF DIVIDE INTO BEING UNSTRING
*FROM ITEM DATA-NAME IF MOVE VERB BEING UNSTRING
            88  CORR-PHASE                  VALUE
                                              "CORRESPONDING"
                                                    "CORR".
            88  PROGRAM-WORD                VALUE "PROGRAM".
            88  RUN-WORD                    VALUE "RUN".
        03  WORD-3               PIC X(30)  USAGE DISPLAY.
            88  BY-WORD                     VALUE "BY".
            88  INTO-WORD                   VALUE "INTO".
            88  PICTURE-CLAUSE              VALUE "PICTURE"
                                                    "PIC".
            88  TO-WORD                     VALUE "TO".
        03  WORD-4               PIC X(30)  USAGE DISPLAY.
*DIVISOR IF DIVIDE BY VERB  BEING UNSTRING
*TO ITEM DATA-NAME IF MOVE VERB BEING UNSTRING
        03  WORD-4-BYTES REDEFINES WORD-4
            04  FILLER           PIC X      USAGE DISPLAY.
                88  SIGN-BYTE               VALUE "S".
            04  FILLER           PIC X(29)  USAGE DISPLAY.
        03  WORD-5               PIC X(30)  USAGE DISPLAY.
*MUST CONTAIN ALPHA IF ANALYZING GO TO DEPENDING ON
*STATEMENT
            88  NOT-PROCEDURE-NAME          VALUE SPACES.
        03  WORD-6               PIC X(30)  USAGE DISPLAY.
        03  WORD-7               PIC X(30)  USAGE DISPLAY.
        03  WORD-8               PIC X(30)  USAGE DISPLAY.
     02  WORD-DELIMITERS.
        03  WORD-DELIMITER-1     PIC X      USAGE DISPLAY.
        03  WORD-DELIMITER-2     PIC X      USAGE DISPLAY.
        03  WORD-DELIMITER-3     PIC X      USAGE DISPLAY.
        03  WORD-DELIMITER-4     PIC X      USAGE DISPLAY.
        03  WORD-DELIMITER-5     PIC X      USAGE DISPLAY.
        03  WORD-DELIMITER-6     PIC X      USAGE DISPLAY.
        03  WORD-DELIMITER-7     PIC X      USAGE DISPLAY.
        03  WORD-DELIMITER-8     PIC X      USAGE DISPLAY.
*8 WORDS ARE USED TO ENSURE FULL STOP (.) IS FOUND
```

```
 01           PABORT-PARAGRAPH-NAME.
     02       FILLER                  PIC X(7)      USAGE DISPLAY
                                                    VALUE "PABORT-".
     02       ODOMETER-DISPLAY    PIC 9(4)      USAGE DISPLAY.
     02       ODEMETER REDEFINES ODOMETER-DISPLAY
                                  PIC S9(4)V   USAGE COMP
                                                    VALUE ZERO.

 01-NEGATIVE-OR-ZERO-TRAP.
     02 FILLER                      PIC X(8)      USAGE DISPLAY
                                                    VALUE "D IF ".
*ACTIVE DEFENSIVE TRAP; D DISABLES UNTIL ANSI DEBUG TURNED ON
     02 TRAP-DATA-NAME          PIC X(30)     USAGE DISPLAY
                                                    VALUE SPACES.
     02 FILLER                      PIC X         USAGE DISPLAY
                                                    VALUE SPACE.
     02 TRAP-TYPE                 PIC X(8)      USAGE DISPLAY
                                                    VALUE SPACES.

     EJECT
```

```
 PROCEDURE DIVISION.

 DECLARATIVES.

 DEBUG SECTION.

     USE FOR DEBUGGING ON ALL PROCEDURES.

 DEBUG-PROGRAM-FLOW.

     DISPLAY        DEBUG-LINE
                    DEBUG-NAME
                    DEBUG-CONTENTS.

 DEBUG-BREAKPOINT.

*    ACCEPT            breakpoint   FROM mnemonic-name.
* * USED TO DISABLE ACCEPT EVEN IF DEBUG MODULE IS ACTIVE
* * IS DELETED WHEN INTERACTIVE BREAKPOINTS ARE REQUIRED

 END DECLARATIVES.

 P101-INITIATION.
```

```
        OPEN INPUT     COBOLIN

        OPEN OUTPUT    COBOLOUT

        DISPLAY        "INSEXIT PROGRAM START."

        GO TO          P102-IDENTIFICATION-DIVISION.

    P102-IDENTIFICATION-DIVISION.

        PERFORM        PC01-READ-COBOLIN
        THRU           PC01-X.

*FIND IDENTIFICATION DIVISION
        IF             IDENTIFICATION-DIVISION
           NEXT SENTENCE
        ELSE           GO TO P102-IDENTIFICATION-DIVISION.

        MOVE           "FOUND"
        TO             ID-SWITCH

*PROGRAM-ID MUST BE NEXT STATEMENT LINE
        PERFORM        PC01-READ-COBOLIN
        THRU           PC01-X.

*FIND WORDS IN AREA B
        PERFORM        PCO3-FIND-WORDS
        THRU           PC03-X.

*WORD-2 MUST BE PROGRAM NAME
        DISPLAY        "TARGET PROGRAM IS "
                       WORD-2

*TURN AUTO COPY OFF
        MOVE           "READ"
        TO             COPY-SWITCH

        GO TO          P103-ENVIROMENT-DIVISION.

    P103-ENVIRONMENT-DIVISION.
*FIND ENVIRONMENT DIVISION

        PERFORM        PC01-READ-COBLPROG
        THRU           PC01-X.

        IF             ENVIRONMENT-DIVISION
```

```
                          MOVE    "FOUND"
                          TO      ENVIRONMENT-SWITCH
                          PERFORM P231-CONFIGURATION-SECTION
                          THRU P231-X
                          MOVE    "COPY"
                          TO      COPY-SWITCH
                          GO TO P104-WORKING-STORAGE
            ELSE NEXT SENTENCE.

*COBOL 85 DOES NOT REQUIRE ENVIRONMENT DIVISION. IF DATA
*DIVISION FOUND BEFORE ENVIRONMENT DIVISION THEN INSERT
*ENVIRONMENT
            IF              DATA-DIVISION
                          MOVE    "FOUND"
                          TO      DATA-SWITCH
                          PERFORM P232-ENVIRONMENT-DIVISION
                          THRU P232-X
                          MOVE    "COPY"
                          TO      COPY-SWITCH
                          GO TO P104-WORKING-STORAGE
            ELSE          GO TO P103-ENVIRONMENT-DIVISION.

  P104-WORKING-STORAGE.
 *NEED TO FIND WORKING-STORAGE TO INSERT 77 ITEMS

       PERFORM       PC01-READ-COBLPROG
       THRU          PC01-X.

       IF            WORKING-STORAGE
                     MOVE    "FOUND"
                     TO      WORKING-STORAGE-SWITCH
                     PERFORM P233-77-ITEMS
                     THRU P233-X
                     GO TO P105-PROCEDURE-DIVISION
       ELSE          GO TO P104-WORKING-STORAGE.

P105-PROCEDURE-DIVISION.

       PERFORM       PC01-READ-COBLPROG
       THRU          PC01-X.

       IF        PROCEDURE-FOUND
          NEXT SENTENCE
       ELSE          GO TO P105-PROCEDURE-DIVISION.

       MOVE          "FOUND"
       TO            PROCEDURE-SWITCH
```

```
    MOVE            "NEW"
    TO              WRITE-SWITCH

    MOVE            "READ"
    TO              COPY-SWITCH

*INSERT USE FOR DEBUGGING IF REQUIRED
    PERFORM         PC01-READ-COBOLIN
    THRU            PC01-X.

*DECLARATIVES. IF PRESENT MUST BE NEXT LINE
    IF              DECLARE
                    PERFORM P254-DECLARATIVES
                    THRU P254-X
    ELSE            GO TO P106-USE-FOR-DEBUGGING.

 P106-USE-FOR-DEBUGGING.
*NO DECLARATIVES - INSERT

    MOVE            "NEW"
    TO              WRITE-SWITCH

    MOVE            "DECLARATIVES."
    TO              NEW-AREA-AB

    PERFORM         PC02-WRITE-COBOLOUT
    THRU            PCO2-X.

    MOVE            SPACES
    TO              NEW-SOURCE-LINE

    PERFORM         PC02-WRITE-COBOLOUT
    THRU            PCO2-X.

    MOVE            "DEBUG SECTION."
    TO              NEW-AREA-AB

    PERFORM         PC02-WRITE-COBOLOUT
    THRU            PCO2-X.

    MOVE            SPACES
    TO              NEW-SOURCE-LINE

    PERFORM         PC02-WRITE-COBOLOUT
    THRU            PCO2-X.
```

```
MOVE              "USE FOR DEBUGGING ON ALL PROCEDURES."
TO                NEW-AREA-B

PERFORM           PC02-WRITE-COBOLOUT
THRU              PCO2-X.

MOVE              SPACES
TO                NEW-SOURCE-LINE

PERFORM           PC02-WRITE-COBOLOUT
THRU              PCO2-X.

MOVE              "DEBUG-PROGRAM-FLOW."
TO                NEW-AREA-AB

PERFORM           PC02-WRITE-COBOLOUT
THRU              PCO2-X.

MOVE              SPACES
TO                NEW-SOURCE-LINE

PERFORM           PC02-WRITE-COBOLOUT
THRU              PCO2-X.

MOVE              "DISPLAY     DEBUG-LINE"
TO                NEW-AREA-B

PERFORM           PC02-WRITE-COBOLOUT
THRU              PCO2-X.

MOVE              "DEBUG-NAME"
TO                NEW-AREA-B

PERFORM           PC02-WRITE-COBOLOUT
THRU              PCO2-X.

MOVE              "DEBUG-CONTENTS."
TO                NEW-AREA-B

PERFORM           PC02-WRITE-COBOLOUT
THRU              PCO2-X.

MOVE              SPACES
TO                NEW-SOURCE-LINE

PERFORM           PC02-WRITE-COBOLOUT
```

```
THRU          PCO2-X.

MOVE          "DISPLAY UPON LOCAL-PRINTER"
*LOCAL PRINTER IS THE PROGRAMMER'S PRINTER
TO            NEW-AREA-B

PERFORM       PC02-WRITE-COBOLOUT
THRU          PCO2-X.

MOVE          "DEBUG-LINE"
TO            NEW-AREA-B

PERFORM       PC02-WRITE-COBOLOUT
THRU          PCO2-X.

MOVE          "DEBUG-NAME"
TO            NEW-AREA-B

PERFORM       PC02-WRITE-COBOLOUT
THRU          PCO2-X.

MOVE          "DEBUG-CONTENTS."
TO            NEW-AREA-B

PERFORM       PC02-WRITE-COBOLOUT
THRU          PCO2-X.

MOVE          SPACES
TO            NEW-SOURCE-LINE

PERFORM       PC02-WRITE-COBOLOUT
THRU          PCO2-X.

MOVE          "DEBUG-BREAKPOINT."
TO            NEW-AREA-AB

PERFORM       PC02-WRITE-COBOLOUT
THRU          PCO2-X.

MOVE          SPACES
TO            NEW-SOURCE-LINE

PERFORM       PC02-WRITE-COBOLOUT
THRU          PCO2-X.

MOVE          "*ACCEPT BREAKPOINT FROM TERMINAL
```

```
*BREAKPOINT IS 77 THAT ALLOWS PROGRAMMER TO ABEND DEBUG
*SESSION; TERMINAL IS PROGRAMMER'S TERMINAL
     TO             NEW-INDICATOR-A-B

     PERFORM        PC02-WRITE-COBOLOUT
     THRU           PCO2-X.

     MOVE           SPACES
     TO             NEW-SOURCE-LINE

     PERFORM        PC02-WRITE-COBOLOUT
     THRU           PCO2-X.

*USE SWITCH TO DETERMINE IF END DECLARATIVES HAS TO BE
*INSERTED
     IF             DECLARATIVES-FOUND
                    GO TO P107-COPY-PROGRAM
     ELSE NEXT SENTENCE.

     MOVE           "END DECLARATIVES."
     TO             NEW-AREA-AB

     PERFORM        PC02-WRITE-COBOLOUT
     THRU           PCO2-X.

     MOVE           SPACES
     TO             NEW-SOURCE-LINE

     PERFORM        PC02-WRITE-COBOLOUT
     THRU           PCO2-X.

     GO TO          P107-COPY-PROGRAM.

 P107-COPY-PROGRAM.
*COPY REST OF COBOL PROGRAM

     PERFORM        PC01-READ-COBOLIN
     THRU           PCO1-X.

     GO TO          P107-COPY-PROGRAM.
*INFINITE LOOP BROKEN BY READ AT END

 PEOJ.

     CLOSE          COBOLIN
                    COBOLOUT.
```

```
IF              ID-NOT-FOUND
                DISPLAY "NO IDENTIFICATION DIVISION"
ELSE
IF              PROCEDURE-NOT-FOUND
                DISPLAY "NO PROCEDURE DIVISION"
ELSE NEXT SENTENCE.

DISPLAY         "INSANSI PROGRAM EOJ."

STOP RUN.

EJECT
```

```
P231-CONFIGURATION-SECTION.
*ENVIRONMENT DIVISION FOUND; CONFIGURATION SECTION NEXT IF
*PRESENT

    PERFORM     PC01-READ-COBOLIN
    THRU        PC01-X.

    IF              CONFIGURATION-SECTION
        NEXT SENTENCE
    ELSE            PERFORM PC10-WRITE-CONFIGURATION
                    THRU   PC10-X
*WRITE OUT CONFIGURATION SECTION. IF NOT PRESENT
                GO TO P231-X.

    PERFORM     PC01-READ-COBOLIN
    THRU        PC01-X.

*SOURCE-COMPUTER NEXT IF PRESENT
    IF              SOURCE-COMP
                    PERFORM PC02-WRITE-COBOLOUT
                    THRU   PC02-X
    ELSE            PERFORM PC11-WRITE-SOURCE-COMPUTER
                    THRU   PC11-X
                    GO TO  P231-X.

*CHECK FOR WITH DEBUGGING MODE; ASSUMES ON SAME SOURCE LINE
    MOVE        ZERO
    TO          TALLY-COUNTER

    INSPECT     AREA-B
    TALLYING    TALLY-COUNTER
```

```
        FOR ALL        "DEBUGGING"

        IF             DEBUG
                       DISPLAY "RUN ABORTED - WITH DEBUGGING
  -                    "MODE FOUND AT SOURCE LINE "
                       SEQUENCE-NUMBER
                       GO TO PEOJ.
        ELSE           PEFFORM PC12-WRITE-DEBUGGING-MODE
                       THRU   PC12-X
                       GO TO  P231-X.


  P231-X. EXIT.


  PABORT-P231.
 *RUNAWAY CODE ABEND

        DISPLAY        "RUN ABORTED - RUNAWAY CODE AT P231"

        GO TO          PEOJ.

        EJECT
```

```
  P232-ENVIRONMENT-DIVISION.
 *NO ENVIRONMENT DIVISION.  MUST INSERT IT + CONFIGURATION
 *SECTION + SOURCE-COMPUTER + WITH DEBUGGING MODE

        MOVE           "NEW"
        TO             WRITE-SWITCH

        MOVE           "ENVIRONMENT DIVISION."
        TO             NEW-AREA-AB

        PERFORM        PC02-WRITE-COBOLOUT
        THRU           PC02-X.

        MOVE           SPACES
        TO             NEW-SOURCE-LINE

        PERFORM        PC02-WRITE-COBOLOUT
        THRU           PC02-X.

        PERFORM        PC10-WRITE-CONFIGURATION-SECTION
        THRU           P310-X.

        GO TO          P232-X.
```

```
P232-X. EXIT.
PABORT-P232.
*RUNAWAY CODE ABEND

    DISPLAY        "RUN ABORTED - RUNAWAY CODE AT P232"

    GO TO          PEOJ.

    EJECT
```

```
P233-WORKING-STORAGE.

*INSERT 77 ITEMS TO MAKE ANSI DEBUG MODULE WORK. 77 LEVELS
*USED TO DISTINGUISH FROM NORMAL W-S ITEMS

    MOVE           "77  WS-BEGIN WS-BEGIN WS-BEGIN WS-BEGIN"
    TO             NEW-AREA-AB
*EYECATCHER FOR MEMORY DUMP TO EASILY FIND W-S START

    PERFORM        PC02-WRITE-COBOLOUT
    THRU           PC02-X.

    MOVE           "77 BREAKPOINT  PIC X  USAGE IS DISPLAY."
    TO             NEW-AREA-AB
*USED WITH ACCEPT FOR INTERACTIVE DEBUGGING

    PERFORM        PC02-WRITE-COBOLOUT
    THRU           PC02-X.

    MOVE           "88  DUMP   VALUE IS ""D""."
    TO             NEW-AREA-B
*USED TO ABEND INTERACTIVE DEBUGGING SESSION WITH DUMP

    PERFORM        PC02-WRITE-COBOLOUT
    THRU           PC02-X.

    MOVE           "77  ZERO-LIT  PIC S9V  USAGE IS COMP
-                  "VALUE IS ZERO."
    TO             NEW-AREA-B
*REQUIRED FOR DIVIDE BY ZERO DEFENSIVE TRAP

    PERFORM        PC02-WRITE-COBOLOUT
    THRU           PC02-X.

    MOVE           "77  INFINITY  PIC S9V  USAGE IS COMP
```

```
      -                   "VALUE IS ZERO."
           TO              NEW-AREA-AB
     *REQUIRED FOR DIVIDE BY ZERO DEFENSIVE TRAP

           PERFORM         PC02-WRITE-COBOLOUT
           THRU            PC02-X.

      P233-X. EXIT.

      PABORT-P233.
     *RUNAWAY CODE ABEND

           DISPLAY        "RUN ABORTED - RUNAWAY CODE AT P233"

           GO TO           PEOJ.

           EJECT
```

```
      P254-DECLARATIVES.
     *DECLARATIVES FOUND - CHECK FOR USE FOR DEBUGGING

           MOVE           "FOUND"
           TO              DECLARATIVES-SWITCH

     *DECLARATIVES SECTION MUST BE NEXT LINE - BYPASS
           PERFORM         PC01-READ-COBOLIN
           THRU            PC01-X.

           PERFORM         PC02-WRITE COBOLOUT
           THRU            PC02-X.

           PERFORM         PC01-READ-COBOLIN
           THRU            PC01-X.

     *USE FOR DEBUGGING MUST BE NEXT LINE IF PRESENT
           MOVE            ZERO
           TO              TALLY-COUNTER

           INSPECT         AREA-B
           TALLYING        TALLY-COUNTER
           FOR ALL         "DEBUGGING"

           IF              DEBUG
                           DISPLAY "USE FOR DEBUGGING STATEMENT FOUND"
                           DISPLAY "PROGRAM TERMINATED - USE EDIT"
```

```
                    GO TO PEOJ
     ELSE           GO TO P224-X.


P254-X. EXIT.

PABORT-P254.
*RUNAWAY CODE ABEND

     DISPLAY        "RUN ABORTED - RUNAWAY CODE AT P254"
     GO TO              PEOJ.


     EJECT
```

```
PC01-READ-COBOLIN.

     IF             DO-WRITE
*AUTO COPY OFF; WRITE OUT LAST READ SOURCE LINE BEFORE READ
                    PERFORM PC02-WRITE-COBOLOUT
                    THRU    PC02-X
     ELSE NEXT SENTENCE.

     READ           COBOLIN
     INTO           COBOL-LINE-WS
     AT END         GO TO PEOJ.

     IF             FILE-STATUS-OK
         NEXT SENTENCE
     ELSE           DISPLAY "RUN ABORTED - BAD FILE STATUS OF "
                         COBLPROG-FILE-STATUS
*ASSUMES OUTPUT TO PROGRAMMER'S TERMINAL
                    GO TO PEOJ.


     IF             DO-COPY
*AUTO COPY ON; DO IMMEDIATE WRITE; CANNOT INSERT NEW SOURCE
*LINE BEFORE SOURCE LINE JUST READ
                    PERFORM   PC02-WRITE-COBOLOUT
                    THRU    PC02-X
     IF             DO-READ
*AUTO COPY JUST TURNED OFF; MOVE WRITE TO SWITCH TO ENABLE
*WRITE BEFORE READ
                    MOVE    "WRIT"
                    TO      COPY-SWITCH
     ELSE NEXT SENTENCE.

*BYPASS NON STATEMENT LINE OR BLANK SOURCE LINE
```

```
        IF              NON-STATEMENT-LINE
        OR              BLANK-SOURCE-LINE
                        GO TO PCO1-READ-COBOLIN
        ELSE            GO TO PC01-X.

   PC01-X. EXIT.

   PABORT-PC01.
  *RUNAWAY CODE ABEND

        DISPLAY     "RUN ABORTED - RUNAWAY CODE AT PC01"
        GO TO       PEOJ.

        EJECT
```

```
   PC02-WRITE-COBOLOUT.

  *WRITE-SWITCH USED TO DETERMINE FROM IDENTIFIER
        IF              OLD-SOURCE-LINE
                        WRITE  COBOL-LINE-OUT
                        FROM   COBOL-LINE-WS
        ELSE            WRITE  COBOL-LINE-OUT
                        FROM   NEW-SOURCE-LINE.
  *NEW-SOURCE-LINE

        IF              FILE-STATUS-OK
                        GO TO  PC02-X
        ELSE            DISPLAY "RUN ABORTED - BAD FILE STATUS OF "
                            COBLPROG-FILE-STATUS
  *ASSUMES OUTPUT TO PROGRAMMER'S TERMINAL
                        GO TO PEOJ.

   PC02-X. EXIT.

   PABORT-PC02.
  *RUNAWAY CODE ABEND

        DISPLAY     "RUN ABORTED - RUNAWAY CODE AT PC02"

        GO TO       PEOJ.

        EJECT
```

```
PC03-FIND-WORDS.

    MOVE            SPACES
    TO              B-WORDS
                    WORD-DELIMITERS


    SET             AREA-B-INDEX
                    UNSTRING-POINTER
    TO              1


    SEARCH          AREA-B-BYTES
    VARYING         UNSTRING-POINTER
*AREA-B-BYTES INDEXED BY AREA-B-INDEX; UNSTRING POINTER IS
*KEPT IN SYNC AND WILL POINT TO THE FIRST ALPHA CHARACTER
*IN AREA B
    AT END          DISPLAY "RUN ABORTED - NO ALPHA CHARACTER
-                   "FOUND AT SEQUENCE NUMBER "
                    SEQUENCE-NUMBER
                    GO TO PEOJ
*CAN'T HAPPEN; IT MUST FIND AN ALPHA CHARACTER
    WHEN            ALPHA
        NEXT SENTENCE.
*FIRST ALPHA CHARACTER OF FIRST WORD FOUND


    UNSTRING        AREA-B
    DELIMITED ALL SPACES OR "." OR "," OR ";"
*.,; USED TO STRIP FROM WORD; FULL STOP NEEDED FOR SENTENCE
*END
    INTO            WORD-1
    DELIMITER IN WORD-1-DELIMITER
    INTO            WORD-2
    DELIMITER IN WORD-2-DELIMITER
    INTO            WORD-3
    DELIMITER IN WORD-3-DELIMITER
    INTO            WORD-4
    DELIMITER IN WORD-4-DELIMITER
    INTO            WORD-5
    DELIMITER IN WORD-5-DELIMITER
    INTO            WORD-6
    DELIMITER IN WORD-6-DELIMITER
    INTO            WORD-7
    DELIMITER IN WORD-7-DELIMITER
    INTO            WORD-8
    DELIMITER IN WORD-8-DELIMITER
    WITH POINTER UNSTRING-POINTER
```

```
         ON OVERFLOW   DISPLAY "RUN ABORTED - TOO MANY WORDS IN
-                      "SOURCE LINE AT SEQUENCE NUMBER "
                       SEQUENCE NUMBER
                       GO TO PEOJ.
*OVERFLOW MEANS MORE THEN 8 WORDS IN AREA B - NOT ALLOWED
*INCREASE RECEIVING WORDS IF REQUIRED

         GO TO         PC03-X.

 PCO3-X. EXIT.

 PABORT-PC03.
*RUNAWAY CODE ABEND

         DISPLAY       "RUN ABORTED - RUNAWAY CODE AT PC03"

         GO TO         PEOJ.

         EJECT
```

```
 PC10-WRITE-CONFIGURATION-SECTION.

         MOVE          "NEW"
         TO            WRITE-SWITCH

         MOVE          "CONFIGURATION SECTION."
         TO            NEW-AREA-AB

         PERFORM       PC02-WRITE-COBOLOUT
         THRU          PC02-X.

         MOVE          SPACES
         TO            NEW-SOURCE-LINE

         PERFORM       PC02-WRITE-COBOLOUT
         THRU          PC02-X.

         MOVE "*                 WITH DEBUGGING MODE."
         TO            NEW-INDICATOR-AREA-A-B

         PERFORM       PC02-WRITE-COBOLOUT
         THRU          PC02-X.

         MOVE          SPACES
         TO            NEW-SOURCE-LINE
```

```
        PERFORM         PC02-WRITE-COBOLOUT
        THRU            PC02-X.

        PERFORM         PC11-WRITE-SOURCE-COMPUTER
        THRU            PC11-X.

        GO TO           PC10-X.

  PC10-X. EXIT.

  PABORT-PC10.
*RUNAWAY CODE ABEND

        DISPLAY         "RUN ABORTED - RUNAWAY CODE AT PC10"

        GO TO           PEOJ.

        EJECT
```

```
  PC11-WRITE-SOURCE-COMPUTER.

        MOVE            "NEW"
        TO              WRITE-SWITCH

        MOVE            "SOURCE-COMPUTER."
        TO              NEW-AREA-AB

        PERFORM         PC02-WRITE-COBOLOUT
        THRU            PC02-X.

        MOVE            SPACES
        TO              NEW-SOURCE-LINE

        PERFORM         PC02-WRITE-COBOLOUT
        THRU            PC02-X.

        PERFORM         PC12-WRITE-DEBUGGING-MODE
        THRU            PC12-X.

        GO TO           PC11-X.

  PC11-X. EXIT.

  PABORT-PC11.
*RUNAWAY CODE ABEND
```

```
        DISPLAY         "RUN ABORTED - RUNAWAY CODE AT PC11"

        GO TO           PEOJ.

        EJECT
```

```
    PC12-WRITE-DEBUGGING-MODE.
        MOVE "*                    WITH DEBUGGING MODE."
        TO              NEW-INDICATOR-AREA-A-B

        PERFORM         PC02-WRITE-COBOLOUT
        THRU            PC02-X.

        MOVE            SPACES
        TO              NEW-SOURCE-LINE

        PERFORM         PC02-WRITE-COBOLOUT
        THRU            PC02-X.

        GO TO           PC12-X.

    PC12-X. EXIT.

    PABORT-PC12.
   *RUNAWAY CODE ABEND

        DISPLAY         "RUN ABORTED - RUNAWAY CODE AT PC12"

        GO TO           PEOJ.

        EJECT
```

INSEXIT

```
    IDENTIFICATION DIVISION.

    PROGRAM-ID.       INSEXIT.
   *PROGRAM INSERTS DIVIDE BY ZERO DEFENSIVE TRAP BEFORE EACH
   *EXIT PROGRAM, STOP RUN, & GOBACK [IBM]
   *PROGRAM ALSO INSERTS DEFENSIVE TRAP IF LAST SOURCE LINE IS
   *NOT A TRANSFER OF CONTROL
```

```
AUTHOR.          ERIC GARRIGUE VESELY
                 THE ANALYST WORKBENCH CONSULTING SDN BHD


DATE-WRITTEN. 26 FEBRUARY 1990

DATE-COMPILED.

ENVIRONMENT DIVISION.

CONFIGURATION SECTION.

SOURCE COMPUTER.
*                          WITH DEBUGGING MODE.
*ABOVE * IS SOURCE TIME SWITCH

 INPUT-OUTPUT SECTION.
 FILE CONTROL.
*SIMPLE SEQUENTIAL IO IS USED TO REDUCE COMPLEXITY

 SELECT              COBOLIN
*COBOLIN IS NAME OF FILE CONTAINING COBOL PROGRAM
     ASSIGN TO          SEQINPUT
*SEQINPUT IS NAME THAT COBOLIN IS ASSIGNED TO
     ORGANIZATION IS SEQUENTIAL
     ACCESS MODE  IS SEQUENTIAL
     FILE STATUS  IS    COBLPROG-FILE-STATUS.

 SELECT              COBOLOUT
*COBOLOUT IS NAME OF NEW FILE THAT CONTAINS TRAPPED COBOL
*PROGRAM
     ASSIGN TO          SEQOUTPT
*SEQOUTPT IS NAME THAT COBOLOUT IS ASSIGNED TO
     ORGANIZATION IS SEQUENTIAL
     ACCESS MODE  IS SEQUENTIAL
     FILE STATUS  IS    COBLPROG-FILE-STATUS.

     EJECT
```

```
 DATA DIVISION.

 FILE SECTION.

 FD           COBOLIN              LABEL RECORD STANDARD.

 01 COBOL-LINE-IN                  PIC X(80) USAGE DISPLAY.
```

```
*ASSUMES 80 COLUMN [BYTE] RECORDS

FD              COBOLOUT            LABEL RECORD STANDARD.

01  COBOL-LINE-OUT                 PIC X(80) USAGE DISPLAY.

WORKING-STORAGE SECTION.

01  COBOL-LINE-WS.
    02  SEQUENCE-NUMBER            PIC X(6)  USAGE DISPLAY.
    02  INDICATOR-A-B.
        03  INDICATOR              PIC X     USAGE DISPLAY.
            88  NON-STATEMENT-LINE           VALUE "*"
                                                   "D"
                                                   "/"
                                                   "-".

        03  AREA-AB.
            88  BLANK-SOURCE-LINE            VALUE SPACES.
            04  AREA-A             PIC X(4)  USAGE DISPLAY.
                88  IDENTIFICATION-DIVISION  VALUE "IDEN"
                                                   "ID D".
*IBM ABBREVIATION
                88  ENVIRONMENT-DIVISION     VALUE "ENVI".
                88  SELECT-CLAUSE            VALUE "SELE".
                88  CONFIGURATION-SECTION    VALUE "CONF".
                88  SOURCE-COMP              VALUE "SOUR".
                88  DATA-DIVISION            VALUE "DATA".
                88  WS-SECTION               VALUE "WORK".
                88  LEVEL-77                 VALUE "77  ".
                88  PROCEDURE-DIVISION       VALUE "PROC".
                88  DECLARE                  VALUE "DECL".
                88  BLANK-AREA-A             VALUE SPACES.
            04  AREA-B             PIC X(61) USAGE DISPLAY.
            04  AREA-B-BYTES REDEFINES AREA-B
                                   PIC X     OCCURS 61 TIMES
                                             INDEXED BY
                                             AREA-B-INDEX.
                88  ALPHA                    VALUE "A" THRU
                                                   "Z".
    02  IDEN-AREA                  PIC X(8)  USAGE DISPLAY.

01  COBLPROG-FILE-STATUS.
    02  SK1                        PIC X     USAGE DISPLAY.
        88  FILE-STATUS-OK                   VALUE "0".
    02  SK2                        PIC X     USAGE DISPLAY.

01. NEW-SOURCE-LINE                          VALUE SPACES.
```

```
    02  FILLER                   PIC X(6)  USAGE DISPLAY.
    02  NEW-INDICATOR-A-B.
        03  NEW-INDICATOR        PIC X     USAGE DISPLAY.
        03  NEW-AREA-AB.
            04  NEW-AREA-A        PIC X(4)  USAGE DISPLAY.
            04  NEW-AREA-B        PIC X(61) USAGE DISPLAY.
    02  FILLER                   PIC X(8)  USAGE DISPLAY.


01  DIVISION-PARAGRAPH-SWITCHES.
    02  ID-SWITCH                PIC X(5)  USAGE DISPLAY
                                           VALUE SPACES.
        88  ID-NOT-FOUND                   VALUE SPACES.
        88  ID-FOUND                       VALUE "FOUND".
    02  ENVIRONMENT-SWITCH       PIC X(5)  USAGE DISPLAY
                                           VALUE SPACES.
        88  ENVIRONMENT-NOT-FOUND          VALUE SPACES.
        88  ENVIRONMENT-FOUND              VALUE "FOUND".
    02  CONFIGURATION-SWITCH     PIC X(5)  USAGE DISPLAY
                                           VALUE SPACES.
        88  CONFIGURATION-NOT-FOUND        VALUE SPACES.
        88  CONFIGURATION-FOUND            VALUE "FOUND".
    02  SOURCE-SWITCH            PIC X(5)  USAGE DISPLAY
                                           VALUE SPACES.
        88  SOURCE-NOT-FOUND               VALUE SPACES.
        88  SOURCE-FOUND                   VALUE "FOUND".
    02  SELECT-SWITCH            PIC X(5)  USAGE DISPLAY
                                           VALUE SPACES.
        88  SELECT-NOT-FOUND               VALUE SPACES.
        88  SELECT-FOUND                   VALUE "FOUND".
    02  DATA-SWITCH              PIC X(5)  USAGE DISPLAY
                                           VALUE SPACES.
        88  DATA-NOT-FOUND                 VALUE SPACES.
        88  DATA-FOUND                     VALUE "FOUND".
    02  WS-SWITCH                PIC X(5)  USAGE DISPLAY
                                           VALUE SPACES.
        88  WS-NOT-FOUND                   VALUE SPACES.
        88  WS-FOUND                       VALUE "FOUND".
    02  PROCEDURE-SWITCH         PIC X(5)  USAGE DISPLAY
                                           VALUE SPACES.
        88  PROCEDURE-NOT-FOUND            VALUE SPACES.
        88  PROCEDURE-FOUND                VALUE "FOUND".
    02  DECLARATIVES-SWITCH      PIC X(5)  USAGE DISPLAY
                                           VALUE SPACES.
        88  DECLARATIVES-NOT-FOUND         VALUE SPACES.
        88  DECLARATIVES-FOUND             VALUE "FOUND".


01  COPY-SWITCH                  PIC X(4)  USAGE DISPLAY
```

```
                                                        VALUE "COPY".
        88  DO-COPY                                      VALUE "COPY".
*READ & DO IMMEDIATE WRITE; INSERTION OF NEW SOURCE LINE
*NOT ON
        88  DO-READ                                      VALUE "READ".
*READ ONLY; USED IMMEDIATELY AFTER AUTO COPY TURNED OFF
        88  DO-WRITE                                     VALUE "WRIT".
*AUTO COPY TURNED OFF; WRITE PREVIOUS SOURCE LINE BEFORE
*READ


    01  WRITE-SWITCH              PIC X(3)     USAGE DISPLAY
                                               VALUE "OLD".
        88  OLD-SOURCE-LINE                    VALUE "OLD".
            NEW-SOURCE-LINE                    VALUE "NEW".
    01  BREAKPOINT               PIC X(80)    USAGE DISPLAY.
        88  DUMP                               VALUE "D".


    01  TALLY-COUNTER            PIC S9V      USAGE COMP
                                               VALUE ZERO.
        88  DEBUG                              VALUE 1.
        88  DEFENSIVE-TRAP-FOUND               VALUE 1.
        88  END-DELIMITER                      VALUE 1.
        88  FULLSTOP                           VALUE 1.
        88  STATUS-FOUND                       VALUE 1.


    01  END-SCOPE-DELIMITER.
        02  FILLER               PIC X(4)     USAGE DISPLAY
                                               VALUE "END-".
        02  END-VERB             PIC X(26)    USAGE DISPLAY
                                               VALUE SPACES.


    01  NUMBER-OF-NUMERIC-ITEMS  PIC S999V  VALUE 999.
*OCCURS DEPENDING ON DATA-NAME FOR NUMERIC-ITEM-TABLE;
*IF TOO SMALL THEN CHANGE IT TO REQUIRED NUMBER


    01  NUMERIC-ITEM-TABLE.
        02  NUMERIC-ITEM             PIC X(30)
                                     OCCURS 1 TO 999 TIMES
*SECOND INTEGER MUST BE THE SAME VALUE AS NUMBER-OF-
*NUMERIC-ITEMS

                                     DEPENDING ON
                                     NUMBER-OF-NUMERIC-ITEMS
                                     INDEXED BY
                                     NUMERIC-ITEM-INDEX.


    01  UNSTRING-ITEMS.
        02  UNSTRING-POINTER     PIC S99V    USAGE COMP
```

```
                                            VALUE ZERO.
     02  B-WORDS.
        03  WORD-1                  PIC X(30)  USAGE DISPLAY.
            88  ARITHMETIC-VERB              VALUE "ADD"
                                                   "COMPUTE"
                                                   "DIVIDE"
                                                   "MULTIPLY"
                                                   "SUBTRACT".
            88  CALL-VERB                    VALUE "CALL".
            88  DIVIDE-VERB                  VALUE "DIVIDE".
            88  END-PERFORM-VERB             VALUE
                                             "END-PERFORM."
            88  EVALUATE-VERB                VALUE
                                                   "EVALUATE".
            88  EXIT-VERB                    VALUE "EXIT".
            88  GO-VERB                      VALUE "GO".
            88  GOBACK-VERB                  VALUE "GOBACK".
*IBM
            88  IF-VERB                      VALUE "IF".
            88  IO-VERB                      VALUE "CLOSE"
                                                   "DELETE"
                                                   "OPEN"
                                                   "READ"
                                                   "REWRITE"
                                                   "SEEK"
*IBM
                                                   "WRITE".
*PLACE ANY NON-ANSI I-O VERBS OF YOUR COMPILER IN THIS LIST
            88  MOVE-VERB                    VALUE "MOVE".
            88  PERFORM-VERB                 VALUE "PERFORM".
            88  SEARCH-VERB                  VALUE "SEARCH".
            88  STOP-VERB                    VALUE "STOP".
            88  STRING-UNSTRING-VERB         VALUE "STRING"
                                                   "UNSTRING".
            88  TARGET-VERB                  VALUE "ADD"
                                                   "CALL"
                                                   "COMPUTE"
                                                   "DIVIDE"
                                                   "EVALUATE"
                                                   "GO"
                                                   "MULTIPLY"
                                                   "SEARCH"
                                                   "STRING"
                                                   "SUBTRACT"
                                                   "UNSTRING".
            88  VERB                         VALUE "ACCEPT"
                                                   "ADD"
```

"ALTER"

*OBSOLETE

"CALL"
"CANCEL"
"CLOSE"
"COMPUTE"
"CONTINUE"

*COBOL-85

"COPY"

*TREATED LIKE A VERB

"DELETE"
"DISABLE"
"DISPLAY"
"DIVIDE"
"ELSE"

*TREATED LIKE A VERB

"ENABLE"
"ENTER"

*OBSOLETE

"EVALUATE"

*COBOL-85

"EXAMINE"

*COBOL-68

"EXIT"
"GENERATE"
"GO"
"GOBACK"

*IBM

"IF"

"INITIALIZE"

*COBOL-85

"INITIATE"
"INSPECT"
"MERGE"
"MOVE"
"MULTIPLY"
"OPEN"
"PERFORM"
"PURGE"
"READ"
"RECEIVE"
"RELEASE"
"REPLACE"

*COBOL-85; TREATED LIKE A VERB

"RETURN"
"REWRITE"

```
                                                     "SEARCH"
                                                     "SEEK"

*IBM
                                                     "SEND"
                                                     "SET"
                                                     "SORT"
                                                     "START"
                                                     "STOP"
                                                     "STRING"
                                                     "SUBTRACT"
                                                     "SUPPRESS"
                                                     "TERMINATE"
                                                     "TRANSFORM"

*IBM
                                                     "UNSTRING"
                                                     "USE"
                                                     "WRITE".
        03  WORD-2                PIC X(30)  USAGE DISPLAY.
*MUST CONTAIN PROGRAM-NAME FOR PROGRAM-ID PARAGRAPH
*ITEM DATA-NAME IF DATA DIVISION  BEING UNSTRING
*DIVISOR IF DIVIDE INTO BEING UNSTRING
*FROM ITEM DATA-NAME IF MOVE VERB BEING  UNSTRING
            88  CORR-PHASE                    VALUE
                                             "CORRESPONDING"
                                                       "CORR".

            88  PROGRAM-WORD                 VALUE "PROGRAM".
            88  RUN-WORD                     VALUE "RUN".
        03  WORD-3                PIC X(30)  USAGE DISPLAY.
            88  BY-WORD                      VALUE "BY".
            88  INTO-WORD                    VALUE "INTO".
            88  PICTURE-CLAUSE               VALUE "PICTURE"
                                                   "PIC".

            88  TO-WORD                      VALUE "TO".
        03  WORD-4                PIC X(30)  USAGE DISPLAY.
*DIVISOR IF DIVIDE BY VERB       BEING UNSTRING
*TO ITEM DATA-NAME IF MOVE VERB BEING UNSTRING
        03  WORD-4-BYTES REDEFINES WORD-4
            04  FILLER            PIC X      USAGE DISPLAY.
                88  SIGN-BYTE                VALUE "S".
            04  FILLER            PIC X(29)  USAGE DISPLAY.
        03  WORD-5                PIC X(30)  USAGE DISPLAY.
*MUST CONTAIN ALPHA IF ANALYZING GO TO DEPENDING ON
*STATEMENT
            88  NOT-PROCEDURE-NAME           VALUE SPACES.
        03  WORD-6                PIC X(30)  USAGE DISPLAY.
        03  WORD-7                PIC X(30)  USAGE DISPLAY.
```

```
            03  WORD-8                PIC X(30)  USAGE DISPLAY.
        02  WORD-DELIMITERS.
            03  WORD-DELIMITER-1      PIC X      USAGE DISPLAY.
            03  WORD-DELIMITER-2      PIC X      USAGE DISPLAY.
            03  WORD-DELIMITER-3      PIC X      USAGE DISPLAY.
            03  WORD-DELIMITER-4      PIC X      USAGE DISPLAY.
            03  WORD-DELIMITER-5      PIC X      USAGE DISPLAY.
            03  WORD-DELIMITER-6      PIC X      USAGE DISPLAY.
            03  WORD-DELIMITER-7      PIC X      USAGE DISPLAY.
            03  WORD-DELIMITER-8      PIC X      USAGE DISPLAY.
    *8 WORDS ARE USED TO ENSURE FULL STOP (.) IS FOUND


     01              PABORT-PARAGRAPH-NAME.
        02           FILLER           PIC X(7)   USAGE DISPLAY
                                                 VALUE "PABORT-".
        02           ODOMETER-DISPLAY PIC 9(4)   USAGE DISPLAY.
        02           ODOMETER REDEFINES ODOMETER-DISPLAY
                                      PIC S9(4)V USAGE COMP
                                                 VALUE ZERO.

    01-NEGATIVE-OR-ZERO-TRAP.
        02  FILLER                    PIC X(8)   USAGE DISPLAY
                                                 VALUE "D     IF ".
    *ACTIVE DEFENSIVE TRAP; D DISABLES UNTIL ANSI DEBUG TURNED
    *ON
        02  TRAP-DATA-NAME            PIC X(30)  USAGE DISPLAY
                                                 VALUE SPACES.
        02  FILLER                    PIC X      USAGE DISPLAY
                                                 VALUE SPACE.
        02  TRAP-TYPE                 PIC X(8)   USAGE DISPLAY
                                                 VALUE SPACES.


        EJECT
```

```
    PROCEDURE DIVISION.

    DECLARATIVES.

    DEBUG SECTION.

        USE FOR DEBUGGING ON ALL PROCEDURES.

    DEBUG-PROGRAM-FLOW.

        DISPLAY       DEBUG-LINE
```

```
                DEBUG-NAME
                DEBUG-CONTENTS.

 DEBUG-BREAKPOINT.

 *    ACCEPT        breakpoint   FROM mnemonic-name.
 * * USED TO DISABLE ACCEPT EVEN IF DEBUG MODULE IS ACTIVE
 * * IS DELETED WHEN INTERACTIVE BREAKPOINTS ARE REQUIRED


 END DECLARATIVES.

 P101-INITIATION.
      OPEN INPUT    COBOLIN

      OPEN OUTPUT   COBOLOUT

      DISPLAY       "INSEXIT PROGRAM START."

      GO TO         P102-IDENTIFICATION-DIVISION.

 P102-IDENTIFICATION-DIVISION.

      PERFORM       PC01-READ-COBOLIN
      THRU          PC01-X.

 *FIND IDENTIFICATION DIVISION
      IF            IDENTIFICATION-DIVISION
         NEXT SENTENCE
      ELSE          GO TO P102-IDENTIFICATION-DIVISION.

      MOVE          "FOUND"
      TO            ID-SWITCH

 *PROGRAM-ID MUST BE NEXT SOURCE LINE
      PERFORM       PC01-READ-COBOLIN
      THRU          PC01-X.

 *FIND FIRST WORD IN AREA B
      PERFORM       PCO3-FIND-WORDS
      THRU          PC03-X.

 *WORD-2 MUST BE PROGRAM NAME
      DISPLAY       "TARGET PROGRAM IS "
                    WORD-2

      GO TO         P103-PROCEDURE-DIVISION.
```

```
    P103-PROCEDURE-DIVISION.

        PERFORM        PC01-READ-COBOLIN
        THRU           PC01-X.

   *FIND PROCEDURE DIVISION
       IF              PROCEDURE-DIVISION
           NEXT SENTENCE
       ELSE            GO TO P103-PROCEDURE-DIVISION.

        MOVE           "FOUND"
        TO             PROCEDURE-SWITCH

        MOVE           "READ"
        TO             COPY-SWITCH

        GO TO          P104-EXIT-STOP-GOBACK-VERB.

    P104-EXIT-STOP-GOBACK-VERB.
   *FIND EXIT OR STOP OR GOBACK [IBM] VERB

        PERFORM        PC01-READ-COBOLIN
        THRU           PC01-X.

   *FIND FIRST TWO WORDS
        PERFORM        PC03-FIND-WORDS
        THRU           PC03-X.

        IF             GOBACK-VERB
                       PERFORM   PC10-INSERT-DIVIDE-ZERO-TRAP
                       THRU      PC10-X
                       GO TO    P104-EXIT-STOP-GOBACK-VERB
        ELSE
        IF             EXIT-VERB
        AND            PROGRAM-WORD
   *ASSUMES THAT EXIT & PROGRAM ON SAME SOURCE LINE
                       PERFORM PC10-INSERT-DIVIDE-ZERO-TRAP
                       THRU      PC10-X
                       GO TO    P104-EXIT-STOP-GOBACK-VERB
        ELSE
        IF             STOP-VERB
        AND            RUN-WORD
   *ASSUMES THAT STOP & RUN ON SAME SOURCE LINE
                       PERFORM PC10-INSERT-DIVIDE-ZERO-TRAP
                       THRU      PC10-X
                       GO TO    P104-EXIT-STOP-GOBACK-VERB
```

```
      ELSE            GO TO   P104-EXIT-STOP-GOBACK-VERB.

  PEOJ.

      IF              ID-NOT-FOUND
                      DISPLAY "NO IDENTIFICATION DIVISION"
      ELSE
      IF              PROCEDURE-NOT-FOUND
                      DISPLAY "NO PROCEDURE DIVISION"
                      GO TO PEOJ-1
      ELSE NEXT SENTENCE.

*LAST SOURCE LINE MUST CONTAIN EXIT PROGRAM, GO TO, GOBACK
*OR STOP RUN OTHERWISE PROGRAM FALLS INTO NEVER NEVER LAND
      IF              GO-VERB
      OR              GOBACK-VERB
                      GO TO  PEOJ-1
      ELSE
      IF              EXIT-VERB
      AND             PROGRAM-VERB
                      GO TO  PEOJ-1
      ELSE
      IF              STOP-VERB
      AND             RUN-VERB
                      GO TO    PEOJ-1
      ELSE
                      PERFORM PC10-INSERT-DIVIDE-ZERO-TRAP
                      THRU    PC10-X
                      GO TO    PEOJ-1.

   PEOJ-1.

      CLOSE           COBOLIN
                      COBOLOUT.

      DISPLAY         "INSEXIT PROGRAM EOJ."

      STOP RUN.

      EJECT
```

```
  PC01-READ-COBOLIN.

      IF              DO-WRITE
```

```
*AUTO COPY OFF; WRITE OUT LAST READ SOURCE LINE BEFORE READ
                    PERFORM  PC02-WRITE-COBOLOUT
                    THRU     PC02-X
     ELSE NEXT SENTENCE.
     READ           COBOLIN
     INTO           COBOL-LINE-WS
     AT END         GO TO PEOJ.


     IF             FILE-STATUS-OK
         NEXT SENTENCE
     ELSE           DISPLAY "RUN ABORTED - BAD FILE STATUS OF "
                        COBLPROG-FILE-STATUS
*ASSUMES OUTPUT TO PROGRAMMER'S TERMINAL
                    GO TO   PEOJ.


     IF             DO-COPY
*AUTO COPY ON; DO IMMEDIATE WRITE; CANNOT INSERT NEW SOURCE
*LINE BEFORE SOURCE LINE JUST READ
                    PERFORM  PC02-WRITE-COBOLOUT
                    THRU     PC02-X
     IF             DO-READ
*AUTO COPY JUST TURNED OFF; MOVE WRITE TO SWITCH TO ENABLE
*WRITE BEFORE READ
                    MOVE     "WRIT"
                    TO       COPY-SWITCH
     ELSE NEXT SENTENCE.


*BYPASS NON STATEMENT LINE OR BLANK SOURCE LINE
     IF             NON-STATEMENT-LINE
     OR             BLANK-SOURCE-LINE
                    GO TO    PCO1-READ-COBOLIN
     ELSE           GO TO    PC01-X.


 PC01-X. EXIT.


 PABORT-PC01.
*RUNAWAY CODE ABEND


     DISPLAY        "RUN ABORTED - RUNAWAY CODE AT PC01"


     GO TO          PEOJ.


     EJECT
```

```
 PC02-WRITE-COBOLOUT.

*WRITE-SWITCH USED TO DETERMINE FROM IDENTIFIER
     IF          OLD-SOURCE-LINE
                 WRITE    COBOL-LINE-OUT
                 FROM     COBOL-LINE-WS
     ELSE        WRITE    COBOL-LINE-OUT
                 FROMNEW-SOURCE-LINE.
*NEW-SOURCE-LINE

     IF          FILE-STATUS-OK
                 GO TO     PC02-X
     ELSE        DISPLAY "RUN ABORTED - BAD FILE STATUS OF "
                             COBLPROG-FILE-STATUS
*ASSUMES OUTPUT TO PROGRAMMER'S TERMINAL
                 GO TO PEOJ.

 PC02-X. EXIT.

 PABORT-PC02.
*RUNAWAY CODE ABEND

     DISPLAY        "RUN ABORTED - RUNAWAY CODE AT PC02"

     GO TO          PEOJ.

     EJECT
```

```
 PC03-FIND-WORDS.

     MOVE           SPACES
     TO             B-WORDS
                    WORD-DELIMITERS

     SET            AREA-B-INDEX
                    UNSTRING-POINTER
     TO             1

     SEARCH         AREA-B-BYTES
     VARYING        UNSTRING-POINTER
*AREA-B-BYTES INDEXED BY AREA-B-INDEX; UNSTRING POINTER IS
*KEPT IN SYNC AND WILL POINT TO THE FIRST ALPHA CHARACTER IN
*AREA B
     AT END         DISPLAY "RUN ABORTED - NO ALPHA CHARACTER
     -                "FOUND AT SEQUENCE NUMBER "
                    SEQUENCE-NUMBER
```

```
                         GO TO PEOJ
         *CAN'T HAPPEN; IT MUST FIND AN ALPHA CHARACTER
             WHEN        ALPHA
                 NEXT SENTENCE.
         *FIRST ALPHA CHARACTER OF FIRST WORD FOUND

             UNSTRING     AREA-B
             DELIMITED ALLSPACES OR "." OR "," OR ";"
         *.,; USED TO STRIP FROM WORD; FULL STOP NEEDED FOR
         *SENTENCE END
             INTO         WORD-1
             DELIMITER IN WORD-1-DELIMITER
             INTO         WORD-2
             DELIMITER IN WORD-2-DELIMITER
             INTO         WORD-3
             DELIMITER IN WORD-3-DELIMITER
             INTO         WORD-4
             DELIMITER IN WORD-4-DELIMITER
             INTO         WORD-5
             DELIMITER IN WORD-5-DELIMITER
             INTO         WORD-6
             DELIMITER IN WORD-6-DELIMITER
             INTO         WORD-7
             DELIMITER IN WORD-7-DELIMITER
             INTO         WORD-8
             DELIMITER IN WORD-8-DELIMITER
             WITH POINTER UNSTRING-POINTER
             ON OVERFLOW  DISPLAY "RUN ABORTED - TOO MANY WORDS IN
         -                "SOURCE LINE AT SEQUENCE NUMBER "
                          SEQUENCE NUMBER
                          GO TO PEOJ.
         *OVERFLOW MEANS MORE THEN 8 WORDS IN AREA B - NOT ALLOWED
         *INCREASE RECEIVING WORDS IF REQUIRED

             GO TO        PC03-X.

         PCO3-X. EXIT.

         PABORT-PC03.
         *RUNAWAY CODE ABEND

             DISPLAY      "RUN ABORTED - RUNAWAY CODE AT PC03"

             GO TO        PEOJ.

             EJECT
```

```
PC10-INSERT-DIVIDE-ZERO-TRAP.

      MOVE            "NEW"
      TO              WRITE-SWITCH

      MOVE            SPACES
      TO              NEW-SOURCE-LINE

      PERFORM         PC02-WRITE-COBOLOUT
      THRU            PC02-X.

      MOVE            "DIVIDE ZERO-LIT BY ZERO-LIT GIVING
                      "INFINITY."
      TO              NEW-AREA-B

      PERFORM         PC02-WRITE-COBOLOUT
      THRU            PC02-X.

      MOVE            "*DEFENSIVE TRAP INSERTED TO FORCE ABEND"
      TO              NEW-INDICATOR-A-B

      PERFORM         PC02-WRITE-COBOLOUT
      THRU            PC02-X.

      MOVE            SPACES
      TO              NEW-SOURCE-LINE

      PERFORM         PC02-WRITE-COBOLOUT
      THRU            PC02-X.

      MOVE            "OLD"
      TO              WRITE-SWITCH

      GO TO           PC10-X.

  PC10-X.   EXIT.

  PABORT-PC10.
 *RUNAWAY CODE ABEND

      DISPLAY         "RUN ABORTED - RUNAWAY CODE AT PC10"

      GO TO           PEOJ.

      EJECT
```

ISNEG

```
 IDENTIFICATION DIVISION.

 PROGRAM-ID.        INSNEG.
*PROGRAM INSERTS IF NEGATIVE DEFENSIVE TEST ON MOVE;
*ONLY SIMPLE SYNTAX OF MOVE ITEM TO ITEM ON ONE LINE IS
*PROCESSED
*PROGRAM INSERTS IF ZERO DEFENSIVE TEST ON DIVIDE;
*ONLY SIMPLE SYNTAX OF DIVIDE BY/INTO ON ONE LINE IS
*PROCESSED

 AUTHOR.            ERIC GARRIGUE VESELY
                    THE ANALYST WORKBENCH CONSULTING SDN BHD

 DATE-WRITTEN.    26 FEBRUARY 1990

 DATE-COMPILED.

 ENVIRONMENT DIVISION.

 CONFIGURATION SECTION.

 SOURCE COMPUTER.
*                    WITH DEBUGGING MODE.
*ABOVE * IS SOURCE TIME SWITCH

 SPECIAL-NAMES.    IMPLEMENTOR-NAME
                    MNEMONIC-NAME
*SETUP SPECIAL-NAMES TO PRINT TO LOCAL PRINTER ON DISPLAY
*UPON

 FILE CONTROL.
*SIMPLE SEQUENTIAL IO IS USED TO REDUCE COMPLEXITY

 SELECT            COBOLIN
*COBOLIN IS NAME OF FILE CONTAINING COBOL PROGRAM
    ASSIGN TO      SEQINPUT
*SEQINPUT IS NAME THAT COBOLIN IS ASSIGNED TO
    ORGANIZATION IS SEQUENTIAL
    ACCESS MODE   IS SEQUENTIAL
    FILE STATUS   IS  COBLPROG-FILE-STATUS.

 SELECT            COBOLOUT
*COBOLOUT IS NAME OF NEW FILE THAT CONTAINS TRAPPED COBOL
*PROGRAM
    ASSIGN TO      SEQOUTPT
```

```
*SEQOUTPT IS NAME THAT COBOLOUT IS ASSIGNED TO
     ORGANIZATION IS SEQUENTIAL
     ACCESS MODE  IS SEQUENTIAL
     FILE STATUS  IS COBLPROG-FILE-STATUS.

     EJECT
```

```
DATA DIVISION.

FILE SECTION.

FD           COBOLIN              LABEL RECORD STANDARD.

01 COBOL-LINE-IN                  PIC X(80) USAGE DISPLAY.
*ASSUMES 80 COLUMN [BYTE] RECORDS

FD           COBOLOUT             LABEL RECORD STANDARD.

01 COBOL-LINE-OUT                 PIC X(80) USAGE DISPLAY.

WORKING-STORAGE SECTION.

01 COBOL-LINE-WS.
   02 SEQUENCE-NUMBER             PIC X(6)  USAGE DISPLAY.
   02 INDICATOR-A-B.
      03 INDICATOR                PIC X     USAGE DISPLAY.
         88 NON-STATEMENT-LINE              VALUE "*"
                                                  "D"
                                                  "/"
                                                  "-".

      03 AREA-AB.
         88 BLANK-SOURCE-LINE               VALUE SPACES.
         04 AREA-A               PIC X(4)   USAGE DISPLAY.
            88 IDENTIFICATION-DIVISION      VALUE "IDEN"
                                                  "ID D".

*IBM ABBREVIATION
            88 ENVIRONMENT-DIVISION         VALUE "ENVI".
            88 SELECT-CLAUSE                VALUE "SELE".
            88 CONFIGURATION-SECTION        VALUE "CONF".
            88 SOURCE-COMP                  VALUE "SOUR".
            88 DATA-DIVISION                VALUE "DATA".
            88 WS-SECTION                   VALUE "WORK".
            88 LEVEL-77                     VALUE "77  ".
            88 PROCEDURE-DIVISION           VALUE "PROC".
            88 DECLARE                      VALUE "DECL".
```

```
                88  BLANK-AREA-A                VALUE SPACES.
          04  AREA-B                    PIC X(61) USAGE DISPLAY.
          04  AREA-B-BYTES REDEFINES AREA-B
                                        PIC X     OCCURS 61 TIMES
                                                  INDEXED BY
                                                  AREA-B-INDEX.
                88  ALPHA                         VALUE "A" THRU
                                                        "Z".
      02  IDEN-AREA                     PIC X(8)  USAGE DISPLAY.


  01  COBLPROG-FILE-STATUS.
      02  SK1                           PIC X     USAGE DISPLAY.
          88  FILE-STATUS-OK                      VALUE "0".
      02  SK2                           PIC X     USAGE DISPLAY.


  01  NEW-SOURCE-LINE                             VALUE SPACES.
      02  FILLER                        PIC X(6)  USAGE DISPLAY.
      02  NEW-INDICATOR-A-B.
          03  NEW-INDICATOR             PIC X     USAGE DISPLAY.
          03  NEW-AREA-AB.
              04  NEW-AREA-A            PIC X(4)  USAGE DISPLAY.
              04  NEW-AREA-B            PIC X(61) USAGE DISPLAY.
      02  FILLER                        PIC X(8)  USAGE DISPLAY.


  01  DIVISION-PARAGRAPH-SWITCHES.
      02  ID-SWITCH                     PIC X(5)  USAGE DISPLAY
                                                  VALUE SPACES.
          88  ID-NOT-FOUND                        VALUE SPACES.
          88  ID-FOUND                            VALUE "FOUND".
      02  ENVIRONMENT-SWITCH            PIC X(5)  USAGE DISPLAY
                                                  VALUE SPACES.
          88  ENVIRONMENT-NOT-FOUND               VALUE SPACES.
          88  ENVIRONMENT-FOUND                   VALUE "FOUND".
      02  CONFIGURATION-SWITCH          PIC X(5)  USAGE DISPLAY
                                                  VALUE SPACES.
          88  CONFIGURATION-NOT-FOUND             VALUE SPACES.
          88  CONFIGURATION-FOUND                 VALUE "FOUND".
      02  SOURCE-SWITCH                 PIC X(5)  USAGE DISPLAY
                                                  VALUE SPACES.
          88  SOURCE-NOT-FOUND                    VALUE SPACES.
          88  SOURCE-FOUND                        VALUE "FOUND".
      02  SELECT-SWITCH                 PIC X(5)  USAGE DISPLAY
                                                  VALUE SPACES.
          88  SELECT-NOT-FOUND                    VALUE SPACES.
          88  SELECT-FOUND                        VALUE "FOUND".
```

```
   02  DATA-SWITCH                          PIC X(5)  USAGE DISPLAY
                                                      VALUE SPACES.
       88  DATA-NOT-FOUND                              VALUE SPACES.
       88  DATA-FOUND                                  VALUE "FOUND".
   02  WS-SWITCH                            PIC X(5)  USAGE DISPLAY
                                                      VALUE SPACES.
       88  WS-NOT-FOUND                                VALUE SPACES.
       88  WS-FOUND                                    VALUE "FOUND".
   02  PROCEDURE-SWITCH                     PIC X(5)  USAGE DISPLAY
                                                      VALUE SPACES.
       88  PROCEDURE-NOT-FOUND                         VALUE SPACES.
       88  PROCEDURE-FOUND                             VALUE "FOUND".
   02  DECLARATIVES-SWITCH                  PIC X(5)  USAGE DISPLAY
                                                      VALUE SPACES.
       88  DECLARATIVES-NOT-FOUND                      VALUE SPACES.
       88  DECLARATIVES-FOUND                          VALUE "FOUND".


 01  COPY-SWITCH                            PIC X(4)  USAGE DISPLAY
                                                      VALUE "COPY".
       88  DO-COPY                                     VALUE "COPY".
*READ & DO IMMEDIATE WRITE; INSERTION OF NEW SOURCE LINE NOT
*ON
       88  DO-READ                                     VALUE "READ".
*READ ONLY; USED IMMEDIATELY AFTER AUTO COPY TURNED OFF
       88  DO-WRITE                                    VALUE "WRIT".
*AUTO COPY TURNED OFF; WRITE PREVIOUS SOURCE LINE BEFORE
*READ

 01  WRITE-SWITCH                           PIC X(3)  USAGE DISPLAY
                                                      VALUE "OLD".
       88  OLD-SOURCE-LINE                             VALUE "OLD".
           NEW-SOURCE-LINE                             VALUE "NEW".


 01  BREAKPOINT                             PIC X(80) USAGE DISPLAY.
       88  DUMP                                        VALUE "D".


 01  TALLY-COUNTER                          PIC S9V   USAGE COMP
                                                      VALUE ZERO.
       88  DEBUG                                       VALUE 1.
       88  DEFENSIVE-TRAP-FOUND                        VALUE 1.
       88  END-DELIMITER                               VALUE 1.
       88  FULLSTOP                                    VALUE 1.
       88  STATUS-FOUND                                VALUE 1.
 01  END-SCOPE-DELIMITER.
     02  FILLER                             PIC X(4)  USAGE DISPLAY
```

```
                                                  VALUE "CLOSE"
        02  END-VERB              PIC X(26) USAGE DISPLAY
                                                  VALUE SPACES.


    01  NUMBER-OF-NUMERIC-ITEMS   PIC S999V VALUE 999.
    *OCCURS DEPENDING ON DATA-NAME FOR NUMERIC-ITEM-TABLE;
    *IF TOO SMALL THEN CHANGE IT TO REQUIRED NUMBER


    01  NUMERIC-ITEM-TABLE.
        02  NUMERIC-ITEM          PIC X(30)
                                    OCCURS 1 TO 999 TIMES
    *SECOND INTEGER MUST BE THE SAME VALUE AS NUMBER-OF-NUMERIC-
    *ITEMS
                                    DEPENDING ON
                                    NUMBER-OF-NUMERIC-ITEMS
                                    INDEXED BY
                                    NUMERIC-ITEM-INDEX.


    01  UNSTRING-ITEMS.
        02  UNSTRING-POINTER      PIC S99V  USAGE COMP
                                            VALUE ZERO.

        02  B-WORDS.
            03  WORD-1            PIC X(30) USAGE DISPLAY.
                88  LEVEL-NUMBER             VALUE "02 THRU 49".
                88  ARITHMETIC-VERB          VALUE "ADD"
                                                   "COMPUTE"
                                                   "DIVIDE"
                                                   "MULTIPLY"
                                                   "SUBTRACT".
                88  CALL-VERB                VALUE "CALL".
                88  DIVIDE-VERB              VALUE "DIVIDE".
                88  END-PERFORM-VERB         VALUE "END-PERFORM."

                88  EVALUATE-VERB            VALUE "EVALUATE".
                88  EXIT-VERB                VALUE "EXIT".
                88  GO-VERB                  VALUE "GO".
                88  GOBACK-VERB              VALUE "GOBACK".
    *IBM
                88  IF-VERB                  VALUE "IF".
                88  IO-VERB                  VALUE "CLOSE"
                                                   "DELETE"
                                                   "OPEN"
                                                   "READ"
                                                   "REWRITE"
                                                   "SEEK"
```

```
*IBM
                                           "WRITE".
*PLACE ANY NON-ANSI I-O VERBS OF YOUR COMPILER IN THIS LIST
            88  MOVE-VERB              VALUE "MOVE".
            88  PERFORM-VERB           VALUE "PERFORM".
            88  SEARCH-VERB            VALUE "SEARCH".
            88  STOP-VERB              VALUE "STOP".
            88  STRING-UNSTRING-VERB   VALUE "STRING"
                                             "UNSTRING".

            88  TARGET-VERB            VALUE "ADD"
                                             "CALL"
                                             "COMPUTE"
                                             "DIVIDE"
                                             "EVALUATE"
                                             "GO"
                                             "MULTIPLY"
                                             "SEARCH"
                                             "STRING"
                                             "SUBTRACT"
                                             "UNSTRING".

                88  VERB               VALUE "ACCEPT"
                                             "ADD"
                                             "ALTER"

    *OBSOLETE
                                             "CALL"
                                             "CANCEL"
                                             "CLOSE"
                                             "COMPUTE"
                                             "CONTINUE"

    *COBOL-85
                                             "COPY"

    *TREATED LIKE A VERB
                                             "DELETE"
                                             "DISABLE"
                                             "DISPLAY"
                                             "DIVIDE"
                                             "ELSE"

    *TREATED LIKE A VERB
                                             "ENABLE"
                                             "ENTER"

    *OBSOLETE
                                             "EVALUATE"

    *COBOL-85
                                             "EXAMINE"

    *COBOL-68
                                             "EXIT"
```

"GENERATE"
"GO"
"GOBACK"

*IBM

"IF"

"INITIALIZE"

*COBOL-85

"INITIATE"
"INSPECT"
"MERGE"
"MOVE"
"MULTIPLY"
"OPEN"
"PERFORM"
"PURGE"
"READ"
"RECEIVE"
"RELEASE"
"REPLACE"

*COBOL-85; TREATED LIKE A VERB

"RETURN"
"REWRITE"
"SEARCH"
"SEEK"

*IBM

"SEND"
"SET"
"SORT"
"START"
"STOP"
"STRING"
"SUBTRACT"
"SUPPRESS"
"TERMINATE"
"TRANSFORM"

*IBM

"UNSTRING"
"USE"
"WRITE".
      03 WORD-2   PIC X(30) USAGE DISPLAY.
*MUST CONTAIN PROGRAM-NAME FOR PROGRAM-ID PARAGRAPH
*ITEM DATA-NAME IF DATA DIVISION BEING UNSTRING
*DIVISOR IF DIVIDE INTO BEING UNSTRING
*FROM ITEM DATA-NAME IF MOVE VERB BEING UNSTRING
         88 CORR-PHASE   VALUE

```
                                        "CORRESPONDING"
                                              "CORR".
      88  PROGRAM-WORD              VALUE "PROGRAM".
      88  RUN-WORD                  VALUE "RUN".
   03  WORD-3            PIC X(30)  USAGE DISPLAY.
      88  BY-WORD                   VALUE "BY".
      88  INTO-WORD                 VALUE "INTO".
      88  PICTURE-CLAUSE            VALUE "PICTURE"
                                          "PIC".
      88  TO-WORD                   VALUE "TO".
   03  WORD-4            PIC X(30)  USAGE DISPLAY.
*DIVISOR IF DIVIDE BY VERB    BEING UNSTRING
*TO ITEM DATA-NAME IF MOVE VERB BEING UNSTRING
   03  WORD-4-BYTES REDEFINES WORD-4
      04  FILLER         PIC X      USAGE DISPLAY.
         88  SIGN-BYTE             VALUE "S".
      04  FILLER         PIC X(29)  USAGE DISPLAY.
   03  WORD-5            PIC X(30)  USAGE DISPLAY.
*MUST CONTAIN ALPHA IF ANALYZING GO TO DEPENDING ON
*STATEMENT
      88  NOT-PROCEDURE-NAME        VALUE SPACES.
   03  WORD-6            PIC X(30)  USAGE DISPLAY.
   03  WORD-7            PIC X(30)  USAGE DISPLAY.
   03  WORD-8           `PIC X(30)  USAGE DISPLAY.
 02  WORD-DELIMITERS.
   03  WORD-DELIMITER-1   PIC X     USAGE DISPLAY.
   03  WORD-DELIMITER-2   PIC X     USAGE DISPLAY.
   03  WORD-DELIMITER-3   PIC X     USAGE DISPLAY.
   03  WORD-DELIMITER-4   PIC X     USAGE DISPLAY.
   03  WORD-DELIMITER-5   PIC X     USAGE DISPLAY.
   03  WORD-DELIMITER-6   PIC X     USAGE DISPLAY.
   03  WORD-DELIMITER-7   PIC X     USAGE DISPLAY.
   03  WORD-DELIMITER-8   PIC X     USAGE DISPLAY.
*8 WORDS ARE USED TO ENSURE FULL STOP (.) IS FOUND


 01       PABORT-PARAGRAPH-NAME.
   02     FILLER             PIC X(7)   USAGE DISPLAY
                                        VALUE "PABORT-".
   02     ODOMETER-DIS PLAY  PIC 9(4)   USAGE DISPLAY.
   02     ODOMETER REDEFINES ODOMETER-DISPLAY
                             PIC S9(4)V USAGE COMP
                                        VALUE ZERO.


01-NEGATIVE-OR-ZERO-TRAP.
  02 FILLER                  PIC X(8)   USAGE DISPLAY
                                        VALUE "D    IF ".
```

```
*ACTIVE DEFENSIVE TRAP; D DISABLES UNTIL ANSI DEBUG TURNED
*ON
    02  TRAP-DATA-NAME          PIC X(30)   USAGE DISPLAY
                                            VALUE SPACES.
    02  FILLER                  PIC X       USAGE DISPLAY
                                            VALUE SPACE.
    02  TRAP-TYPE               PIC X(8)    USAGE DISPLAY
                                            VALUE SPACES.

    EJECT
```

```
PROCEDURE DIVISION.

    DECLARATIVES.

    DEBUG SECTION.

        USE FOR DEBUGGING ON ALL PROCEDURES.

    DEBUG-PROGRAM-FLOW.

        DISPLAY         DEBUG-LINE
                        DEBUG-NAME
                        DEBUG-CONTENTS.

    DEBUG-BREAKPOINT.

*       ACCEPT          breakpoint      FROM mnemonic-name.
* *  USED TO DISABLE ACCEPT EVEN IF DEBUG MODULE IS ACTIVE
* *  IS DELETED WHEN INTERACTIVE BREAKPOINTS ARE REQUIRED

    END DECLARATIVES.

    P101-INITIATION.

        OPEN INPUT      COBOLIN

        DISPLAY         "INSNEG PROGRAM START."

        SET             NUMERIC-ITEM-INDEX
        TO              1

        GO TO           P102-IDENTIFICATION-DIVISION.

    P102-IDENTIFICATION-DIVISION.
```

```
         PERFORM        PC10-READ-COBOLIN
         THRU           PC10-X.

*FIND IDENTIFICATION DIVISION
         IF             IDENTIFICATION-DIVISION
             NEXT SENTENCE
         ELSE           GO TO P102-IDENTIFICATION-DIVISION.

         MOVE           "FOUND"
         TO             ID-SWITCH

*PROGRAM-ID MUST BE NEXT STATEMENT LINE
         PERFORM        PC10-READ-COBOLIN
         THRU           PC10-X.

*FIND WORDS IN AREA B
         PERFORM        PCO3-FIND-WORDS
         THRU           PC03-X.

*WORD-2 MUST BE PROGRAM NAME
         DISPLAY        "TARGET PROGRAM IS "
                        WORD-2

         GO TO          P103-DATA-DIVISION.

  P103-DATA-DIVISION.
*FIND DATA DIVISION

         PERFORM        PC10-READ-COBLPROG
         THRU           PC10-X.

         IF             DATA-DIVISION
                        MOVE   "FOUND"
                        TO     DATA-SWITCH
                        GO TO  P104-FIND-ITEMS
         ELSE           GO TO  P103-DATA-DIVISION.

  P104-FIND-ITEMS.
*FIND SIGNED NUMERIC ITEMS (PIC CONTAINS S9...)

         PERFORM        PC10-READ-COBLPROG
         THRU           PC10-X.

         IF             PROCEDURE-DIVISION
                        MOVE   "FOUND"
                        TO     PROCEDURE-SWITCH
```

```
                    MOVE     "READ"
                    TO       COPY-SWITCH
 *TURN AUTO COPY OFF
                    GO TO P105-FIND-DIVIDE-OR-MOVE-VERB
     ELSE   NEXT SENTENCE.


 *FIND WORDS IN AREA B
     PERFORM      PCO3-FIND-WORDS
     THRU         PC03-X.


     IF           LEVEL-NUMBER
        NEXT SENTENCE
     ELSE         GO TO  P104-FIND-ITEMS.

 *ITEM FORMAT MUST BE LEVEL-NUMBER, DATA-NAME, [PIC], [PIC
 *STRING] DETERMINE IF ELEMENTARY ITEM (HAS PIC)
     IF           PICTURE-CLAUSE
        NEXT SENTENCE
     ELSE         GO TO  P104-FIND-ITEMS.

     *DETERMINE IF SIGNED NUMERIC (S IN FIRST BYTE)
     IF           SIGN-BYTE
        NEXT SENTENCE
     ELSE         GO TO  P104-FIND-ITEMS.

 *MOVE ITEM DATA-NAME (WORD 2) TO NUMERIC ITEM TABLE
     MOVE         WORD-2
     TO           NUMERIC-ITEM-TABLE(NUMERIC-ITEM-INDEX)

     SET          NUMERIC-ITEM-INDEX
     UP BY        1

 *VET NUMERIC-ITEM FOR IN RANGE

     IF           NUMERIC-ITEM-INDEX
     >            NUMBER-OF-NUMERIC-ITEMS
                  DISPLAY "RUN ABORTED - TOO MANY ITEMS"
 *ASSUMES OUTPUT TO PROGRAMMER'S TERMINAL
                  GO TO  PEOJ
     ELSE         GO TO  P104-FIND-ITEMS.


 P105-FIND-DIVIDE-OR-MOVE-VERB.
 *DETERMINE IF MOVE IS MOVING SIGNED NUMERIC TO UNSIGNED;
 *INSTALL IF NEGATIVE DEFENSIVE TRAP IF YES
     PERFORM      PC10-READ-COBLPROG
     THRU         PC10-X.


 *FIND WORDS IN AREA-B
```

```
        PERFORM        PC03-FIND-WORDS
        THRU           PC03-X.

        IF             DIVIDE-VERB
                       PERFORM   P251-DIVIDE-VERB
                       THRU   P251-X
                       GO TO  P105-FIND-DIVIDE-OR-MOVE-VERB
        ELSE   NEXT SENTENCE.

        IF             MOVE-VERB
                       PERFORM   P252-MOVE-VERB
                       THRU   P252-X
                       GO TO  P105-FIND-DIVIDE-OR-MOVE-VERB
        ELSE           GO TO  P105-FIND-DIVIDE-OR-MOVE-VERB.

    PEOJ.

        CLOSE          COBOLIN.

        IF             ID-NOT-FOUND
                       DISPLAY "NO IDENTIFICATION DIVISION"
        ELSE
        IF             DATA-NOT-FOUND
                       DISPLAY "NO DATA DIVISION"
        ELSE NEXT SENTENCE.

        DISPLAY        "INSNEG PROGRAM EOJ."

        STOP RUN.

        EJECT
```

```
     P251-DIVIDE-VERB.
    *INSERT IF ZERO DIVIDE DEFENSIVE TEST ON ONE LINE DIVIDE
    *STATEMENT; SYNTAX IS DIVIDE DATA-ITEM-1 BY/INTO DATA-
    *ITEM-2

        IF             BY-WORD
                       MOVE   WORD-4
                       TO     TRAP-DATA-NAME
    *WORD-4 MUST BE DIVISOR
        IF             INTO-WORD
                       MOVE   WORD-2
                       TO     TRAP-DATA-NAME
    *WORD-2 MUST BE DIVISOR
```

```
     ELSE              DISPLAY"COMPLEX DIVIDE AT "
                             SEQUENCE-NUMBER
                       GO TO   P251-X.
   *DIVIDE STATEMENT NOT ON ONE LINE - WARN PROGRAMMER

       MOVE              "NEW"
       TO                WRITE-SWITCH

       MOVE              "ZERO"
       TO                TRAP-TYPE

       MOVE              DEFENSIVE-TRAP
       TO                NEW-INDICATOR-A-B

       PERFORM           PC02-WRITE-COBLPROG
       THRU              PC02-X.

       MOVE              "D"
       TO                NEW-INDICATOR
   *DISABLE ACTIVE DEFENSIVE TRAP FOR PRODUCTION

       MOVE              "DIVIDE ZERO-LIT BY ZERO-LIT GIVING
   -                     "INFINITY"
       TO                NEW-AREA-B

       PERFORM           PC02-WRITE-COBLPROG
       THRU              PC02-X.

       MOVE              "*ACTIVATE TO TRAP ZERO DIVISOR
       TO                NEW-INDICATOR-A-B

       PERFORM           PC02-WRITE-COBLPROG
       THRU              PC02-X.

       GO TO             P251-X.

   P251-X.   EXIT.

   PABORT-P251.
   *RUNAWAY CODE ABEND

       DISPLAY           "RUN ABORTED - RUNAWAY CODE AT P251"

       GO TO             PEOJ.

       EJECT
```

```
 P252-MOVE-VERB.
*INSERT IF NEGATIVE IF TO DATA-NAME IS UNSIGNED
*ONLY SIMPLE MOVE SYNTAX OF MOVE ITEM TO ITEM IS PROCESSED

*BYPASS MOVE CORR
    IF            CORR-PHASE
                  DISPLAY"MOVE CORRESPONDING AT "
                        SEQUENCE-NUMBER
                  GO TO   P105-FIND-MOVE-VERB
    ELSE   NEXT SENTENCE.

    SEARCH        NUMERIC-ITEM-TABLE
    VARYING       NUMERIC-ITEM-INDEX
    AT END        GO TO P252-X
*FROM ITEM IS NON NUMERIC - BYPASS
    WHEN          WORD-2
    =             NUMERIC-ITEM-TABLE
        NEXT SENTENCE.

    IF            TO-WORD
        NEXT SENTENCE
    ELSE          DISPLAY"COMPLEX MOVE AT "
                        SEQUENCE-NUMBER
*TO IS NOT THIRD WORD; WARN PROGRAMMER
                  GO TO   P105-FIND-MOVE-VERB
    ELSE   NEXT SENTENCE.

    SEARCH        NUMERIC-ITEM-TABLE
    VARYING       NUMERIC-ITEM-INDEX
    AT END        PERFORM P321-INSERT-IF-NEGATIVE
                  THRU    P321-X
*TO ITEM IS NON NUMERIC - INSERT IF NEGATIVE TRAP
    WHEN          WORD-4
    =             NUMERIC-ITEM-TABLE
                  GO TO  P252-X.
*TO ITEM IS NUMERIC - BYPASS

 P252-X.   EXIT.
 PABORT-P252.
*RUNAWAY CODE ABEND

    DISPLAY       "RUN ABORTED - RUNAWAY CODE AT P252"

    GO TO         PEOJ.

    EJECT
```

```
    P321-INSERT-IF-NEGATIVE.

        MOVE            "NEW"
        TO              WRITE-SWITCH

        MOVE            "WORD-2"
        TO              TRAP-DATA-NAME

        MOVE            "NEGATIVE"
        TO              TRAP-TYPE

        MOVE            DEFENSIVE-TRAP
        TO              NEW-INDICATOR-A-B

        PERFORM         PC02-WRITE-COBLPROG
        THRU            PC02-X.

        MOVE            "D"
        TO              NEW-INDICATOR
*DISABLE ACTIVE DEFENSIVE TRAP FOR PRODUCTION
        MOVE            "DIVIDE ZERO-LIT BY ZERO-LIT GIVING
                            INFINITY"
        TO              NEW-AREA-B

        PERFORM         PC02-WRITE-COBLPROG
        THRU            PC02-X.

        MOVE            "*ACTIVATE TO TRAP LOSS OF MINUS SIGN
        TO              NEW-INDICATOR-A-B

        PERFORM         PC02-WRITE-COBLPROG
        THRU            PC02-X.

        GO TO           P321-X.

    P321-X.   EXIT.

    PABORT-P321.
*RUNAWAY CODE ABEND

        DISPLAY         "RUN ABORTED - RUNAWAY CODE AT P321"

        GO TO           PEOJ.

        EJECT
```

```
PC01-READ-COBOLIN.

    IF              DO-WRITE
*AUTO COPY OFF; WRITE OUT LAST READ SOURCE LINE BEFORE READ
                PERFORM PC02-WRITE-COBOLOUT
                THRU     PC02-X
    ELSE NEXT SENTENCE.


    READ            COBOLIN
    INTO            COBOL-LINE-WS
    AT END          GO TO PEOJ.


    IF              FILE-STATUS-OK
        NEXT SENTENCE
    ELSE            DISPLAY "RUN ABORTED - BAD FILE STATUS OF "
                        COBLPROG-FILE-STATUS
*ASSUMES OUTPUT TO PROGRAMMER'S TERMINAL
                GO TO PEOJ.
    IF              DO-COPY
*AUTO COPY ON; DO IMMEDIATE WRITE; CANNOT INSERT NEW SOURCE
*LINE BEFORE SOURCE LINE JUST READ
                PERFORM   PC02-WRITE-COBOLOUT
                THRU    PC02-X
    IF              DO-READ
*AUTO COPY JUST TURNED OFF; MOVE WRITE TO SWITCH TO ENABLE
*WRITE BEFORE READ
                MOVE    "WRIT"
                TO      COPY-SWITCH
    ELSE NEXT SENTENCE.

*BYPASS NON STATEMENT LINE OR BLANK SOURCE LINE
    IF              NON-STATEMENT-LINE
    OR              BLANK-SOURCE-LINE
                GO TO PC01-READ-COBOLIN
    ELSE            GO TO PC01-X.

 PC01-X. EXIT.

 PABORT-PC01.
*RUNAWAY CODE ABEND

    DISPLAY         "RUN ABORTED - RUNAWAY CODE AT PC01"

    GO TO           PEOJ.

    EJECT
```

```
    PC02-WRITE-COBOLOUT.

*WRITE-SWITCH USED TO DETERMINE FROM IDENTIFIER
    IF            OLD-SOURCE-LINE
                  WRITE  COBOL-LINE-OUT
                  FROM   COBOL-LINE-WS
    ELSE          WRITE  COBOL-LINE-OUT
                  FROM   NEW-SOURCE-LINE.
*NEW-SOURCE-LINE

    IF            FILE-STATUS-OK
                  GO TO  PC02-X
    ELSE          DISPLAY "RUN ABORTED - BAD FILE STATUS OF "
                      COBLPROG-FILE-STATUS
*ASSUMES OUTPUT TO PROGRAMMER'S TERMINAL
                  GO TO PEOJ.

    PC02-X. EXIT.
    PABORT-PC02.
*RUNAWAY CODE ABEND

    DISPLAY       "RUN ABORTED - RUNAWAY CODE AT PC02"

    GO TO         PEOJ.

    EJECT
```

```
    PC03-FIND-WORDS.

    MOVE          SPACES
    TO            B-WORDS
                  WORD-DELIMITERS

    SET           AREA-B-INDEX
                  UNSTRING-POINTER
    TO            1

    SEARCH        AREA-B-BYTES
    VARYING       UNSTRING-POINTER
*AREA-B-BYTES INDEXED BY AREA-B-INDEX; UNSTRING POINTER IS
*KEPT IN SYNC AND WILL POINT TO THE FIRST ALPHA CHARACTER IN
*AREA B
    AT END        DISPLAY "RUN ABORTED - NO ALPHA CHARACTER
-                 "FOUND AT SEQUENCE NUMBER "
                  SEQUENCE-NUMBER
```

```
                    GO TO PEOJ
*CAN'T HAPPEN; IT MUST FIND AN ALPHA CHARACTER
     WHEN         ALPHA
        NEXT SENTENCE.
*FIRST ALPHA CHARACTER OF FIRST WORD FOUND

     UNSTRING     AREA-B
     DELIMITED ALLSPACES OR "." OR "," OR ";"
*.,; USED TO STRIP FROM WORD; FULL STOP NEEDED FOR SENTENCE
*END
     INTO         WORD-1
     DELIMITER IN WORD-1-DELIMITER
     INTO         WORD-2
     DELIMITER IN WORD-2-DELIMITER
     INTO         WORD-3
     DELIMITER IN WORD-3-DELIMITER
     INTO         WORD-4
     DELIMITER IN WORD-4-DELIMITER
     INTO         WORD-5
     DELIMITER IN WORD-5-DELIMITER
     INTO         WORD-6
     DELIMITER IN WORD-6-DELIMITER
     INTO         WORD-7
     DELIMITER IN WORD-7-DELIMITER
     INTO         WORD-8
     DELIMITER IN WORD-8-DELIMITER
     WITH POINTER UNSTRING-POINTER
     ON OVERFLOW  DISPLAY "RUN ABORTED - TOO MANY WORDS IN
   -               "SOURCE LINE AT SEQUENCE NUMBER "
                  SEQUENCE NUMBER
                  GO TO PEOJ.
*OVERFLOW MEANS MORE THEN 8 WORDS IN AREA B - NOT ALLOWED
*INCREASE RECEIVING WORDS IF REQUIRED

     GO TO        PC03-X.

  PCO3-X. EXIT.

  PABORT-PC03.
*RUNAWAY CODE ABEND

     DISPLAY      "RUN ABORTED - RUNAWAY CODE AT PC03"

     GO TO        PEOJ.

     EJECT
```

INSRUNAB

```
IDENTIFICATION DIVISION.

 PROGRAM-ID.        INSRUNAB.
*INSERTS RUNAWAY ABEND PARAGRAPH AFTER EXIT PARAGRAPH

 AUTHOR.            ERIC GARRIGUE VESELY
                    THE ANALYST WORKBENCH CONSULTING SDN BHD

 DATE-WRITTEN.   26 FEBRUARY 1990

 DATE-COMPILED.


 ENVIRONMENT DIVISION.
 CONFIGURATION SECTION.

 SOURCE COMPUTER.
 *                        WITH DEBUGGING MODE.
 *ABOVE * IS SOURCE TIME SWITCH

 INPUT-OUTPUT SECTION.

 FILE CONTROL.
*SIMPLE SEQUENTIAL IO USED TO REDUCE COMPLEXITY

 SELECT              COBOLIN
*COBOLIN IS NAME OF FILE CONTAINING COBOL PROGRAM
     ASSIGN TO        SEQINPUT
*SEQINPUT IS NAME THAT COBOLIN IS ASSIGNED TO
     ORGANIZATION IS SEQUENTIAL
     ACCESS MODE  IS SEQUENTIAL
     FILE STATUS  IS  COBLPROG-FILE-STATUS.


 SELECT              COBOLOUT
*COBOLOUT IS NAME OF NEW FILE THAT CONTAINS TRAPPED COBOL
*PROGRAM
     ASSIGN TO        SEQOUTPT
*SEQOUTPT IS NAME THAT COBOLOUT IS ASSIGNED TO
     ORGANIZATION IS SEQUENTIAL
     ACCESS MODE  IS SEQUENTIAL
     FILE STATUS  IS  COBLPROG-FILE-STATUS.

     EJECT
```

```
DATA DIVISION.

FILE SECTION.

FD          COBOLIN          LABEL RECORD STANDARD.


01 COBOL-LINE-IN             PIC X(80) USAGE DISPLAY.
*ASSUMES 80 COLUMN [BYTE] RECORDS

FD          COBOLOUT         LABEL RECORD STANDARD.


01 COBOL-LINE-OUT            PIC X(80) USAGE DISPLAY.



WORKING-STORAGE SECTION.
01 COBOL-LINE-WS.
   02 SEQUENCE-NUMBER         PIC X(6)  USAGE DISPLAY.
   02 INDICATOR-A-B.
      03 INDICATOR            PIC X     USAGE DISPLAY.
         88 NON-STATEMENT-LINE          VALUE "*"
                                              "D"
                                              "/"
                                              "-".


      03 AREA-AB.
         88 BLANK-SOURCE-LINE           VALUE SPACES.
         04 AREA-A             PIC X(4) USAGE DISPLAY.
            88 IDENTIFICATION-DIVISION  VALUE "IDEN"
                                              "ID D".

*IBM ABBREVIATION
            88 ENVIRONMENT-DIVISION     VALUE "ENVI".
            88 SELECT-CLAUSE            VALUE "SELE".
            88 CONFIGURATION-SECTION    VALUE "CONF".
            88 SOURCE-COMP              VALUE "SOUR".
            88 DATA-DIVISION            VALUE "DATA".
            88 WS-SECTION               VALUE "WORK".
            88 LEVEL-77                 VALUE "77  ".
            88 PROCEDURE-DIVISION       VALUE "PROC".
            88 DECLARE                  VALUE "DECL".
            88 BLANK-AREA-A             VALUE SPACES.
         04 AREA-B              PIC X(61) USAGE DISPLAY.
         04 AREA-B-BYTES REDEFINES AREA-B
                                PIC X     OCCURS 61 TIMES
                                          INDEXED BY
                                          AREA-B-INDEX.
            88 ALPHA                     VALUE "A" THRU
                                              "Z".
```

```
    02  IDEN-AREA                   PIC X(8)   USAGE DISPLAY.


01  COBLPROG-FILE-STATUS.
    02  SK1                         PIC X      USAGE DISPLAY.
        88  FILE-STATUS-OK                     VALUE "0".
    02  SK2                         PIC X      USAGE DISPLAY.


01  NEW-SOURCE-LINE                            VALUE SPACES.
    02  FILLER                      PIC X(6)   USAGE DISPLAY.
    02  NEW-INDICATOR-A-B.
        03  NEW-INDICATOR           PIC X      USAGE DISPLAY.
        03  NEW-AREA-AB.
            04  NEW-AREA-A          PIC X(4)   USAGE DISPLAY.
            04  NEW-AREA-B          PIC X(61)  USAGE DISPLAY.
    02  FILLER                      PIC X(8)   USAGE DISPLAY.
01  DIVISION-PARAGRAPH-SWITCHES.
    02  ID-SWITCH                   PIC X(5)   USAGE DISPLAY
                                               VALUE SPACES.
        88  ID-NOT-FOUND                       VALUE SPACES.
        88  ID-FOUND                           VALUE "FOUND".
    02  ENVIRONMENT-SWITCH          PIC X(5)   USAGE DISPLAY
                                               VALUE SPACES.
        88  ENVIRONMENT-NOT-FOUND              VALUE SPACES.
        88  ENVIRONMENT-FOUND                  VALUE "FOUND".
    02  CONFIGURATION-SWITCH        PIC X(5)   USAGE DISPLAY
                                               VALUE SPACES.
        88  CONFIGURATION-NOT-FOUND            VALUE SPACES.
        88  CONFIGURATION-FOUND                VALUE "FOUND".
    02  SOURCE-SWITCH               PIC X(5)   USAGE DISPLAY
                                               VALUE SPACES.
        88  SOURCE-NOT-FOUND                   VALUE SPACES.
        88  SOURCE-FOUND                       VALUE "FOUND".
    02  SELECT-SWITCH               PIC X(5)   USAGE DISPLAY
                                               VALUE SPACES.
        88  SELECT-NOT-FOUND                   VALUE SPACES.
        88  SELECT-FOUND                       VALUE "FOUND".
    02  DATA-SWITCH                 PIC X(5)   USAGE DISPLAY
                                               VALUE SPACES.
        88  DATA-NOT-FOUND                     VALUE SPACES.
        88  DATA-FOUND                         VALUE "FOUND".
    02  WS-SWITCH                   PIC X(5)   USAGE DISPLAY
                                               VALUE SPACES.
        88  WS-NOT-FOUND                       VALUE SPACES.
        88  WS-FOUND                           VALUE "FOUND".
    02  PROCEDURE-SWITCH            PIC X(5)   USAGE DISPLAY
                                               VALUE SPACES.
```

```
      88  PROCEDURE-NOT-FOUND                   VALUE SPACES.
      88  PROCEDURE-FOUND                       VALUE "FOUND".
   02  DECLARATIVES-SWITCH        PIC X(5)  USAGE DISPLAY
                                            VALUE SPACES.
      88  DECLARATIVES-NOT-FOUND              VALUE SPACES.
      88  DECLARATIVES-FOUND                  VALUE "FOUND".

 01  COPY-SWITCH                   PIC X(4)  USAGE DISPLAY
                                            VALUE "COPY".
      88  DO-COPY                             VALUE "COPY".
*READ & DO IMMEDIATE WRITE; INSERTION OF NEW SOURCE LINE
*NOT ON
      88  DO-READ                             VALUE "READ".
*READ ONLY; USED IMMEDIATELY AFTER AUTO COPY TURNED OFF
      88  DO-WRITE                            VALUE "WRIT".
*AUTO COPY TURNED OFF; WRITE PREVIOUS SOURCE LINE BEFORE
*READ

 01  WRITE-SWITCH                  PIC X(3)  USAGE DISPLAY
                                            VALUE "OLD".
      88  OLD-SOURCE-LINE                     VALUE "OLD".
          NEW-SOURCE-LINE                     VALUE "NEW".

 01  BREAKPOINT                    PIC X(80) USAGE DISPLAY.
      88  DUMP                                VALUE "D".

 01  TALLY-COUNTER                 PIC S9V   USAGE COMP
                                            VALUE ZERO.
      88  DEBUG                               VALUE 1.
      88  DEFENSIVE-TRAP-FOUND                VALUE 1.
      88  END-DELIMITER                       VALUE 1.
      88  FULLSTOP                            VALUE 1.
      88  STATUS-FOUND                        VALUE 1.

 01  END-SCOPE-DELIMITER.
      02  FILLER                    PIC X(4)  USAGE DISPLAY
                                            VALUE "END-".
      02  END-VERB                  PIC X(26) USAGE DISPLAY
                                            VALUE SPACES.


 01  NUMBER-OF-NUMERIC-ITEMS      PIC S999V VALUE 999.
*OCCURS DEPENDING ON DATA-NAME FOR NUMERIC-ITEM-TABLE; IF
*TOO SMALL THEN CHANGE IT TO REQUIRED NUMBER

 01  NUMERIC-ITEM-TABLE.
      02  NUMERIC-ITEM              PIC X(30)
```

```
                                    OCCURS 1 TO 999 TIMES
*SECOND INTEGER MUST BE THE SAME VALUE AS NUMBER-OF-NUMERIC-
*ITEMS
                                    DEPENDING ON
                                    NUMBER-OF-NUMERIC-ITEMS
                                    INDEXED BY
                                    NUMERIC-ITEM-INDEX.

 01  UNSTRING-ITEMS.
     02  UNSTRING-POINTER          PIC S99V  USAGE COMP
                                             VALUE ZERO.
     02  B-WORDS.
         03  WORD-1                PIC X(30) USAGE DISPLAY.
             88  ARITHMETIC-VERB             VALUE "ADD"
                                                   "COMPUTE"
                                                   "DIVIDE"
                                                   "MULTIPLY"
                                                   "SUBTRACT".
             88  CALL-VERB                   VALUE "CALL".
             88  DIVIDE-VERB                 VALUE "DIVIDE".
             88  END-PERFORM-VERB            VALUE "END-PERFORM."
             88  EVALUATE-VERB               VALUE "EVALUATE".
             88  EXIT-VERB                   VALUE "EXIT".
             88  GO-VERB                     VALUE "GO".
             88  GOBACK-VERB                 VALUE "GOBACK".
*IBM
             88  IF-VERB                     VALUE "IF".
             88  IO-VERB                     VALUE "CLOSE"
                                                   "DELETE"
                                                   "OPEN"
                                                   "READ"
                                                   "REWRITE"
                                                   "SEEK"
*IBM
                                                   "WRITE".
*PLACE ANY NON-ANSI I-O VERBS OF YOUR COMPILER IN THIS LIST
             88  MOVE-VERB                   VALUE "MOVE".
             88  PERFORM-VERB                VALUE "PERFORM".
             88  SEARCH-VERB                 VALUE "SEARCH".
             88  STOP-VERB                   VALUE "STOP".
             88  STRING-UNSTRING-VERB        VALUE "STRING"
                                                   "UNSTRING".
             88  TARGET-VERB                 VALUE "ADD"
                                                   "CALL"
                                                   "COMPUTE"
                                                   "DIVIDE"
```

```
                                              "EVALUATE"
                                              "GO"
                                              "MULTIPLY"
                                              "SEARCH"
                                              "STRING"
                                              "SUBTRACT"
                                              "UNSTRING".
              88  VERB            VALUE  "ACCEPT"
                                              "ADD"
                                              "ALTER"
*OBSOLETE

                                              "CALL"
                                              "CANCEL"
                                              "CLOSE"
                                              "COMPUTE"
                                              "CONTINUE"
*COBOL-85
                                              "COPY"
*TREATED LIKE A VERB
                                              "DELETE"
                                              "DISABLE"
                                              "DISPLAY"
                                              "DIVIDE"
                                              "ELSE"

*TREATED LIKE A VERB
                                              "ENABLE"
                                              "ENTER"
*OBSOLETE
                                              "EVALUATE"
*COBOL-85
                                              "EXAMINE"
*COBOL-68
                                              "EXIT"
                                              "GENERATE"
                                              "GO"
                                              "GOBACK"
*IBM
                                              "IF"

                                              "INITIALIZE"
*COBOL-85
                                              "INITIATE"
                                              "INSPECT"
                                              "MERGE"
                                              "MOVE"
                                              "MULTIPLY"
```

```
                                                    "OPEN"
                                                    "PERFORM"
                                                    "PURGE"
                                                    "READ"
                                                    "RECEIVE"
                                                    "RELEASE"
                                                    "REPLACE"

      *COBOL-85; TREATED LIKE A VERB

                                                    "RETURN"
                                                    "REWRITE"
                                                    "SEARCH"
                                                    "SEEK"

      *IBM

                                                    "SEND"
                                                    "SET"
                                                    "SORT"
                                                    "START"
                                                    "STOP"
                                                    "STRING"
                                                    "SUBTRACT"
                                                    "SUPPRESS"
                                                    "TERMINATE"
                                                    "TRANSFORM"

      *IBM

                                                    "UNSTRING"
                                                    "USE"
                                                    "WRITE".
            03  WORD-2               PIC X(30) USAGE DISPLAY.
      *MUST CONTAIN PROGRAM-NAME FOR PROGRAM-ID PARAGRAPH
      *ITEM DATA-NAME IF DATA DIVISION  BEING UNSTRING
      *DIVISOR IF DIVIDE INTO BEING UNSTRING
      *FROM ITEM DATA-NAME IF MOVE VERB BEING UNSTRING
                88  CORR-PHASE                 VALUE
                                               "CORRESPONDING"
                                                     "CORR".

                88  PROGRAM-WORD           VALUE "PROGRAM".
                88  RUN-WORD               VALUE "RUN".
            03  WORD-3               PIC X(30) USAGE DISPLAY.
                88  BY-WORD                VALUE "BY".
                88  INTO-WORD              VALUE "INTO".
                88  PICTURE-CLAUSE         VALUE "PICTURE"
                                                "PIC".

                88  TO-WORD                VALUE "TO".
            03  WORD-4               PIC X(30) USAGE DISPLAY.
      *DIVISOR IF DIVIDE BY VERB      BEING UNSTRING
```

```
*TO ITEM DATA-NAME IF MOVE VERB BEING UNSTRING
       03 WORD-4-BYTES REDEFINES WORD-4
          04 FILLER            PIC X       USAGE DISPLAY.
             88 SIGN-BYTE                  VALUE "S".
          04 FILLER            PIC X(29)   USAGE DISPLAY.
       03 WORD-5               PIC X(30)   USAGE DISPLAY.
*MUST CONTAIN ALPHA IF ANALYZING GO TO DEPENDING ON
*STATEMENT
             88 NOT-PROCEDURE-NAME         VALUE SPACES.
       03 WORD-6               PIC X(30)   USAGE DISPLAY.
       03 WORD-7               PIC X(30)   USAGE DISPLAY.
       03 WORD-8               PIC X(30)   USAGE DISPLAY.
    02 WORD-DELIMITERS.
       03 WORD-DELIMITER-1     PIC X       USAGE DISPLAY.
       03 WORD-DELIMITER-2     PIC X       USAGE DISPLAY.
       03 WORD-DELIMITER-3     PIC X       USAGE DISPLAY.
       03 WORD-DELIMITER-4     PIC X       USAGE DISPLAY.
       03 WORD-DELIMITER-5     PIC X       USAGE DISPLAY.
       03 WORD-DELIMITER-6     PIC X       USAGE DISPLAY.
       03 WORD-DELIMITER-7     PIC X       USAGE DISPLAY.
       03 WORD-DELIMITER-8     PIC X       USAGE DISPLAY.
*8 WORDS ARE USED TO ENSURE FULL STOP (.) IS FOUND


  01          PABORT-PARAGRAPH-NAME.
    02        FILLER           PIC X(7)    USAGE DISPLAY
                                           VALUE "PABORT-".
    02        ODOMETER-DISPLAY PIC 9(4)    USAGE DISPLAY.
    02        ODOMETER REDEFINES ODOMETER-DISPLAY
                               PIC S9(4)V USAGE COMP
                                           VALUE ZERO.


  01-NEGATIVE-OR-ZERO-TRAP.
    02 FILLER                  PIC X(8)    USAGE DISPLAY
                                           VALUE "D    IF ".
*ACTIVE DEFENSIVE TRAP; D DISABLES UNTIL ANSI DEBUG TURNED
*ON
    02 TRAP-DATA-NAME          PIC X(30)   USAGE DISPLAY
                                           VALUE SPACES.
    02 FILLER                  PIC X       USAGE DISPLAY
                                           VALUE SPACE.
    02 TRAP-TYPE               PIC X(8)    USAGE DISPLAY
                                           VALUE SPACES.

    EJECT
```

```
PROCEDURE DIVISION.

DECLARATIVES.

DEBUG SECTION.

    USE FOR DEBUGGING ON ALL PROCEDURES.

DEBUG-PROGRAM-FLOW.

    DISPLAY       DEBUG-LINE
                  DEBUG-NAME
                  DEBUG-CONTENTS.

DEBUG-BREAKPOINT.
*    ACCEPT        breakpoint    FROM mnemonic-name.
*  * USED TO DISABLE ACCEPT EVEN IF DEBUG MODULE IS ACTIVE
*  * IS DELETED WHEN INTERACTIVE BREAKPOINTS ARE REQUIRED

END DECLARATIVES.

P101-INITIATION.

    OPEN INPUT    COBOLIN

    OPEN OUTPUT   COBOLOUT

    DISPLAY       "INSRUNAB PROGRAM START."

    GO TO         P102-IDENTIFICATION-DIVISION.

 P102-IDENTIFICATION-DIVISION.

    PERFORM       PC01-READ-COBOLIN
    THRU          PC01-X.

*FIND IDENTIFICATION DIVISION
    IF         IDENTIFICATION-DIVISION
       NEXT SENTENCE
    ELSE          GO TO P102-IDENTIFICATION-DIVISION.

    MOVE          "FOUND"
    TO            ID-SWITCH

*PROGRAM-ID MUST BE NEXT STATEMENT LINE
    PERFORM       PC01-READ-COBOLIN
```

```
        THRU          PC01-X.

*FIND WORDS IN AREA B
    PERFORM       PCO3-FIND-WORDS
    THRU          PC03-X.

*WORD-2 MUST BE PROGRAM NAME
    DISPLAY       "TARGET PROGRAM IS "
                  WORD-2

    GO TO         P103-PROCEDURE-DIVISION.

 P103-PROCEDURE-DIVISION.

    PERFORM       PC01-READ-COBLPROG
    THRU          PC01-X.

    IF            PROCEDURE-FOUND
        NEXT SENTENCE
    ELSE          GO TO P105-PROCEDURE-DIVISION.

    MOVE          "FOUND"
    TO            PROCEDURE-SWITCH

    GO TO         P104-FIND-EXIT.

 P104-FIND-EXIT.
*FIND EXIT PARAGRAPH

    PERFORM       PC01-READ-COBLPROG
    THRU          PC01-X.

*ASSUMES THAT EXIT IS ON SAME LINE AS PARAGRAPH NAME;
*CHECK FOR SOMETHING IN A AREA
    IF            BLANK-AREA-A
                  GO TO  P104-FIND-EXIT
    ELSE NEXT SENTENCE.

*EXIT MUST BE SECOND WORD IF IT IS AN EXIT PARAGRAPH
    PERFORM       PC03-FIND-WORDS
    THRU          PCO3-EXIT.

    IF            EXIT-VERB
        NEXT SENTENCE
    ELSE          GO TO  P104-FIND-EXIT.
```

```
MOVE            "NEW"
TO              WRITE-SWITCH

MOVE            SPACES
TO              NEW-SOURCE-LINE

PERFORM         PC02-WRITE-COBOLOUT
THRU            PC02-X.

ADD             1
TO              ODOMETER
ON SIZE ERROR DIVIDE ZERO-LIT BY ZERO-LIT GIVING
INFINITY

MOVE            PABORT-PARAGRAPH-NAME
TO              NEW-AREA-AB

PERFORM         PC02-WRITE-COBOLOUT
THRU            PC02-X.

MOVE            "*RUNAWAY CODE ABEND"
TO              NEW-INDICATOR-A-B

PERFORM         PC02-WRITE-COBOLOUT
THRU            PC02-X.

MOVE            SPACES
TO              NEW-SOURCE-LINE

PERFORM         PC02-WRITE-COBOLOUT
THRU            PC02-X.

MOVE            "DISPLAY - 'RUNAWAY CODE AT ODOMETER' "
                ODOMETER
TO              NEW-AREA-B

PERFORM         PC02-WRITE-COBOLOUT
THRU            PC02-X.

MOVE            SPACES
TO              NEW-SOURCE-LINE

PERFORM         PC02-WRITE-COBOLOUT
THRU            PC02-X.

MOVE            "DIVIDE ZERO-LIT BY
```

```
-                     "ZERO-LIT GIVING INFINITY"
        TO           NEW-AREA-B

        PERFORM      PC02-WRITE-COBOLOUT
        THRU         PC02-X.

        MOVE         SPACES
        TO           NEW-SOURCE-LINE

        PERFORM      PC02-WRITE-COBOLOUT
        THRU         PC02-X.

        MOVE         "OLD"
        TO           WRITE-SWITCH

        GO TO        P104-FIND-EXIT.

   PEOJ.

        CLOSE        COBOLIN
                     COBOLOUT.

        IF           ID-NOT-FOUND
                     DISPLAY "NO IDENTIFICATION DIVISION"
        ELSE
        IF           PROCEDURE-NOT-FOUND
                     DISPLAY "NO PROCEDURE DIVISION"
        ELSE NEXT SENTENCE.

        DISPLAY      "INSRUNAB PROGRAM EOJ."

        STOP RUN.

        EJECT
```

```
   PC01-READ-COBOLIN.

        IF           DO-WRITE
   *AUTO COPY OFF; WRITE OUT LAST READ SOURCE LINE BEFORE READ
                     PERFORM PC02-WRITE-COBOLOUT
                     THRU    PC02-X
        ELSE NEXT SENTENCE.

        READ         COBOLIN
        INTO         COBOL-LINE-WS
```

```
      AT END           GO TO PEOJ.


      IF               FILE-STATUS-OK
         NEXT SENTENCE
      ELSE             DISPLAY "RUN ABORTED - BAD FILE STATUS OF"
                              COBLPROG-FILE-STATUS
*ASSUMES OUTPUT TO PROGRAMMER'S TERMINAL
                  GO TO PEOJ.


      IF               DO-COPY
*AUTO COPY ON; DO IMMEDIATE WRITE; CANNOT INSERT NEW SOURCE
*LINE BEFORE SOURCE LINE JUST READ
                  PERFORM    PC02-WRITE-COBOLOUT
                  THRU       PC02-X


      IF               DO-READ
*AUTO COPY JUST TURNED OFF; MOVE WRITE TO SWITCH TO ENABLE
*WRITE BEFORE READ
                  MOVE       "WRIT"
                  TO         COPY-SWITCH
      ELSE NEXT SENTENCE.


*BYPASS NON STATEMENT LINE OR BLANK SOURCE LINE
      IF               NON-STATEMENT-LINE
      OR               BLANK-SOURCE-LINE
                  GO TO PCO1-READ-COBOLIN
      ELSE             GO TO PC01-X.

  PC01-X. EXIT.

  PABORT-PC01.
*RUNAWAY CODE ABEND

      DISPLAY        "RUN ABORTED - RUNAWAY CODE AT PC01"

      GO TO          PEOJ.

      EJECT
```

```
  PC02-WRITE-COBOLOUT.

*WRITE-SWITCH USED TO DETERMINE FROM IDENTIFIER
      IF               OLD-SOURCE-LINE
                  WRITE  COBOL-LINE-OUT
```

```
                    FROM    COBOL-LINE-WS
      ELSE          WRITE   COBOL-LINE-OUT
                    FROM    NEW-SOURCE-LINE.
*NEW-SOURCE-LINE

      IF            FILE-STATUS-OK
                    GO TO  PC02-X
      ELSE          DISPLAY "RUN ABORTED - BAD FILE STATUS OF "
                            COBLPROG-FILE-STATUS
*ASSUMES OUTPUT TO PROGRAMMER'S TERMINAL
                    GO TO PEOJ.


   PC02-X. EXIT.

   PABORT-PC02.
*RUNAWAY CODE ABEND

      DISPLAY       "RUN ABORTED - RUNAWAY CODE AT PC02"

      GO TO         PEOJ.

      EJECT
```

```
   PC03-FIND-WORDS.

      MOVE          SPACES
      TO            B-WORDS
                    WORD-DELIMITERS

      SET           AREA-B-INDEX
                    UNSTRING-POINTER
      TO            1

      SEARCH        AREA-B-BYTES
      VARYING       UNSTRING-POINTER
*AREA-B-BYTES INDEXED BY AREA-B-INDEX; UNSTRING POINTER IS
*KEPT IN SYNC AND WILL POINT TO THE FIRST ALPHA CHARACTER IN
*AREA B
      AT END        DISPLAY "RUN ABORTED - NO ALPHA CHARACTER
    -                 "FOUND AT SEQUENCE NUMBER "
                    SEQUENCE-NUMBER
                    GO TO PEOJ
*CAN'T HAPPEN; IT MUST FIND AN ALPHA CHARACTER
      WHEN          ALPHA
```

```
            NEXT SENTENCE.
   *FIRST ALPHA CHARACTER OF FIRST WORD FOUND
        UNSTRING      AREA-B
        DELIMITED ALLSPACES OR "." OR "," OR ";"
   *.,; USED TO STRIP FROM WORD; FULL STOP NEEDED FOR SENTENCE
   *END
        INTO          WORD-1
        DELIMITER IN  WORD-1-DELIMITER
        INTO          WORD-2
        DELIMITER IN  WORD-2-DELIMITER
        INTO          WORD-3
        DELIMITER IN  WORD-3-DELIMITER
        INTO          WORD-4
        DELIMITER IN  WORD-4-DELIMITER
        INTO          WORD-5
        DELIMITER IN  WORD-5-DELIMITER
        INTO          WORD-6
        DELIMITER IN  WORD-6-DELIMITER
        INTO          WORD-7
        DELIMITER IN  WORD-7-DELIMITER
        INTO          WORD-8
        DELIMITER IN  WORD-8-DELIMITER
        WITH POINTER  UNSTRING-POINTER
        ON OVERFLOW   DISPLAY "RUN ABORTED - TOO MANY WORDS IN
   -                  "SOURCE LINE AT SEQUENCE NUMBER "
                      SEQUENCE NUMBER
                      GO TO PEOJ.
   *OVERFLOW MEANS MORE THEN 8 WORDS IN AREA B - NOT ALLOWED
   *INCREASE RECEIVING WORDS IF REQUIRED

        GO TO         PC03-X.

    PCO3-X. EXIT.

    PABORT-PC03.
   *RUNAWAY CODE ABEND

        DISPLAY       "RUN ABORTED - RUNAWAY CODE AT PC03"

        GO TO         PEOJ.

        EJECT
```

INSSIZE

```
 IDENTIFICATION DIVISION.

 PROGRAM-ID.        INSSIZE.
*PROGRAM INSERTS ON SIZE ERROR INTO ARITHMETIC STATEMENTS;
*ON EXCEPTION INTO CALL STATEMENTS; ON OVERFLOW INTO STRING
*& UNSTRING STATEMENTS; AT END INTO SEARCH STATEMENTS; WHEN
*OTHER INTO EVALUATE STATEMENTS; DIVIDE ZERO BY ZERO INTO GO
*TO DEPENDING ON

 AUTHOR.            ERIC GARRIGUE VESELY
                    THE ANALYST WORKBENCH CONSULTING SDN BHD

 DATE-WRITTEN.    26 FEBRUARY 1990

 DATE-COMPILED.

*REMARKS.        !WARNING! COBOL-85 REQUIRED; NEEDS END- SCOPE
*                 DELIMITED VERB
 ENVIRONMENT DIVISION.

 CONFIGURATION SECTION.

 SOURCE COMPUTER.

*                    WITH DEBUGGING MODE.
*ABOVE * IS SOURCE TIME SWITCH

 INPUT-OUTPUT SECTION.

 FILE CONTROL.
*SIMPLE SEQUENTIAL IO IS USED TO REDUCE COMPLEXITY

 SELECT            COBOLIN
*COBOLIN IS NAME OF FILE CONTAINING COBOL PROGRAM
     ASSIGN TO     SEQINPUT
*SEQINPUT IS NAME THAT COBOLIN IS ASSIGNED TO
     ORGANIZATION IS SEQUENTIAL
     ACCESS MODE  IS SEQUENTIAL
     FILE STATUS  IS COBLPROG-FILE-STATUS.

 SELECT            COBOLOUT
*COBOLOUT IS NAME OF NEW FILE THAT CONTAINS TRAPPED COBOL
*PROGRAM
     ASSIGN TO     SEQOUTPT
```

```
*SEQOUTPT IS NAME THAT COBOLOUT IS ASSIGNED TO
      ORGANIZATION IS SEQUENTIAL
      ACCESS MODE  IS SEQUENTIAL
      FILE STATUS  IS  COBLPROG-FILE-STATUS.

      EJECT
```

```
DATA DIVISION.

FILE SECTION.

FD            COBOLIN          LABEL RECORD STANDARD.
01 COBOL-LINE-IN              PIC X(80)  USAGE DISPLAY.
*ASSUMES 80 COLUMN [BYTE] RECORDS

FD            COBOLOUT         LABEL RECORD STANDARD.

01 COBOL-LINE-OUT             PIC X(80)  USAGE DISPLAY.

WORKING-STORAGE SECTION.

01 COBOL-LINE-WS.
   02 SEQUENCE-NUMBER         PIC X(6)   USAGE DISPLAY.
   02 INDICATOR-A-B.
      03 INDICATOR            PIC X      USAGE DISPLAY.
         88 NON-STATEMENT-LINE           VALUE "*"
                                              "D"
                                              "/"
                                              "-".

      03 AREA-AB.
         88 BLANK-SOURCE-LINE            VALUE SPACES.
         04 AREA-A            PIC X(4)   USAGE DISPLAY.
            88 IDENTIFICATION-DIVISION VALUE "IDEN"
                                             "ID D".
*IBM ABBREVIATION
            88 ENVIRONMENT-DIVISION     VALUE "ENVI".
            88 SELECT-CLAUSE            VALUE "SELE".
            88 CONFIGURATION-SECTION    VALUE "CONF".
            88 SOURCE-COMP              VALUE "SOUR".
            88 DATA-DIVISION            VALUE "DATA".
            88 WS-SECTION               VALUE "WORK".
            88 LEVEL-77                 VALUE "77  ".
            88 PROCEDURE-DIVISION       VALUE "PROC".
            88 DECLARE                  VALUE "DECL".
            88 BLANK-AREA-A             VALUE SPACES.
```

```
          04  AREA-B            PIC X(61)   USAGE DISPLAY.
          04  AREA-B-BYTES REDEFINES AREA-B
                                PIC X       OCCURS 61 TIMES
                                            INDEXED BY
                                            AREA-B-INDEX.
              88  ALPHA                     VALUE "A" THRU
                                                  "Z".
      02  IDEN-AREA             PIC X(8)    USAGE DISPLAY.


  01  COBLPROG-FILE-STATUS.
      02  SK1                   PIC X       USAGE DISPLAY.
          88  FILE-STATUS-OK                VALUE "0".
      02  SK2                   PIC X       USAGE DISPLAY.
  01  NEW-SOURCE-LINE                       VALUE SPACES.
      02  FILLER                PIC X(6)    USAGE DISPLAY.
      02  NEW-INDICATOR-A-B.
          03  NEW-INDICATOR     PIC X       USAGE DISPLAY.
          03  NEW-AREA-AB.
              04  NEW-AREA-A    PIC X(4)    USAGE DISPLAY.
              04  NEW-AREA-B    PIC X(61)   USAGE DISPLAY.
      02  FILLER                PIC X(8)    USAGE DISPLAY.


  01  DIVISION-PARAGRAPH-SWITCHES.
      02  ID-SWITCH             PIC X(5)    USAGE DISPLAY
                                            VALUE SPACES.

          88  ID-NOT-FOUND                  VALUE SPACES.
          88  ID-FOUND                      VALUE "FOUND".
      02  ENVIRONMENT-SWITCH    PIC X(5)    USAGE DISPLAY
                                            VALUE SPACES.

          88  ENVIRONMENT-NOT-FOUND         VALUE SPACES.
          88  ENVIRONMENT-FOUND             VALUE "FOUND".
      02  CONFIGURATION-SWITCH  PIC X(5)    USAGE DISPLAY
                                            VALUE SPACES.

          88  CONFIGURATION-NOT-FOUND       VALUE SPACES.
          88  CONFIGURATION-FOUND           VALUE "FOUND".
      02  SOURCE-SWITCH         PIC X(5)    USAGE DISPLAY
                                            VALUE SPACES.

          88  SOURCE-NOT-FOUND              VALUE SPACES.
          88  SOURCE-FOUND                  VALUE "FOUND".
      02  SELECT-SWITCH         PIC X(5)    USAGE DISPLAY
                                            VALUE SPACES.

          88  SELECT-NOT-FOUND              VALUE SPACES.
          88  SELECT-FOUND                  VALUE "FOUND".
      02  DATA-SWITCH           PIC X(5)    USAGE DISPLAY
                                            VALUE SPACES.

          88  DATA-NOT-FOUND                VALUE SPACES.
```

```
        88  DATA-FOUND                          VALUE "FOUND".
    02  WS-SWITCH                PIC X(5)    USAGE DISPLAY
                                             VALUE SPACES.
        88  WS-NOT-FOUND                     VALUE SPACES.
        88  WS-FOUND                         VALUE "FOUND".
    02  PROCEDURE-SWITCH         PIC X(5)    USAGE DISPLAY
                                             VALUE SPACES.
        88  PROCEDURE-NOT-FOUND              VALUE SPACES.
        88  PROCEDURE-FOUND                  VALUE "FOUND".
    02  DECLARATIVES-SWITCH      PIC X(5)    USAGE DISPLAY
                                             VALUE SPACES.
        88  DECLARATIVES-NOT-FOUND           VALUE SPACES.
        88  DECLARATIVES-FOUND               VALUE "FOUND".

 01  COPY-SWITCH                 PIC X(4)    USAGE DISPLAY
                                             VALUE "COPY".
        88  DO-COPY                          VALUE "COPY".
*READ & DO IMMEDIATE WRITE; INSERTION OF NEW SOURCE LINE
*NOT ON
        88  DO-READ                          VALUE "READ".
*READ ONLY; USED IMMEDIATELY AFTER AUTO COPY TURNED OFF
        88  DO-WRITE                         VALUE "WRIT".
*AUTO COPY TURNED OFF; WRITE PREVIOUS SOURCE LINE BEFORE
*READ

 01  WRITE-SWITCH                PIC X(3)    USAGE DISPLAY
                                             VALUE "OLD".
        88  OLD-SOURCE-LINE                  VALUE "OLD".
            NEW-SOURCE-LINE                  VALUE "NEW".

 01  BREAKPOINT                  PIC X(80)   USAGE DISPLAY.
        88  DUMP                             VALUE "D".

 01  TALLY-COUNTER               PIC S9V     USAGE COMP
                                             VALUE ZERO.
        88  DEBUG                            VALUE 1.
        88  DEFENSIVE-TRAP-FOUND             VALUE 1.
        88  END-DELIMITER                    VALUE 1.
        88  FULLSTOP                         VALUE 1.
        88  STATUS-FOUND                     VALUE 1.

 01  END-SCOPE-DELIMITER.
    02  FILLER                   PIC X(4)    USAGE DISPLAY
                                             VALUE "END-".
    02  END-VERB                 PIC X(26)   USAGE DISPLAY
                                             VALUE SPACES.
```

```
          88  GOTO                           VALUE "GO".


 01  NUMBER-OF-NUMERIC-ITEMS   PIC S999V VALUE 999.
*OCCURS DEPENDING ON DATA-NAME FOR NUMERIC-ITEM-TABLE; IF
*TOO SMALL THEN CHANGE IT TO REQUIRED NUMBER


 01  NUMERIC-ITEM-TABLE.
     02  NUMERIC-ITEM               PIC X(30)
                                    OCCURS 1 TO 999 TIMES
*SECOND INTEGER MUST BE THE SAME VALUE AS NUMBER-OF-NUMERIC-
*ITEMS
                                    DEPENDING ON
                                    NUMBER-OF-NUMERIC-ITEMS
                                    INDEXED BY
                                    NUMERIC-ITEM-INDEX.

 01  UNSTRING-ITEMS.
     02  UNSTRING-POINTER       PIC S99V   USAGE COMP
                                           VALUE ZERO.

     02  B-WORDS.
         03  WORD-1                 PIC X(30) USAGE DISPLAY.
             88  ARITHMETIC-VERB              VALUE "ADD"
                                                    "COMPUTE"
                                                    "DIVIDE"
                                                    "MULTIPLY"
                                                    "SUBTRACT".

             88  CALL-VERB                    VALUE "CALL".
             88  DIVIDE-VERB                  VALUE "DIVIDE".
             88  END-PERFORM-VERB             VALUE "END-PERFORM."
             88  EVALUATE-VERB                VALUE "EVALUATE".
             88  EXIT-VERB                    VALUE "EXIT".
             88  GO-VERB                      VALUE "GO".
             88  GOBACK-VERB                  VALUE "GOBACK".
 *IBM
             88  IF-VERB                      VALUE "IF".
             88  IO-VERB                      VALUE "CLOSE"
                                                    "DELETE"
                                                    "OPEN"
                                                    "READ"
                                                    "REWRITE"
                                                    "SEEK"
 *IBM
                                                    "WRITE".
*PLACE ANY NON-ANSI I-O VERBS OF YOUR COMPILER IN THIS LIST
             88  MOVE-VERB                    VALUE "MOVE".
             88  PERFORM-VERB                 VALUE "PERFORM".
             88  SEARCH-VERB                  VALUE "SEARCH".
```

```
              88  STOP-VERB                    VALUE  "STOP".
              88  STRING-UNSTRING-VERB         VALUE  "STRING"
                                                      "UNSTRING".
              88  TARGET-VERB                  VALUE  "ADD"
                                                      "CALL"
                                                      "COMPUTE"
                                                      "DIVIDE"
                                                      "EVALUATE"
                                                      "GO"
                                                      "MULTIPLY"
                                                      "SEARCH"
                                                      "STRING"
                                                      "SUBTRACT"
                                                      "UNSTRING".
              88  VERB                         VALUE  "ACCEPT"
                                                      "ADD"
                                                      "ALTER"
*OBSOLETE
                                                      "CALL"
                                                      "CANCEL"
                                                      "CLOSE"
                                                      "COMPUTE"
                                                      "CONTINUE"
*COBOL-85
                                                      "COPY"
*TREATED LIKE A VERB
                                                      "DELETE"
                                                      "DISABLE"
                                                      "DISPLAY"
                                                      "DIVIDE"
                                                      "ELSE"
*TREATED LIKE A VERB
                                                      "ENABLE"
                                                      "ENTER"
*OBSOLETE
                                                      "EVALUATE"
*COBOL-85
                                                      "EXAMINE"
*COBOL-68
                                                      "EXIT"
                                                      "GENERATE"
                                                      "GO"
                                                      "GOBACK"
*IBM
                                                      "IF"
```

```
                                                      "INITIALIZE"
*COBOL-85
                                                      "INITIATE"
                                                      "INSPECT"
                                                      "MERGE"
                                                      "MOVE"
                                                      "MULTIPLY"
                                                      "OPEN"
                                                      "PERFORM"
                                                      "PURGE"
                                                      "READ"
                                                      "RECEIVE"
                                                      "RELEASE"
                                                      "REPLACE"
*COBOL-85; TREATED LIKE A VERB
                                                      "RETURN"
                                                      "REWRITE"
                                                      "SEARCH"
                                                      "SEEK"
*IBM
                                                      "SEND"
                                                      "SET"
                                                      "SORT"
                                                      "START"
                                                      "STOP"
                                                      "STRING"
                                                      "SUBTRACT"
                                                      "SUPPRESS"
                                                      "TERMINATE"
                                                      "TRANSFORM"
*IBM
                                                      "UNSTRING"
                                                      "USE"
                                                      "WRITE".
          03 WORD-2              PIC X(30) USAGE DISPLAY.
*MUST CONTAIN PROGRAM-NAME FOR PROGRAM-ID PARAGRAPH
*ITEM DATA-NAME IF DATA DIVISION  BEING UNSTRING
*DIVISOR IF DIVIDE INTO BEING UNSTRING
*FROM ITEM DATA-NAME IF MOVE VERB BEING UNSTRING
          88 CORR-PHASE                   VALUE
                                          "CORRESPONDING"
                                                     "CORR".

          88 PROGRAM-WORD        VALUE "PROGRAM".
          88 RUN-WORD            VALUE "RUN".
       03 WORD-3                 PIC X(30) USAGE DISPLAY.
```

```
              88  BY-WORD                        VALUE "BY".
              88  INTO-WORD                      VALUE "INTO".
              88  PICTURE-CLAUSE                 VALUE "PICTURE"
                                                        "PIC".
              88  TO-WORD                        VALUE "TO".
          03  WORD-4            PIC X(30)  USAGE DISPLAY.
*DIVISOR IF DIVIDE BY VERB      BEING UNSTRING
*TO ITEM DATA-NAME IF MOVE VERB BEING UNSTRING
          03  WORD-4-BYTES REDEFINES WORD-4
              04  FILLER        PIC X      USAGE DISPLAY.
                  88  SIGN-BYTE                  VALUE "S".
              04  FILLER        PIC X(29)  USAGE DISPLAY.
          03  WORD-5            PIC X(30)  USAGE DISPLAY.
*MUST CONTAIN ALPHA IF ANALYZING GO TO DEPENDING ON
*STATEMENT
              88  NOT-PROCEDURE-NAME             VALUE SPACES.
          03  WORD-6            PIC X(30)  USAGE DISPLAY.
          03  WORD-7            PIC X(30)  USAGE DISPLAY.
          03  WORD-8            PIC X(30)  USAGE DISPLAY.
      02  WORD-DELIMITERS.
          03  WORD-DELIMITER-1  PIC X      USAGE DISPLAY.
          03  WORD-DELIMITER-2  PIC X      USAGE DISPLAY.
          03  WORD-DELIMITER-3  PIC X      USAGE DISPLAY.
          03  WORD-DELIMITER-4  PIC X      USAGE DISPLAY.
          03  WORD-DELIMITER-5  PIC X      USAGE DISPLAY.
          03  WORD-DELIMITER-6  PIC X      USAGE DISPLAY.
          03  WORD-DELIMITER-7  PIC X      USAGE DISPLAY.
          03  WORD-DELIMITER-8  PIC X      USAGE DISPLAY.
*8 WORDS ARE USED TO ENSURE FULL STOP (.) IS FOUND


01            PABORT-PARAGRAPH-NAME.
    02        FILLER            PIC X(7)   USAGE DISPLAY
                                           VALUE "PABORT-".
    02        ODOMETER-DISPLAY  PIC 9(4)   USAGE DISPLAY.
    02        ODOMETER REDEFINES ODOMETER-DISPLAY
                                 PIC S9(4)V USAGE COMP
                                           VALUE ZERO.


01-NEGATIVE-OR-ZERO-TRAP.
    02  FILLER                  PIC X(8)   USAGE DISPLAY
                                           VALUE "D     IF ".
*ACTIVE DEFENSIVE TRAP; D DISABLES UNTIL ANSI DEBUG
*TURNED ON
    02  TRAP-DATA-NAME          PIC X(30)  USAGE DISPLAY
                                           VALUE SPACES.
    02  FILLER                  PIC X      USAGE DISPLAY
```

```
                                      VALUE SPACE.
      02  TRAP-TYPE              PIC X(8)  USAGE DISPLAY
                                      VALUE SPACES.


      EJECT
```

```
PROCEDURE DIVISION.

DECLARATIVES.

DEBUG SECTION.

      USE FOR DEBUGGING ON ALL PROCEDURES.

DEBUG-PROGRAM-FLOW.

      DISPLAY       DEBUG-LINE
                    DEBUG-NAME
                    DEBUG-CONTENTS.

DEBUG-BREAKPOINT.

*     ACCEPT        breakpoint   FROM mnemonic-name.
* *  USED TO DISABLE ACCEPT EVEN IF DEBUG MODULE IS ACTIVE
* *  IS DELETED WHEN INTERACTIVE BREAKPOINTS ARE REQUIRED

END DECLARATIVES.

P101-INITIATION.

      OPEN INPUT    COBOLIN

      OPEN OUTPUT   COBOLOUT

      DISPLAY       "INSSIZE PROGRAM START."

      GO TO         P102-IDENTIFICATION-DIVISION.

P102-IDENTIFICATION-DIVISION.

      PERFORM       PC01-READ-COBOLIN
      THRU          PC01-X.

*FIND IDENTIFICATION DIVISION
      IF            IDENTIFICATION-DIVISION
```

```
                 NEXT SENTENCE
        ELSE            GO TO P102-IDENTIFICATION-DIVISION.

        MOVE            "FOUND"
        TO              ID-SWITCH

   *PROGRAM-ID MUST BE NEXT STATEMENT LINE
        PERFORM         PC01-READ-COBOLIN
        THRU            PC01-X.

   *FIND WORDS IN AREA B
        PERFORM         PCO3-FIND-WORDS
        THRU            PC03-X.

   *WORD-2 MUST BE PROGRAM NAME
        DISPLAY         "TARGET PROGRAM IS "
                        WORD-2

        GO TO           P103-PROCEDURE-DIVISION.

    P103-PROCEDURE-DIVISION.

        PERFORM         PC01-READ-COBLPROG
        THRU            PC01-X.

        IF              PROCEDURE-FOUND
           NEXT SENTENCE
        ELSE            GO TO P105-PROCEDURE-DIVISION.

        MOVE            "FOUND"
        TO              PROCEDURE-SWITCH

        MOVE            "READ"
        TO              COPY-SWITCH

        GO TO           P104-FIND-TARGET-VERB.

    P104-FIND-TARGET-VERB.

        PERFORM         PC01-READ-COBLPROG
        THRU            PC01-X.

   *FIND TARGET-VERB
        PERFORM         PCO3-FIND-WORDS
        THRU            PC03-X.

        IF              TARGET-VERB
```

```
*ASSUMES THAT VERB IF PRESENT IS FIRST WORD IN AREA B
        NEXT SENTENCE
     ELSE          GO TO  P104-FIND-TARGET-VERB.


     IF            GO-VERB
     AND           NOT-PROCEDURE-NAME
*GO TO WITHOUT DEPENDING ON; START OVER
                   GO TO     P104-FIND-TARGET-VERB.
     ELSE   NEXT SENTENCE.


*SETUP END- SCOPE DELIMITER STATEMENT
     MOVE          WORD-1
     TO            END-VERB


     GO TO          P105-DEFENSIVE-TRAP-PRESENT


 P105-DEFENSIVE-TRAP-PRESENT.
*ASSUMES TRAP OR TERMINATOR ON DIFFERENT SOURCE LINE


     PERFORM       PC01-READ-COBLPROG
     THRU          PC01-X.


*DETERMINE IF DEFENSIVE TRAP PRESENT


     MOVE          ZERO
     TO            TALLY-COUNTER


     INSPECT       B-WORDS
     TALLYING      TALLY-COUNTER
     FOR ALL       "SIZE "
                   "OVERFLOW "
                   "EXCEPTION "
                   "OTHER "
                   "END "
*SPACE REQUIRED TO ISOLATE THE COBOL RESERVED WORK


     IF            TRAP-FOUND
                   GO TO  P104-FIND-TARGET-VERB
*STATEMENT CONTAINS DEFENSIVE TRAP; DOESN'T NEED ANOTHER
     ELSE   NEXT SENTENCE.


*DETERMINE IF FULL STOP PRESENT
     MOVE          ZERO
     TO            TALLY-COUNTER


     INSPECT       WORD-DELIMITERS
     TALLYING      TALLY-COUNTER
```

```
      FOR ALL         ". "

      IF              FULLSTOP
      NEXT SENTENCE
      ELSE            GO TO P106-FIND-TERMINATOR.

 *FULL STOP REPLACED BY END- EXCEPT FOR GO TO
      IF              GOTO
         NEXT SENTENCE
      ELSE INSPECT REPLACING ALL ". " BY SPACES.

 *WRITE OUT CURRENT SOURCE LINE BEFORE INSERTING TRAP
      PERFORM         PC02-WRITE-COBOLOUT
      THRU            PC02-X.

      PERFORM PC10-INSERT-DEFENSIVE-TRAP
      THRU            PC10-X.

      IF              GOTO
                      GO TO  P104-FIND-TARGET-VERBS
 *GO TO DOESN'T HAVE END- SCOPE TERMINATOR
      ELSE            GO TO  P107-WRITE-END-X.

  P106-FIND-TERMINATOR
 *FIND TERMINATION OF TARGET VERB

 *DETERMINE IF END- SCOPE DELIMINATER PRESENT
      MOVE            ZERO
      TO              TALLY-COUNTER

      INSPECT         B-WORDS
      TALLYING        TALLY-COUNTER
      FOR ALL         "END-"

      IF              END-DELIMITER
 *END-VERB FOUND; STATEMENT TERMINATED INSERT DEFENSIVE TRAP
                      PERFORM PC10-INSERT-DEFENSIVE-TRAP
                      THRU PC10-X
                      GO TO  P104-FIND-TARGET-VERB
 *NO NEED TO WRITE ANOTHER END-; START OVER
      ELSE   NEXT SENTENCE.

      IF              VERB
 *VERB FOUND; STATEMENT TERMINATED INSERT DEFENSIVE TRAP
                      PERFORM PC10-INSERT-DEFENSIVE-TRAP
                      THRU   PC10-X
                      GO TO  P107-WRITE-END-X.
```

```
          ELSE NEXT SENTENCE.


      IF NOT        BLANK-AREA-A
*AREA A ENTRY FOUND; STATEMENT TERMINATED INSERT DEFENSIVE
*TRAP
                    PERFORM PC10-INSERT-DEFENSIVE-TRAP
                    THRU   PC10-X
                    GO TO  P107-WRITE-END-X
      ELSE          GO TO  P105-DEFENSIVE-TRAP-PRESENT.
*NO TERMINATOR; GET NEXT SOURCE LINE


 P107-WRITE-END-X.
*WRITE END- SCOPE DELIMITER.


      MOVE          "NEW"
      TO            WRITE-SWITCH

      MOVE          END-SCOPE-DELIMITER
      TO            NEW-AREA-B

      PERFORM       PC02-WRITE-COBOLOUT
      THRU          PC02-X.

      MOVE          SPACES
      TO            NEW-SOURCE-LINE

      PERFORM       PC02-WRITE-COBOLOUT
      THRU          PC02-X.

      MOVE          "OLD"
      TO            WRITE-SWITCH

      GO TO         P104-FIND-TARGET-VERB.

 PEOJ.

      CLOSE         COBOLIN
                    COBOLOUT.

      IF            ID-NOT-FOUND
                    DISPLAY "NO IDENTIFICATION DIVISION"
      ELSE
      IF            PROCEDURE-NOT-FOUND
                    DISPLAY "NO PROCEDURE DIVISION"
      ELSE   NEXT SENTENCE.
```

```
        DISPLAY        "INSSIZE PROGRAM EOJ."

        STOP RUN.

        EJECT
```

```
  PC01-READ-COBOLIN.

      IF             DO-WRITE
*AUTO COPY OFF; WRITE OUT LAST READ SOURCE LINE BEFORE READ
                   PERFORM PC02-WRITE-COBOLOUT
                   THRU     PC02-X
      ELSE NEXT SENTENCE.

      READ           COBOLIN
      INTO           COBOL-LINE-WS
      AT END         GO TO PEOJ.

      IF             FILE-STATUS-OK
          NEXT SENTENCE
      ELSE           DISPLAY "RUN ABORTED - BAD FILE STATUS OF "
                             COBLPROG-FILE-STATUS
*ASSUMES OUTPUT TO PROGRAMMER'S TERMINAL
                   GO TO PEOJ.

      IF             DO-COPY
*AUTO COPY ON; DO IMMEDIATE WRITE; CANNOT INSERT NEW SOURCE
*LINE BEFORE SOURCE LINE JUST READ
                   PERFORM   PC02-WRITE-COBOLOUT
                   THRU      PC02-X
      IF             DO-READ
*AUTO COPY JUST TURNED OFF; MOVE WRITE TO SWITCH TO ENABLE
*WRITE BEFORE READ
                   MOVE   "WRIT"
                   TO     COPY-SWITCH
      ELSE NEXT SENTENCE.

*BYPASS NON STATEMENT LINE OR BLANK SOURCE LINE
      IF             NON-STATEMENT-LINE
      OR             BLANK-SOURCE-LINE
                     GO TO PCO1-READ-COBOLIN
      ELSE           GO TO PC01-X.

  PC01-X. EXIT.
```

```
PABORT-PC01.
*RUNAWAY CODE ABEND

    DISPLAY         "RUN ABORTED - RUNAWAY CODE AT PC01"

    GO TO           PEOJ.

    EJECT
```

```
PC02-WRITE-COBOLOUT.

*WRITE-SWITCH USED TO DETERMINE FROM IDENTIFIER
    IF              OLD-SOURCE-LINE
                    WRITE   COBOL-LINE-OUT
                    FROM    COBOL-LINE-WS
    ELSE            WRITE   COBOL-LINE-OUT
                    FROM    NEW-SOURCE-LINE.
*NEW-SOURCE-LINE

    IF              FILE-STATUS-OK
                    GO TO  PC02-X
    ELSE            DISPLAY "RUN ABORTED - BAD FILE STATUS OF "
                            COBLPROG-FILE-STATUS
*ASSUMES OUTPUT TO PROGRAMMER'S TERMINAL
                    GO TO PEOJ.
  PC02-X. EXIT.

  PABORT-PC02.
*RUNAWAY CODE ABEND

    DISPLAY         "RUN ABORTED - RUNAWAY CODE AT PC02"

    GO TO           PEOJ.

    EJECT
```

```
PC03-FIND-WORDS.

    MOVE            SPACES
    TO              B-WORDS
                    WORD-DELIMITERS

    SET             AREA-B-INDEX
```

```
                        UNSTRING-POINTER
        TO              1


        SEARCH          AREA-B-BYTES
        VARYING         UNSTRING-POINTER
   *AREA-B-BYTES INDEXED BY AREA-B-INDEX; UNSTRING POINTER IS
   *KEPT IN SYNC AND WILL POINT TO THE FIRST ALPHA CHARACTER IN
   *AREA B
        AT END          DISPLAY "RUN ABORTED - NO ALPHA CHARACTER
    -                   "FOUND AT SEQUENCE NUMBER "
                        SEQUENCE-NUMBER
                        GO TO PEOJ
   *CAN'T HAPPEN; IT MUST FIND AN ALPHA CHARACTER
        WHEN            ALPHA
            NEXT SENTENCE.
   *FIRST ALPHA CHARACTER OF FIRST WORD FOUND


        UNSTRING        AREA-B
        DELIMITED ALL SPACES OR "." OR "," OR ";"
   *.,; USED TO STRIP FROM WORD; FULL STOP NEEDED FOR SENTENCE
   *END
        INTO            WORD-1
        DELIMITER IN    WORD-1-DELIMITER
        INTO            WORD-2
        DELIMITER IN    WORD-2-DELIMITER
        INTO            WORD-3
        DELIMITER IN    WORD-3-DELIMITER
        INTO            WORD-4
        DELIMITER IN    WORD-4-DELIMITER
        INTO            WORD-5
        DELIMITER IN    WORD-5-DELIMITER
        INTO            WORD-6
        DELIMITER IN    WORD-6-DELIMITER
        INTO            WORD-7
        DELIMITER IN    WORD-7-DELIMITER
        INTO            WORD-8
        DELIMITER IN    WORD-8-DELIMITER
        WITH POINTER    UNSTRING-POINTER
        ON OVERFLOW     DISPLAY "RUN ABORTED - TOO MANY WORDS IN
    -                   "SOURCE LINE AT SEQUENCE NUMBER "
                        SEQUENCE NUMBER
                        GO TO PEOJ.
   *OVERFLOW MEANS MORE THAN 8 WORDS IN AREA B - NOT ALLOWED
   *INCREASE RECEIVING WORDS IF REQUIRED


        GO TO           PC03-X.
```

```
PCO3-X.  EXIT.

PABORT-PC03.
*RUNAWAY CODE ABEND

     DISPLAY         "RUN ABORTED - RUNAWAY CODE AT PC03"

     GO TO           PEOJ.

     EJECT
```

```
PC10-INSERT-DEFENSIVE-TRAP.
*TRAP WORDS DEPENDS ON TARGET-VERB

     MOVE            "NEW"
     TO              WRITE-SWITCH

     IF              ARITHMETIC-VERB
                     MOVE   "ON SIZE ERROR DIVIDE ZERO-LIT BY
 -                   "ZERO-LIT GIVING INFINITY"
                     TO     NEW-AREA-B
     ELSE
     IF              CALL-VERB
                     MOVE   "ON EXCEPTION DIVIDE ZERO-LIT BY
 -                   "ZERO-LIT GIVING INFINITY"
                     TO     NEW-AREA-B
     ELSE
     IF              GO-VERB
                     MOVE   "DIVIDE ZERO-LIT BY
 -                   "ZERO-LIT GIVING INFINITY"
                     TO     NEW-AREA-B
     ELSE
     IF              EVALUATE-VERB
                     MOVE   "WHEN OTHER DIVIDE ZERO-LIT BY
 -                   "ZERO-LIT GIVING INFINITY"
                     TO     NEW-AREA-B
     ELSE
     IF              SEARCH-VERB
                     MOVE   "AT END DIVIDE ZERO-LIT BY
 -                   "ZERO-LIT GIVING INFINITY"
                     TO     NEW-AREA-B
     ELSE
     IF              STRING-UNSTRING-VERB
                     MOVE   "ON OVERFLOW DIVIDE ZERO-LIT BY
 -                   "ZERO-LIT GIVING INFINITY"
```

```
                              TO      NEW-AREA-B
             ELSE             DISPLAY "RUN ABORTED - TARGET VERB NOT
                              FOUND"
                              GO TO  PEOJ.


             PERFORM          PC02-WRITE-COBOLOUT
             THRU             PC02-X.


             MOVE             "*DEFENSIVE TRAP INSERTED TO FORCE ABEND"
             TO               NEW-INDICATOR-A-B


             PERFORM          PC02-WRITE-COBOLOUT
             THRU             PC02-X.


             MOVE             "OLD"
             TO               WRITE-SWITCH


             GO TO            PC10-X.


     PC10-X.   EXIT.
     PABORT-PC10.
    *RUNAWAY CODE ABEND


         DISPLAY         "RUN ABORTED - RUNAWAY CODE AT PC10"


         GO TO           PEOJ.


         EJECT
```

INSTOC

```
     IDENTIFICATION DIVISION.


     PROGRAM-ID.      INSTOC.
    *PROGRAM INSERTS ON TRANSFER OF CONTROL COUNTERS TO TRAP
    *RUNAWAY


     AUTHOR.          ERIC GARRIGUE VESELY
                      THE ANALYST WORKBENCH CONSULTING SDN BHD


     DATE-WRITTEN.    26 FEBRUARY 1990


     DATE-COMPILED.
```

```
ENVIRONMENT DIVISION.
CONFIGURATION SECTION.

SOURCE COMPUTER.
*                        WITH DEBUGGING MODE.
*ABOVE * IS SOURCE TIME SWITCH


INPUT-OUTPUT SECTION.

FILE CONTROL.
*SIMPLE SEQUENTIAL IO IS USED TO REDUCE COMPLEXITY

SELECT               COBOLIN
*COBOLIN IS NAME OF FILE CONTAINING COBOL PROGRAM
    ASSIGN TO         SEQINPUT
*SEQINPUT IS NAME THAT COBOLIN IS ASSIGNED TO
    ORGANIZATION IS SEQUENTIAL
    ACCESS MODE  IS SEQUENTIAL
    FILE STATUS  IS    COBLPROG-FILE-STATUS.

SELECT               COBOLOUT
*COBOLOUT IS NAME OF NEW FILE THAT CONTAINS TRAPPED COBOL
*PROGRAM
    ASSIGN TO         SEQOUTPT
*SEQOUTPT IS NAME THAT COBOLOUT IS ASSIGNED TO
    ORGANIZATION IS SEQUENTIAL
    ACCESS MODE  IS SEQUENTIAL
    FILE STATUS  IS    COBLPROG-FILE-STATUS.

    EJECT
```

```
DATA DIVISION.

FILE SECTION.

FD           COBOLIN          LABEL RECORD STANDARD.

01 COBOL-LINE-IN              PIC X(80)  USAGE DISPLAY.
*ASSUMES 80 COLUMN [BYTE] RECORDS

FD           COBOLOUT         LABEL RECORD STANDARD.

01 COBOL-LINE-OUT            PIC X(80)  USAGE DISPLAY.
```

```
      WORKING-STORAGE SECTION.


      01  COBOL-LINE-WS.
          02  SEQUENCE-NUMBER         PIC X(6)    USAGE DISPLAY.
          02  INDICATOR-A-B.
              03  INDICATOR           PIC X       USAGE DISPLAY.
                  88  NON-STATEMENT-LINE           VALUE "*"
                                                         "D"
                                                         "/"
                                                         "-".

              03  AREA-AB.
                  88  BLANK-SOURCE-LINE            VALUE SPACES.
                  04  AREA-A          PIC X(4)    USAGE DISPLAY.
                      88  IDENTIFICATION-DIVISION VALUE "IDEN"
                                                        "ID D".
     *IBM ABBREVIATION
                      88  ENVIRONMENT-DIVISION     VALUE "ENVI".
                      88  SELECT-CLAUSE            VALUE "SELE".
                      88  CONFIGURATION-SECTION    VALUE "CONF".
                      88  SOURCE-COMP              VALUE "SOUR".
                      88  DATA-DIVISION            VALUE "DATA".
                      88  WS-SECTION               VALUE "WORK".
                      88  LEVEL-77                 VALUE "77  ".
                      88  PROCEDURE-DIVISION       VALUE "PROC".
                      88  DECLARE                  VALUE "DECL".
                      88  BLANK-AREA-A             VALUE SPACES.
                  04  AREA-B          PIC X(61)   USAGE DISPLAY.
                  04  AREA-B-BYTES REDEFINES AREA-B
                                      PIC X       OCCURS 61 TIMES
                                                  INDEXED BY
                                                  AREA-B-INDEX.
                      88  ALPHA                    VALUE "A" THRU
                                                         "Z".
          02  IDEN-AREA               PIC X(8)    USAGE DISPLAY.


      01  COBLPROG-FILE-STATUS.
          02  SK1                     PIC X       USAGE DISPLAY.
              88  FILE-STATUS-OK                   VALUE "0".
          02  SK2                     PIC X       USAGE DISPLAY.


      01  NEW-SOURCE-LINE                          VALUE SPACES.
          02  FILLER                  PIC X(6)    USAGE DISPLAY.
          02  NEW-INDICATOR-A-B.
              03  NEW-INDICATOR       PIC X       USAGE DISPLAY.
              03  NEW-AREA-AB.
                  04  NEW-AREA-A      PIC X(4)    USAGE DISPLAY.
```

```
        04  NEW-AREA-B          PIC X(61)    USAGE DISPLAY.
   02  FILLER                   PIC X(8)     USAGE DISPLAY.
01 DIVISION-PARAGRAPH-SWITCHES.
   02  ID-SWITCH                PIC X(5)     USAGE DISPLAY
                                             VALUE SPACES.

       88  ID-NOT-FOUND                      VALUE SPACES.
       88  ID-FOUND                          VALUE "FOUND".
   02  ENVIRONMENT-SWITCH       PIC X(5)     USAGE DISPLAY
                                             VALUE SPACES.

       88  ENVIRONMENT-NOT-FOUND             VALUE SPACES.
       88  ENVIRONMENT-FOUND                 VALUE "FOUND".
   02  CONFIGURATION-SWITCH     PIC X(5)     USAGE DISPLAY
                                             VALUE SPACES.

       88  CONFIGURATION-NOT-FOUND           VALUE SPACES.
       88  CONFIGURATION-FOUND               VALUE "FOUND".
   02  SOURCE-SWITCH            PIC X(5)     USAGE DISPLAY
                                             VALUE SPACES.

       88  SOURCE-NOT-FOUND                  VALUE SPACES.
       88  SOURCE-FOUND                      VALUE "FOUND".
   02  SELECT-SWITCH            PIC X(5)     USAGE DISPLAY
                                             VALUE SPACES.

       88  SELECT-NOT-FOUND                  VALUE SPACES.
       88  SELECT-FOUND                      VALUE "FOUND".
   02  DATA-SWITCH              PIC X(5)     USAGE DISPLAY
                                             VALUE SPACES.

       88  DATA-NOT-FOUND                    VALUE SPACES.
       88  DATA-FOUND                        VALUE "FOUND".
   02  WS-SWITCH                PIC X(5)     USAGE DISPLAY
                                             VALUE SPACES.

       88  WS-NOT-FOUND                      VALUE SPACES.
       88  WS-FOUND                          VALUE "FOUND".
   02  PROCEDURE-SWITCH         PIC X(5)     USAGE DISPLAY
                                             VALUE SPACES.

       88  PROCEDURE-NOT-FOUND               VALUE SPACES.
       88  PROCEDURE-FOUND                   VALUE "FOUND".
   02  DECLARATIVES-SWITCH      PIC X(5)     USAGE DISPLAY
                                             VALUE SPACES.

       88  DECLARATIVES-NOT-FOUND            VALUE SPACES.
       88  DECLARATIVES-FOUND                VALUE "FOUND".

 01 COPY-SWITCH                 PIC X(4)     USAGE DISPLAY
                                             VALUE "COPY".

      88 DO-COPY                             VALUE "COPY".
*READ & DO IMMEDIATE WRITE; INSERTION OF NEW SOURCE LINE
*NOT ON
      88 DO-READ                             VALUE "READ".
```

```
*READ ONLY; USED IMMEDIATELY AFTER AUTO COPY TURNED OFF
      88 DO-WRITE                           VALUE "WRIT".
*AUTO COPY TURNED OFF; WRITE PREVIOUS SOURCE LINE BEFORE
*READ

   01 WRITE-SWITCH                PIC X(3)   USAGE DISPLAY
                                             VALUE "OLD".
      88 OLD-SOURCE-LINE                     VALUE "OLD".
         NEW-SOURCE-LINE                     VALUE "NEW".

   01 BREAKPOINT                   PIC X(80)  USAGE DISPLAY.
      88 DUMP                                 VALUE "D".

   01 TALLY-COUNTER                PIC S9V    USAGE COMP
                                              VALUE ZERO.
      88 DEBUG                                VALUE 1.
      88 DEFENSIVE-TRAP-FOUND                 VALUE 1.
      88 END-DELIMITER                        VALUE 1.
      88 FULLSTOP                             VALUE 1.
      88 STATUS-FOUND                         VALUE 1.

   01 END-SCOPE-DELIMITER.
      02 FILLER                    PIC X(4)   USAGE DISPLAY
                                              VALUE "END-".
      02 END-VERB                  PIC X(26)  USAGE DISPLAY
                                              VALUE SPACES.

  01   NUMBER-OF-NUMERIC-ITEMS   PIC S999V  VALUE 999.
*OCCURS DEPENDING ON DATA-NAME FOR NUMERIC-ITEM-TABLE; IF
*TOO SMALL THEN CHANGE IT TO REQUIRED NUMBER

   01 NUMERIC-ITEM-TABLE.
      02 NUMERIC-ITEM             PIC X(30)
                                  OCCURS 1 TO 999 TIMES
*SECOND INTEGER MUST BE THE SAME VALUE AS NUMBER-OF-NUMERIC-
*ITEMS
                                  DEPENDING ON
                                  NUMBER-OF-NUMERIC-ITEMS
                                  INDEXED BY
                                  NUMERIC-ITEM-INDEX.

   01 UNSTRING-ITEMS.
      02 UNSTRING-POINTER         PIC S99V   USAGE COMP
                                             VALUE ZERO.
      02 B-WORDS.
         03 WORD-1                PIC X(30)  USAGE DISPLAY.
```

```
        88  ARITHMETIC-VERB              VALUE "ADD"
                                               "COMPUTE"
                                         VALUE ZERO.
                                               "DIVIDE"
                                               "MULTIPLY"
                                               "SUBTRACT".
        88  CALL-VERB                    VALUE "CALL".
        88  DIVIDE-VERB                  VALUE "DIVIDE".
        88  END-PERFORM-VERB             VALUE "END-PERFORM."
        88  EVALUATE-VERB                VALUE "EVALUATE".
        88  EXIT-VERB                    VALUE "EXIT".
        88  GO-VERB                      VALUE "GO".
        88  GOBACK-VERB                  VALUE "GOBACK".
*IBM
        88  IF-VERB                      VALUE "IF".
        88  IO-VERB                      VALUE "CLOSE"
                                               "DELETE"
                                               "OPEN"
                                               "READ"
                                               "REWRITE"
                                               "SEEK"
*IBM
                                               "WRITE".
*PLACE ANY NON-ANSI I-O VERBS OF YOUR COMPILER IN THIS LIST
        88  MOVE-VERB                    VALUE "MOVE".
        88  PERFORM-VERB                 VALUE "PERFORM".
        88  SEARCH-VERB                  VALUE "SEARCH".
        88  STOP-VERB                    VALUE "STOP".
        88  STRING-UNSTRING-VERB         VALUE "STRING"
                                               "UNSTRING".
        88  TARGET-VERB                  VALUE "ADD"
                                               "CALL"
                                               "COMPUTE"
                                               "DIVIDE"
                                               "EVALUATE"
                                               "GO"
                                               "MULTIPLY"
                                               "SEARCH"
                                               "STRING"
                                               "SUBTRACT"
                                               "UNSTRING".
        88  VERB                         VALUE "ACCEPT"
                                               "ADD"
                                               "ALTER"
*OBSOLETE
                                               "CALL"
```

"CANCEL"
"CLOSE"
"COMPUTE"
"CONTINUE"

*COBOL-85   "COPY"

*TREATED LIKE A VERB   "DELETE"
                                                    "DISABLE"
                                                    "DISPLAY"
                                                    "DIVIDE"
                                                    "ELSE"

*TREATED LIKE A VERB   "ENABLE"
                                                    "ENTER"

*OBSOLETE   "EVALUATE"

*COBOL-85   "EXAMINE"

*COBOL-68   "EXIT"
                                                    "GENERATE"
                                                    "GO"
                                                    "GOBACK"

*IBM   "IF"

                                                    "INITIALIZE"

*COBOL-85   "INITIATE"
                                                    "INSPECT"
                                                    "MERGE"
                                                    "MOVE"
                                                    "MULTIPLY"
                                                    "OPEN"
                                                    "PERFORM"
                                                    "PURGE"
                                                    "READ"
                                                    "RECEIVE"
                                                    "RELEASE"
                                                    "REPLACE"

*COBOL-85; TREATED LIKE A VERB   "RETURN"
                                                    "REWRITE"
                                                    "SEARCH"
                                                    "SEEK"

*IBM

                                                                                "SEND"
  "SET"
  "SORT"
  "START"
  "STOP"
  "STRING"
  "SUBTRACT"
  "SUPPRESS"
  "TERMINATE"
  "TRANSFORM"

*IBM

  "UNSTRING"
  "USE"
  "WRITE".

```
          03  WORD-2                 PIC X(30) USAGE DISPLAY.
*MUST CONTAIN PROGRAM-NAME FOR PROGRAM-ID PARAGRAPH
*ITEM DATA-NAME IF DATA DIVISION  BEING UNSTRING
*DIVISOR IF DIVIDE INTO BEING UNSTRING
*FROM ITEM DATA-NAME IF MOVE VERB BEING UNSTRING
              88  CORR-PHASE                VALUE
                                            "CORRESPONDING"
                                                  "CORR".

              88  PROGRAM-WORD              VALUE "PROGRAM".
              88  RUN-WORD                  VALUE "RUN".
          03  WORD-3                 PIC X(30) USAGE DISPLAY.
              88  BY-WORD                   VALUE "BY".
              88  INTO-WORD                 VALUE "INTO".
              88  PICTURE-CLAUSE            VALUE "PICTURE"
                                                  "PIC".

              88  TO-WORD                   VALUE "TO".
          03  WORD-4                 PIC X(30) USAGE DISPLAY.
*DIVISOR IF DIVIDE BY VERB      BEING UNSTRING
*TO ITEM DATA-NAME IF MOVE VERB BEING UNSTRING
          03  WORD-4-BYTES REDEFINES WORD-4
              04  FILLER            PIC X      USAGE DISPLAY.
                  88  SIGN-BYTE               VALUE "S".
              04  FILLER            PIC X(29) USAGE DISPLAY.
          03  WORD-5                 PIC X(30) USAGE DISPLAY.
*MUST CONTAIN ALPHA IF ANALYZING GO TO DEPENDING ON STATEMENT
              88  NOT-PROCEDURE-NAME        VALUE SPACES.
          03  WORD-6                 PIC X(30) USAGE DISPLAY.
          03  WORD-7                 PIC X(30) USAGE DISPLAY.
          03  WORD-8                 PIC X(30) USAGE DISPLAY.
      02  WORD-DELIMITERS.
          03  WORD-DELIMITER-1   PIC X      USAGE DISPLAY.
```

```
        03  WORD-DELIMITER-2     PIC X      USAGE DISPLAY.
        03  WORD-DELIMITER-3     PIC X      USAGE DISPLAY.
        03  WORD-DELIMITER-4     PIC X      USAGE DISPLAY.
        03  WORD-DELIMITER-5     PIC X      USAGE DISPLAY.
        03  WORD-DELIMITER-6     PIC X      USAGE DISPLAY.
        03  WORD-DELIMITER-7     PIC X      USAGE DISPLAY.
        03  WORD-DELIMITER-8     PIC X      USAGE DISPLAY.
 *8 WORDS ARE USED TO ENSURE FULL STOP (.)  IS FOUND


  01            PABORT-PARAGRAPH-NAME.
      02        FILLER               PIC X(7)   USAGE DISPLAY
                                                VALUE "PABORT-".
      02        ODOMETER-DISPLAY  PIC 9(4)   USAGE DISPLAY.
      02        ODOMETER REDEFINES ODOMETER-DISPLAY
                                     PIC S9(4)V USAGE COMP
                                                VALUE ZERO.


  01-NEGATIVE-OR-ZERO-TRAP.
      02 FILLER                     PIC X(8)   USAGE DISPLAY
                                                VALUE "D     IF ".
 *ACTIVE DEFENSIVE TRAP; D DISABLES UNTIL ANSI DEBUG TURNED ON
      02 TRAP-DATA-NAME            PIC X(30)  USAGE DISPLAY
                                                VALUE SPACES.
      02 FILLER                     PIC X      USAGE DISPLAY
                                                VALUE SPACE.
      02 TRAP-TYPE                  PIC X(8)   USAGE DISPLAY
                                                VALUE SPACES.


      EJECT
```

```
  PROCEDURE DIVISION.

  DECLARATIVES.

  DEBUG SECTION.

     USE FOR DEBUGGING ON ALL PROCEDURES.

  DEBUG-PROGRAM-FLOW.

     DISPLAY      DEBUG-LINE
                  DEBUG-NAME
                  DEBUG-CONTENTS.

  DEBUG-BREAKPOINT.
```

```
*     ACCEPT          breakpoint    FROM mnemonic-name.
* * USED TO DISABLE ACCEPT EVEN IF DEBUG MODULE IS ACTIVE
* * IS DELETED WHEN INTERACTIVE BREAKPOINTS ARE REQUIRED

 END DECLARATIVES.

 P101-INITIATION.

      OPEN INPUT    COBOLIN

      OPEN OUTPUT   COBOLOUT

      DISPLAY       "INSTOC PROGRAM START."

      GO TO         P102-IDENTIFICATION-DIVISION.

 P102-IDENTIFICATION-DIVISION.

      PERFORM       PC01-READ-COBOLIN
      THRU          PC01-X.

*FIND IDENTIFICATION DIVISION
      IF            IDENTIFICATION-DIVISION
         NEXT SENTENCE
      ELSE          GO TO P102-IDENTIFICATION-DIVISION.

      MOVE          "FOUND"
      TO            ID-SWITCH

*PROGRAM-ID MUST BE NEXT STATEMENT LINE
      PERFORM       PC01-READ-COBOLIN
      THRU          PC01-X.

*FIND WORDS IN AREA B
      PERFORM       PCO3-FIND-WORDS
      THRU          PC03-X.

*WORD-2 MUST BE PROGRAM NAME
      DISPLAY       "TARGET PROGRAM IS "
                    WORD-2

      GO TO         P103-WORKING-STORAGE.

 P104-WORKING-STORAGE.
*NEED TO FIND WORKING-STORAGE TO INSERT 77 ITEMS

      PERFORM       PC01-READ-COBLPROG
```

```
            THRU            PC01-X.

            IF              WORKING-STORAGE
                            MOVE    "FOUND"
                            TO      WORKING-STORAGE-SWITCH
                            GO TO   P105-FIND-77S
            ELSE            GO TO   P104-WORKING-STORAGE.

        P105-FIND-77S.
       *INSERT PERFORM-RETURN-COUNTER AFTER LAST 77

            PERFORM         PC01-READ-COBLPROG
            THRU            PC01-X.

            IF              LEVEL-77
                            GO TO   P105-FIND-77S
            ELSE    NEXT SENTENCE.

            MOVE            "NEW"
            TO              WRITE-SWITCH

            MOVE            SPACES
            TO              NEW-SOURCE-LINE

            PERFORM         PC02-WRITE-COBOLOUT
            THRU            PC02-X.

            MOVE            "D77  PERFORM-RETURN-COUNTER   PIC S9(4)V
       -                    "USAGE COMP   VALUE ZERO."
            TO              NEW-INDICATOR-A-B
       *D DISABLES EXCEPT WHEN IN DEBUGGING MODE

            PERFORM         PC02-WRITE-COBOLOUT
            THRU            PC02-X.

            MOVE            "D 88 START-OF-PERFORM-PATH  VALUE ZERO."
            TO              NEW-INDICATOR-A-B

            PERFORM         PC02-WRITE-COBOLOUT
            THRU            PC02-X.

            MOVE            "D 88 VALID-TRANSFER-OF-CONTROL   VALUE
       -                    "ZERO."
            TO              NEW-INDICATOR-A-B

            PERFORM         PC02-WRITE-COBOLOUT
```

```
    THRU            PC02-X.

    MOVE            SPACES
    TO              NEW-SOURCE-LINE

    PERFORM         PC02-WRITE-COBOLOUT
    THRU            PC02-X.

    MOVE            "OLD"
    TO              WRITE-SWITCH

    GO TO           P106-PROCEDURE-DIVISION.

P106-PROCEDURE-DIVISION.

    PERFORM         PC01-READ-COBLPROG
    THRU            PC01-X.

    IF              PROCEDURE-FOUND
        NEXT SENTENCE
    ELSE            GO TO P106-PROCEDURE-DIVISION.

    MOVE            "FOUND"
    TO              PROCEDURE-SWITCH

    MOVE            "READ"
    TO              COPY-SWITCH

    GO TO           P107-FIND-PERFORM-VERB.

 P107-FIND-PERFORM-VERB.

    PERFORM         PC01-READ-COBLPROG
    THRU            PC01-X.

*FIND PERFORM-VERB
    PERFORM         PCO3-FIND-WORDS
    THRU            PC03-X.

    IF              PERFORM-VERB
*ASSUMES THAT VERB IF PRESENT IS FIRST WORD IN AREA B
        NEXT SENTENCE
    ELSE            GO TO  P107-FIND-PERFORM-VERB.

    MOVE            "NEW"
    TO              WRITE-SWITCH
```

```
        MOVE              "D     IF NOT START-OF-PERFORM-PATH"
        TO                NEW-INDICATOR-A-B
*D MAKES IT A DEBUGGING LINE - ONLY ACTIVE IN ANSI DEBUG MODE


        PERFORM           PC02-WRITE-COBOLOUT
        THRU              PC02-X.


        MOVE              "D     ALTER RUNAWAY-GOTO TO PROCEED TO
   -                      "NO-RUNAWAY-TEST"
        TO                NEW-INDICATOR-A-B
*D MAKES IT A DEBUGGING LINE - ONLY ACTIVE IN ANSI DEBUG MODE


        PERFORM           PC02-WRITE-COBOLOUT
        THRU              PC02-X.


        MOVE              "D     ELSE NEXT SENTENCE"
        TO                NEW-INDICATOR-A-B
*D MAKES IT A DEBUGGING LINE - ONLY ACTIVE IN ANSI DEBUG MODE


        PERFORM           PC02-WRITE-COBOLOUT
        THRU              PC02-X.


        MOVE              "D     ADD 1 TO PERFORM-RETURN-COUNTER"
        TO                NEW-INDICATOR-A-B
*D MAKES IT A DEBUGGING LINE - ONLY ACTIVE IN ANSI DEBUG MODE


        PERFORM           PC02-WRITE-COBOLOUT
        THRU              PC02-X.


        MOVE              "D     ON SIZE ERROR DIVIDE ZERO-LIT BY
   -                      "ZERO-LIT GIVING INFINITY"
        TO                NEW-INDICATOR-A-B
*D MAKES IT A DEBUGGING LINE - ONLY ACTIVE IN ANSI DEBUG MODE


        PERFORM           PC02-WRITE-COBOLOUT
        THRU              PC02-X.


        MOVE              "OLD"
        TO                WRITE-SWITCH


        GO TO             P108-FIND-TERMINATOR.


    P108-FIND-TERMINATOR.
*DEFENSIVE TRAP PERFORM MUST BE INSERTED AFTER PERFORM.
*TERMINATOR CAN BE PERIOD [.], END-PERFORM, NEW VERB, OR NEW
*MODULE
```

```
       PERFORM         PC02-WRITE-COBOLOUT
       THRU            PC02-X.

       PERFORM         PC03-FIND-WORDS
       THRU            PC03-X.

    IF NOT             BLANK-AREA-A
*AREA A ENTRY FOUND; STATEMENT TERMINATED INSERT DEFENSIVE
*TRAP
                       PERFORM PC10-INSERT-PERFORM
                       THRU    PC10-X
                       GO TO   P107-FIND-PERFORM
       ELSE NEXT SENTENCE.

*DETERMINE IF FULL STOP PRESENT
       MOVE            ZERO
       TO              TALLY-COUNTER

       INSPECT         WORD-DELIMITERS
       TALLYING        TALLY-COUNTER
       FOR ALL         ".".

       IF              FULLSTOP
*FULL STOP FOUND; STATEMENT TERMINATED INSERT DEFENSIVE TRAP
                       PERFORM PC10-INSERT-PERFORM
                       THRU    PC10-X
                       GO TO   P107-FIND-PERFORM
       ELSE NEXT SENTENCE.

       IF              END-PERFORM-VERB
*END-PERFORM FOUND; STATEMENT TERMINATED INSERT DEFENSIVE
*TRAP
                       PERFORM PC10-INSERT-PERFORM
                       THRU    PC10-X
                       GO TO   P107-FIND-PERFORM
       ELSE NEXT SENTENCE.

       IF              VERB
*VERB FOUND; STATEMENT TERMINATED INSERT DEFENSIVE TRAP
                       PERFORM PC10-INSERT-DEFENSIVE-TRAP
                       THRU    PC10-X
                       GO TO   P107-FIND-PERFORM
       ELSE  NEXT SENTENCE.
*TERMINATOR NOT FOUND; CONTINUE LOOKING
       GO TO           P108-FIND-TERMINATOR.

    PEOJ.
```

```
IF              ID-NOT-FOUND
                DISPLAY "NO IDENTIFICATION DIVISION"
ELSE
IF              PROCEDURE-NOT-FOUND
                DISPLAY "NO PROCEDURE DIVISION"
ELSE NEXT SENTENCE.


*INSERT RUNAWAY TEST MODULE AT END OF PROGRAM

     MOVE           "NEW"
     TO             WRITE-SWITCH

     MOVE           "DRUNAWAY-TEST."
     TO             NEW-INDICATOR-A-B

     PERFORM        PC02-WRITE-COBOLOUT
     THRU           PC02-X.

     MOVE           "*TEST FOR RUNAWAY CODE"
     TO             NEW-INDICATOR-A-B

     PERFORM        PC02-WRITE-COBOLOUT
     THRU           PC02-X.

     MOVE           SPACES
     TO             NEW-SOURCE-LINE

     PERFORM        PC02-WRITE-COBOLOUT
     THRU           PC02-X.

     MOVE           "D  SUBTRACT 1 FROM PERFORM-RETURN-COUNTER"
     TO             NEW-INDICATOR-A-B

     PERFORM        PC02-WRITE-COBOLOUT
     THRU           PC02-X.

     MOVE           "D ON SIZE ERROR DIVIDE ZERO-LIT BY
                    "ZERO-LIT GIVING INFINITY"
     TO             NEW-INDICATOR-A-B

     PERFORM        PC02-WRITE-COBOLOUT
     THRU           PC02-X.

     MOVE           SPACES
     TO             NEW-SOURCE-LINE
```

```
PERFORM        PC02-WRITE-COBOLOUT
THRU           PC02-X.

MOVE           "D   GO TO RUNAWAY-GOTO."
TO             NEW-INDICATOR-A-B

PERFORM        PC02-WRITE-COBOLOUT
THRU           PC02-X.

MOVE           SPACES
TO             NEW-SOURCE-LINE

PERFORM        PC02-WRITE-COBOLOUT
THRU           PC02-X.

MOVE           "DRUNAWAY-GOTO."
TO             NEW-INDICATOR-A-B

PERFORM        PC02-WRITE-COBOLOUT
THRU           PC02-X.

MOVE           SPACES
TO             NEW-SOURCE-LINE

PERFORM        PC02-WRITE-COBOLOUT
THRU           PC02-X.

MOVE           "D  GO TO NO-RUNAWAY-TEST."
TO             NEW-INDICATOR-A-B

PERFORM        PC02-WRITE-COBOLOUT
THRU           PC02-X.

MOVE           "*ALTERABLE GOTO; ALTERED TO DO TEST-
               "RUNAWAY IF ROC TO PATH START"
TO             NEW-INDICATOR-A-B

PERFORM        PC02-WRITE-COBOLOUT
THRU           PC02-X.

MOVE           SPACES
TO             NEW-SOURCE-LINE

PERFORM        PC02-WRITE-COBOLOUT
THRU           PC02-X.
```

```
      MOVE          "DTEST-RUNAWAY."
      TO            NEW-INDICATOR-A-B

      PERFORM       PC02-WRITE-COBOLOUT
      THRU          PC02-X.

      MOVE          "*CAN ONLY BE REACHED IF RUNAWAY GOTO
-                   "ALTERED TO TEST-RUNAWAY"
      TO            NEW-INDICATOR-A-B

      PERFORM       PC02-WRITE-COBOLOUT
      THRU          PC02-X.

      MOVE          SPACES
      TO            NEW-SOURCE-LINE

      PERFORM       PC02-WRITE-COBOLOUT
      THRU          PC02-X.

      MOVE          "D   IF   VALID-RETURN-OF-CONTROL"
      TO            NEW-INDICATOR-A-B

      PERFORM       PC02-WRITE-COBOLOUT
      THRU          PC02-X.

      MOVE          SPACES
      TO            NEW-SOURCE-LINE

      PERFORM       PC02-WRITE-COBOLOUT
      THRU          PC02-X.

      MOVE          "D   GO TO RUNAWAY-EXIT"
      TO            NEW-INDICATOR-A-B

      PERFORM       PC02-WRITE-COBOLOUT
      THRU          PC02-X.

      MOVE          "D   DIVIDE ZERO-LIT BY ZERO-LIT
-                   "GIVING INFINITY"
      TO            NEW-INDICATOR-A-B

      PERFORM       PC02-WRITE-COBOLOUT
      THRU          PC02-X.

      MOVE          "*RETURN WAS INCORRECT; THERE IS RUNAWAY
-                   "CODE; ABEND PROGRAM"
```

```
TO              NEW-INDICATOR-A-B

PERFORM         PC02-WRITE-COBOLOUT
THRU            PC02-X.

MOVE            "ONO-RUNAWAY-TEST."
TO              NEW-INDICATOR-A-B

PERFROM         PC02-WRITE-COBOLOUT
THRU            PC02-X.

MOVE            "D   ALTER  RUNAWAY-GOTO TO PROCEED TO"
                "NO-RUNAWAY-TEST"
TO              NEW-INDICATOR-A-B

PERFORM         PC02-WRITE-COBOLOUT
THRU            PC02-X.

MOVE            SPACES
TO              NEW-SOURCE-LINE

PERFORM         PC02-WRITE-COBOLOUT
THRU            PC02-X.

MOVE            "D   GO TO RUNAWAY-EXIT."
TO              NEW-INDICATOR-A-B

PERFORM         PC02-WRITE-COBOLOUT
THRU            PC02-X.

MOVE            SPACES
TO              NEW-SOURCE-LINE

PERFORM         PC02-WRITE-COBOLOUT
THRU            PC02-X.

MOVE            "RUNAYWAY-EXIT.   EXIT."
TO              NEW-INDICATOR-A-B

PERFORM         PC02-WRITE-COBOLOUT
THRU            PC02-X.

MOVE            SPACES
TO              NEW-SOURCE-LINE

PERFORM         PC02-WRITE-COBOLOUT
```

```
       THRU            PC02-X.

*INSERT RUNAWAY PARAGRAPH FOR RUNAWAY TRAP!
       MOVE            "DPABORT-RUNAWAY."
       TO              NEW-INDICATOR-A-B

       PERFORM         PC02-WRITE-COBOLOUT
       THRU            PC02-X.

       MOVE            "*RUNAWAY CODE ABEND"
       TO              NEW-INDICATOR-A-B

       PERFORM         PC02-WRITE-COBOLOUT
       THRU            PC02-X.

       MOVE            SPACES
       TO              NEW-SOURCE-LINE

       PERFORM         PC02-WRITE-COBOLOUT
       THRU            PC02-X.

       MOVE            "D   DISPLAY  'RUN-ABORTED AT RUNAWAY'"
       TO              NEW-INDICATOR-A-B

       PERFORM         PC02-WRITE-COBOLOUT
       THRU            PC02-X.

       MOVE            SPACES
       TO              NEW-SOURCE-LINE

       PERFORM         PC02-WRITE-COBOLOUT
       THRU            PC02-X.

       MOVE            "D   DIVIDE ZERO-LIT BY ZERO-LIT
                       "GIVING INFINITY"
       TO              NEW-INDICATOR-A-B

       PERFORM         PC02-WRITE-COBOLOUT
       THRU            PC02-X.

       MOVE            SPACES
       TO              NEW-SOURCE-LINE

       PERFORM         PC02-WRITE-COBOLOUT
       THRU            PC02-X.
```

```
        MOVE            "EJECT"
        TO              NEW-AREA-B

        PERFORM         PC02-WRITE-COBOLOUT
        THRU            PC02-X.

        MOVE            SPACES
        TO              NEW-SOURCE-LINE

        PERFORM         PC02-WRITE-COBOLOUT
        THRU            PC02-X.

        CLOSE           COBOLIN
                        COBOLOUT.

        DISPLAY         "INSTOC PROGRAM EOJ."

        STOP RUN.

        EJECT
```

```
    PC01-READ-COBOLIN.

        IF              DO-WRITE
*AUTO COPY OFF; WRITE OUT LAST READ SOURCE LINE BEFORE READ
                        PERFORM PC02-WRITE-COBOLOUT
                        THRU    PC02-X
        ELSE NEXT SENTENCE.

        READ            COBOLIN
        INTO            COBOL-LINE-WS
        AT END          GO TO PEOJ.

        IF              FILE-STATUS-OK
            NEXT SENTENCE
        ELSE            DISPLAY "RUN ABORTED - BAD FILE STATUS OF "
                            COBLPROG-FILE-STATUS
*ASSUMES OUTPUT TO PROGRAMMER'S TERMINAL
                        GO TO PEOJ.


        IF              DO-COPY
*AUTO COPY ON; DO IMMEDIATE WRITE; CANNOT INSERT NEW SOURCE
*LINE BEFORE SOURCE LINE JUST READ
                        PERFORM PC02-WRITE-COBOLOUT
```

```
                        THRU    PC02-X
             IF         DO-READ
*AUTO COPY JUST TURNED OFF; MOVE WRITE TO SWITCH TO ENABLE
*WRITE BEFORE READ
                        MOVE    "WRIT"
                        TO      COPY-SWITCH
         ELSE NEXT SENTENCE.


*BYPASS NON STATEMENT LINE OR BLANK SOURCE LINE
         IF             NON-STATEMENT-LINE
         OR             BLANK-SOURCE-LINE
                        GO TO PCO1-READ-COBOLIN
         ELSE           GO TO PC01-X.


      PC01-X. EXIT.


      PABORT-PC01.
*RUNAWAY CODE ABEND


         DISPLAY        "RUN ABORTED - RUNAWAY CODE AT PC01"


         GO TO          PEOJ.


         EJECT
```

```
      PC02-WRITE-COBOLOUT.


*WRITE-SWITCH USED TO DETERMINE FROM IDENTIFIER
         IF             OLD-SOURCE-LINE
                        WRITE   COBOL-LINE-OUT
                        FROM    COBOL-LINE-WS
         ELSE           WRITE   COBOL-LINE-OUT
                        FROM    NEW-SOURCE-LINE.
*NEW-SOURCE-LINE


         IF             FILE-STATUS-OK
                        GO TO   PC02-X
         ELSE           DISPLAY "RUN ABORTED - BAD FILE STATUS OF "
                                COBLPROG-FILE-STATUS
*ASSUMES OUTPUT TO PROGRAMMER'S TERMINAL
                        GO TO PEOJ.


      PC02-X. EXIT.


      PABORT-PC02.
```

```
*RUNAWAY CODE ABEND

    DISPLAY        "RUN ABORTED - RUNAWAY CODE AT PC02"

    GO TO          PEOJ.

    EJECT
```

```
  PC03-FIND-WORDS.

    MOVE           SPACES
    TO             B-WORDS
                   WORD-DELIMITERS

    SET            AREA-B-INDEX
                   UNSTRING-POINTER
    TO             1

    SEARCH         AREA-B-BYTES
    VARYING        UNSTRING-POINTER
*AREA-B-BYTES INDEXED BY AREA-B-INDEX; UNSTRING POINTER IS
*KEPT IN SYNC AND WILL POINT TO THE FIRST ALPHA CHARACTER IN
*AREA B
    AT END         DISPLAY "RUN ABORTED - NO ALPHA CHARACTER
                   "FOUND AT SEQUENCE NUMBER "
-
                   SEQUENCE-NUMBER
                   GO TO PEOJ
*CAN'T HAPPEN; IT MUST FIND AN ALPHA CHARACTER
    WHEN           ALPHA
         NEXT SENTENCE.

*FIRST ALPHA CHARACTER OF FIRST WORD FOUND

    UNSTRING       AREA-B
    DELIMITED ALL SPACES OR "." OR "," OR ";"
*.,; USED TO STRIP FROM WORD; FULL STOP NEEDED FOR SENTENCE
*END
    INTO           WORD-1
    DELIMITER IN WORD-1-DELIMITER
    INTO           WORD-2
    DELIMITER IN WORD-2-DELIMITER
    INTO           WORD-3
    DELIMITER IN WORD-3-DELIMITER
    INTO           WORD-4
    DELIMITER IN WORD-4-DELIMITER
```

```
            INTO              WORD-5
            DELIMITER IN WORD-5-DELIMITER
            INTO              WORD-6
            DELIMITER IN WORD-6-DELIMITER
            INTO              WORD-7
            DELIMITER IN WORD-7-DELIMITER
            INTO              WORD-8
            ON OVERFLOW   DISPLAY "RUN ABORTED - TOO MANY WORDS IN
 -                            "SOURCE LINE AT SEQUENCE NUMBER "
                              SEQUENCE NUMBER
                              GO TO PEOJ.
*OVERFLOW MEANS MORE THEN 8 WORDS IN AREA B - NOT ALLOWED
*INCREASE RECEIVING WORDS IF REQUIRED


            GO TO             PC03-X.


   PCO3-X. EXIT.


   PABORT-PC03.
*RUNAWAY CODE ABEND


       DISPLAY           "RUN ABORTED - RUNAWAY CODE AT PC03"


       GO TO             PEOJ.


       EJECT
```

```
PC10-INSERT-PERFORM.
*INSERT PERFORM TO CHECK FOR VALID TRANSFER OF CONTROL


       MOVE              "NEW"
       TO                WRITE-SWITCH


       MOVE              SPACES
       TO                NEW-SOURCE-LINE


       PERFORM           PC02-WRITE-COBOLOUT
       THRU              PC02-X.


       MOVE              "D   PERFORM RUNAWAY-TEST"
       TO                NEW-INDICATOR-A-B


       PERFORM           PC02-WRITE-COBOLOUT
       THRU              PC02-X.
```

```
      MOVE            "D   THRU RUNAWAY-TEST-EXIT."
      TO              NEW-INDICATOR-A-B

      PERFORM         PC02-WRITE-COBOLOUT
      THRU            PC02-X.

      MOVE            SPACES
      TO              NEW-SOURCE-LINE
      PERFORM         PC02-WRITE-COBOLOUT
      THRU            PC02-X.

      MOVE            "OLD"
      TO              WRITE-SWITCH

      GO TO           PC10-X.

  PC10-X.   EXIT.

  PABORT-PC10.
 *RUNAWAY CODE ABEND

      DISPLAY         "RUN ABORTED - RUNAWAY CODE AT PC10"

      GO TO           PEOJ.

      EJECT
```

OVERMOVE

```
  IDENTIFICATION DIVISION.

  PROGRAM-ID.         OVERMOVE
 *TEST PROGRAM TO SEE WHAT HOST COMPILER DOES WITH AN
 *OVERLAPPING MOVE

  AUTHOR.             ERIC GARRIGUE VESELY
                      THE ANALYST WORKBENCH CONSULTING SDN BHD

  DATE-WRITTEN.    26 FEBRUARY 1990

  DATE-COMPILED.

  ENVIRONMENT DIVISION.
```

```
DATA DIVISION.

WORKING-STORAGE SECTION.

01 OVERLAPPING-MOVE-DATA.
   02 FIRST-THIRTEEN-LETTERS  PIC X(13) USAGE DISPLAY
                                        VALUE
                                        "ABCDEFGHIJKLM".
   02 TEN-DIGITS              PIC X(10) USAGE DISPLAY
                                        VALUE "0123456789".
   02 SECOND-THIRTEEN-LETTERS PIC X(13) USAGE DISPLAY
                                        VALUE
                                        "NOPQRSTUVWXYZ".
   66 FIRST-TEN     RENAMES   FIRST-THIRTEEN-LETTERS
                    THRU      TEN-DIGITS.
   66 TEN-SECOND    RENAMES   TEN-DIGITS
                    THRU      SECOND-THIRTEEN-LETTERS.

PROCEDURE-DIVISION.

   MOVE          FIRST-TEN
   TO            TEN-SECOND

   STOP RUN.

   EJECT
```

SUBFILES

```
IDENTIFICATION DIVISION.

  PROGRAM-ID.        SUBFILES.
 *PROGRAM SUBSTITUTES INSTALLATION STANDARD FILE STATUS COPY
 *FOR PROGRAM FILE STATUS [IF NONE EXISTS THEN IT IS INSERTED]
 *INSTALLATION STANDARD DATA-NAME IS SUBSTITUTED OR INSERTED
 *IN THE FILE-CONTROL-ENTRY OF THE ENVIRONMENT DIVISION AND
 *W-S

  AUTHOR.            ERIC GARRIGUE VESELY
                     THE ANALYST WORKBENCH CONSULTING SDN BHD

  DATE-WRITTEN.    26 FEBRUARY 1990

  DATE-COMPILED.
```

```
 ENVIRONMENT DIVISION.

 CONFIGURATION SECTION.

 SOURCE COMPUTER.
*                           WITH DEBUGGING MODE.
*ABOVE * IS SOURCE TIME SWITCH
 INPUT-OUTPUT SECTION.

 FILE CONTROL.
*SIMPLE SEQUENTIAL IO IS USED TO REDUCE COMPLEXITY

 SELECT              COBOLIN
*COBOLIN IS NAME OF FILE CONTAINING COBOL PROGRAM
     ASSIGN TO       SEQINPUT
*SEQINPUT IS NAME THAT COBOLIN IS ASSIGNED TO
     ORGANIZATION IS SEQUENTIAL
     ACCESS MODE  IS SEQUENTIAL
     FILE STATUS  IS COBLPROG-FILE-STATUS.

 SELECT              COBOLOUT
*COBOLOUT IS NAME OF NEW FILE THAT CONTAINS TRAPPED COBOL
*PROGRAM
     ASSIGN TO       SEQOUTPT
*SEQOUTPT IS NAME THAT COBOLOUT IS ASSIGNED TO
     ORGANIZATION IS SEQUENTIAL
     ACCESS MODE  IS SEQUENTIAL
     FILE STATUS  IS COBLPROG-FILE-STATUS.

     EJECT
```

```
 DATA DIVISION.

 FILE SECTION.

 FD          COBOLIN          LABEL RECORD STANDARD.

 01 COBOL-LINE-IN          PIC X(80)  USAGE DISPLAY.
*ASSUMES 80 COLUMN [BYTE] RECORDS

 FD          COBOLOUT         LABEL RECORD STANDARD.

 01 COBOL-LINE-OUT         PIC X(80)  USAGE DISPLAY.


 WORKING-STORAGE SECTION.
```

```
01  COBOL-LINE-WS.
    02  SEQUENCE-NUMBER          PIC X(6)     USAGE DISPLAY.
    02  INDICATOR-A-B.
        03  INDICATOR            PIC X        USAGE DISPLAY.
            88  NON-STATEMENT-LINE            VALUE "*"
                                                    "D"
                                                    "/"
                                                    "-".
        03  AREA-AB.
            88  BLANK-SOURCE-LINE             VALUE SPACES.
            04  AREA-A           PIC X(4)     USAGE DISPLAY.
                88  IDENTIFICATION-DIVISION VALUE "IDEN"
                                                    "ID D".
*IBM ABBREVIATION
                88  ENVIRONMENT-DIVISION      VALUE "ENVI".
                88  SELECT-CLAUSE             VALUE "SELE".
                88  CONFIGURATION-SECTION     VALUE "CONF".
                88  SOURCE-COMP               VALUE "SOUR".
                88  DATA-DIVISION             VALUE "DATA".
                88  WS-SECTION                VALUE "WORK".
                88  LEVEL-77                  VALUE "77  ".
                88  PROCEDURE-DIVISION        VALUE "PROC".
                88  DECLARE                   VALUE "DECL".
                88  BLANK-AREA-A              VALUE SPACES.
            04  AREA-B           PIC X(61)    USAGE DISPLAY.
            04  AREA-B-BYTES REDEFINES AREA-B
                                 PIC X        OCCURS 61 TIMES
                                              INDEXED BY
                                              AREA-B-INDEX.
                88  ALPHA                     VALUE "A" THRU
                                                    "Z".
    02  IDEN-AREA                PIC X(8)     USAGE DISPLAY.


01  COBLPROG-FILE-STATUS.
    02  SK1                      PIC X        USAGE DISPLAY.
        88  FILE-STATUS-OK                    VALUE "0".
    02  SK2                      PIC X        USAGE DISPLAY.

01  NEW-SOURCE-LINE                           VALUE SPACES.
    02  FILLER                   PIC X(6)     USAGE DISPLAY.
    02  NEW-INDICATOR-A-B.
        03  NEW-INDICATOR        PIC X        USAGE DISPLAY.
        03  NEW-AREA-AB.
            04  NEW-AREA-A       PIC X(4)     USAGE DISPLAY.
            04  NEW-AREA-B       PIC X(61)    USAGE DISPLAY.
    02  FILLER                   PIC X(8)     USAGE DISPLAY.
```

```
01  DIVISION-PARAGRAPH-SWITCHES.
    02  ID-SWITCH                  PIC X(5)    USAGE DISPLAY
                                               VALUE SPACES.

        88  ID-NOT-FOUND                       VALUE SPACES.
        88  ID-FOUND                           VALUE "FOUND".
    02  ENVIRONMENT-SWITCH        PIC X(5)     USAGE DISPLAY
                                               VALUE SPACES.

        88  ENVIRONMENT-NOT-FOUND              VALUE SPACES.
        88  ENVIRONMENT-FOUND                  VALUE "FOUND".
    02  CONFIGURATION-SWITCH      PIC X(5)     USAGE DISPLAY
                                               VALUE SPACES.

        88  CONFIGURATION-NOT-FOUND            VALUE SPACES.
        88  CONFIGURATION-FOUND                VALUE "FOUND".
    02  SOURCE-SWITCH             PIC X(5)     USAGE DISPLAY
                                               VALUE SPACES.

        88  SOURCE-NOT-FOUND                   VALUE SPACES.
        88  SOURCE-FOUND                       VALUE "FOUND".
    02  SELECT-SWITCH             PIC X(5)     USAGE DISPLAY
                                               VALUE SPACES.

        88  SELECT-NOT-FOUND                   VALUE SPACES.
        88  SELECT-FOUND                       VALUE "FOUND".
    02  DATA-SWITCH              PIC X(5)     USAGE DISPLAY
                                               VALUE SPACES.

        88  DATA-NOT-FOUND                     VALUE SPACES.
        88  DATA-FOUND                         VALUE "FOUND".
    02  WS-SWITCH               PIC X(5)      USAGE DISPLAY
                                               VALUE SPACES.

        88  WS-NOT-FOUND                       VALUE SPACES.
        88  WS-FOUND                           VALUE "FOUND".
    02  PROCEDURE-SWITCH         PIC X(5)     USAGE DISPLAY
                                               VALUE SPACES.

        88  PROCEDURE-NOT-FOUND                VALUE SPACES.
        88  PROCEDURE-FOUND                    VALUE "FOUND".
    02  DECLARATIVES-SWITCH      PIC X(5)     USAGE DISPLAY
                                               VALUE SPACES.

        88  DECLARATIVES-NOT-FOUND             VALUE SPACES.
        88  DECLARATIVES-FOUND                 VALUE "FOUND".


  01  COPY-SWITCH                 PIC X(4)    USAGE DISPLAY
                                              VALUE "COPY".

      88  DO-COPY                              VALUE "COPY".
*READ & DO IMMEDIATE WRITE; INSERTION OF NEW SOURCE LINE
*NOT ON
      88  DO-READ                             VALUE "READ".
*READ ONLY; USED IMMEDIATELY AFTER AUTO COPY TURNED OFF
      88  DO-WRITE                            VALUE "WRIT".
```

```
*AUTO COPY TURNED OFF; WRITE PREVIOUS SOURCE LINE BEFORE
*READ


    01  WRITE-SWITCH                  PIC X(3)    USAGE DISPLAY
                                                  VALUE "OLD".
        88  OLD-SOURCE-LINE                       VALUE "OLD".
            NEW-SOURCE-LINE                       VALUE "NEW".


    01  BREAKPOINT                    PIC X(80)   USAGE DISPLAY.
        88  DUMP                                  VALUE "D".


    01  TALLY-COUNTER                 PIC S9V     USAGE COMP
                                                  VALUE ZERO.
        88  DEBUG                                 VALUE 1.
        88  DEFENSIVE-TRAP-FOUND                  VALUE 1.
        88  END-DELIMITER                         VALUE 1.
        88  FULLSTOP                              VALUE 1.
        88  STATUS-FOUND                          VALUE 1.


    01  END-SCOPE-DELIMITER.
        02  FILLER                    PIC X(4)    USAGE DISPLAY
                                                  VALUE "END-".
        02  END-VERB                  PIC X(26)   USAGE DISPLAY
                                                  VALUE SPACES.


   01   NUMBER-OF-NUMERIC-ITEMS        PIC S999V VALUE 999.
*OCCURS DEPENDING ON DATA-NAME FOR NUMERIC-ITEM-TABLE; IF
*TOO SMALL THEN CHANGE IT TO REQUIRED NUMBER


   01   NUMERIC-ITEM-TABLE.
        02  NUMERIC-ITEM              PIC X(30)
                                      OCCURS 1 TO 999 TIMES
*SECOND INTEGER MUST BE THE SAME VALUE AS NUMBER-OF-NUMERIC-
*ITEMS

                                      DEPENDING ON
                                      NUMBER-OF-NUMERIC-ITEMS
                                      INDEXED BY
                                      NUMERIC-ITEM-INDEX.


  01   UNSTRING-ITEMS.
        02  UNSTRING-POINTER          PIC S99V    USAGE COMP
                                                  VALUE ZERO.
        02  B-WORDS.
            03  WORD-1                PIC X(30)   USAGE DISPLAY.
                88  ARITHMETIC-VERB               VALUE "ADD"
                                                       "COMPUTE"
```

```
                                                "DIVIDE"
                                                "MULTIPLY"
                                                "SUBTRACT".
          88 CALL-VERB                VALUE "CALL".
          88 DIVIDE-VERB              VALUE "DIVIDE".
          88 END-PERFORM-VERB         VALUE "END-PERFORM."
          88 EVALUATE-VERB            VALUE "EVALUATE".
          88 EXIT-VERB                VALUE "EXIT".
          88 GO-VERB                  VALUE "GO".
          88 GOBACK-VERB              VALUE "GOBACK".
*IBM
          88 IF-VERB                  VALUE "IF".
          88 IO-VERB                  VALUE "CLOSE"
                                                "DELETE"
                                                "OPEN"
                                                "READ"
                                                "REWRITE"
                                                "SEEK"

*IBM                                            "WRITE".
*PLACE ANY NON-ANSI I-O VERBS OF YOUR COMPILER IN THIS LIST
          88 MOVE-VERB                VALUE "MOVE".
          88 PERFORM-VERB             VALUE "PERFORM".
          88 SEARCH-VERB              VALUE "SEARCH".
          88 STOP-VERB                VALUE "STOP".
          88 STRING-UNSTRING-VERB     VALUE "STRING"
                                                "UNSTRING".
          88 TARGET-VERB              VALUE "ADD"
                                                "CALL"
                                                "COMPUTE"
                                                "DIVIDE"
                                                "EVALUATE"
                                                "GO"
                                                "MULTIPLY"
                                                "SEARCH"
                                                "STRING"
                                                "SUBTRACT"
                                                "UNSTRING".
          88 VERB                     VALUE "ACCEPT"
                                                "ADD"
                                                "ALTER"
*OBSOLETE
                                                "CALL"
                                                "CANCEL"
                                                "CLOSE"
                                                "COMPUTE"
```

"CONTINUE"

*COBOL-85

"COPY"

*TREATED LIKE A VERB

"DELETE"
"DISABLE"
"DISPLAY"
"DIVIDE"
"ELSE"

*TREATED LIKE A VERB

"ENABLE"
"ENTER"

*OBSOLETE

"EVALUATE"

*COBOL-85

"EXAMINE"

*COBOL-68

"EXIT"
"GENERATE"
"GO"
"GOBACK"

*IBM

"IF"

"INITIALIZE"

*COBOL-85

"INITIATE"
"INSPECT"
"MERGE"
"MOVE"
"MULTIPLY"
"OPEN"
"PERFORM"
"PURGE"
"READ"
"RECEIVE"
"RELEASE"
"REPLACE"

*COBOL-85; TREATED LIKE A VERB

"RETURN"
"REWRITE"
"SEARCH"
"SEEK"

*IBM

"SEND"
"SET"

```
                                               "SORT"
                                               "START"
                                               "STOP"
                                               "STRING"
                                               "SUBTRACT"
                                               "SUPPRESS"
                                               "TERMINATE"
                                               "TRANSFORM"

*IBM
                                               "UNSTRING"
                                               "USE"
                                               "WRITE".
        03  WORD-2                PIC X(30)  USAGE DISPLAY.
*MUST CONTAIN PROGRAM-NAME FOR PROGRAM-ID PARAGRAPH
*ITEM DATA-NAME IF DATA DIVISION  BEING UNSTRING
*DIVISOR IF DIVIDE INTO BEING UNSTRING
*FROM ITEM DATA-NAME IF MOVE VERB BEING UNSTRING
            88  CORR-PHASE                  VALUE
                                            "CORRESPONDING"
                                                    "CORR".

            88  PROGRAM-WORD                VALUE "PROGRAM".
            88  RUN-WORD                    VALUE "RUN".
        03  WORD-3                PIC X(30)  USAGE DISPLAY.
            88  BY-WORD                     VALUE "BY".
            88  INTO-WORD                   VALUE "INTO".
            88  PICTURE-CLAUSE              VALUE "PICTURE"
                                                    "PIC".
            88  TO-WORD                     VALUE "TO".
        03  WORD-4                PIC X(30)  USAGE DISPLAY.
*DIVISOR IF DIVIDE BY VERB       BEING UNSTRING
*TO ITEM DATA-NAME IF MOVE VERB BEING UNSTRING
        03  WORD-4-BYTES REDEFINES WORD-4
            04  FILLER            PIC X      USAGE DISPLAY.
                88  SIGN-BYTE               VALUE "S".
            04  FILLER            PIC X(29)  USAGE DISPLAY.
        03  WORD-5                PIC X(30)  USAGE DISPLAY.
*MUST CONTAIN ALPHA IF ANALYZING GO TO DEPENDING ON STATEMENT
            88  NOT-PROCEDURE-NAME          VALUE SPACES.
        03  WORD-6                PIC X(30)  USAGE DISPLAY.
        03  WORD-7                PIC X(30)  USAGE DISPLAY.
        03  WORD-8                PIC X(30)  USAGE DISPLAY.
    02  WORD-DELIMITERS.
        03  WORD-DELIMITER-1      PIC X      USAGE DISPLAY.
        03  WORD-DELIMITER-2      PIC X      USAGE DISPLAY.
        03  WORD-DELIMITER-3      PIC X      USAGE DISPLAY.
        03  WORD-DELIMITER-4      PIC X      USAGE DISPLAY.
```

```
            03 WORD-DELIMITER-5    PIC X      USAGE DISPLAY.
            03 WORD-DELIMITER-6    PIC X      USAGE DISPLAY.
            03 WORD-DELIMITER-7    PIC X      USAGE DISPLAY.
            03 WORD-DELIMITER-8    PIC X      USAGE DISPLAY.
     *8 WORDS ARE USED TO ENSURE FULL STOP (.) IS FOUND


      01         PABORT-PARAGRAPH-NAME.
         02      FILLER            PIC X(7)   USAGE DISPLAY
                                              VALUE "PABORT-".
         02      ODOMETER-DISPLAY  PIC 9(4)   USAGE DISPLAY.
         02      ODOMETER REDEFINES ODOMETER-DISPLAY
                                   PIC S9(4)V USAGE COMP
                                              VALUE ZERO.


      01-NEGATIVE-OR-ZERO-TRAP.
         02 FILLER                 PIC X(8)   USAGE DISPLAY
                                              VALUE "D    IF ".
     *ACTIVE DEFENSIVE TRAP; D DISABLES UNTIL ANSI DEBUG TURNED ON
         02 TRAP-DATA-NAME         PIC X(30)  USAGE DISPLAY
                                              VALUE SPACES.
         02 FILLER                 PIC X      USAGE DISPLAY
                                              VALUE SPACE.
         02 TRAP-TYPE              PIC X(8)   USAGE DISPLAY
                                              VALUE SPACES.


         EJECT
```

```
      PROCEDURE DIVISION.

      DECLARATIVES.

      DEBUG SECTION.

         USE FOR DEBUGGING ON ALL PROCEDURES.

      DEBUG-PROGRAM-FLOW.

         DISPLAY       DEBUG-LINE
                       DEBUG-NAME
                       DEBUG-CONTENTS.

      DEBUG-BREAKPOINT.

     *   ACCEPT          breakpoint   FROM mnemonic-name.
     * * USED TO DISABLE ACCEPT EVEN IF DEBUG MODULE IS ACTIVE
```

```
*  *  IS DELETED WHEN INTERACTIVE BREAKPOINTS ARE REQUIRED

   END DECLARATIVES.

   P101-INITIATION.

        OPEN INPUT    COBOLIN

        OPEN OUTPUT   COBOLOUT

        DISPLAY       "SUBFILES PROGRAM START."

        GO TO         P102-IDENTIFICATION-DIVISION.

    P102-IDENTIFICATION-DIVISION.

        PERFORM       PC01-READ-COBOLIN
        THRU          PC01-X.

   *FIND IDENTIFICATION DIVISION
        IF        IDENTIFICATION-DIVISION
           NEXT SENTENCE
        ELSE          GO TO P102-IDENTIFICATION-DIVISION.

        MOVE          "FOUND"
        TO            ID-SWITCH

   *PROGRAM-ID MUST BE NEXT STATEMENT LINE
        PERFORM       PC01-READ-COBOLIN
        THRU          PC01-X.

   *FIND WORDS IN AREA B
        PERFORM       PCO3-FIND-WORDS
        THRU          PC03-X.

   *WORD-2 MUST BE PROGRAM NAME
        DISPLAY       "TARGET PROGRAM IS "
                      WORD-2

        GO TO         P103-ENVIRONMENT-DIVISION.

    P103-ENVIRONMENT-DIVISION.
    *FIND ENVIRONMENT DIVISION

        PERFORM       PC01-READ-COBLPROG
        THRU          PC01-X.
```

```
      IF              ENVIRONMENT-DIVISION
                      MOVE    "FOUND"
                      TO      ENVIRONMENT-SWITCH
                      GO TO  P104-FIND-SELECT
      ELSE            GO TO  P103-ENVIRONMENT-DIVISION.


  P104-FIND-SELECT.
 *FIND SELECT CLAUSE IN FILE-CONTROL-ENTRY

      PERFORM         PC01-READ-COBLPROG
      THRU            PC01-X.

      IF              DATA-DIVISION
                      MOVE    "FOUND"
                      TO      DATA-SWITCH
                      GO TO  P106-FIND-WS
      ELSE    NEXT SENTENCE.

      IF              SELECT-CLAUSE
                      MOVE    "FOUND"
                      TO      SELECT-SWITCH
                      MOVE    "READ"
                      TO      COPY-SWITCH
 *TURN AUTO COPY OFF
                      GO TO  P105-FIND-SELECT-END
      ELSE            GO TO  P104-FIND-SELECT.


  P105-FIND-SELECT-END.
 *FIND SELECT CLAUSE END WHICH MUST BE A FULLSTOP
 *TERMINATOR (.)

      PERFORM         PC01-READ-COBLPROG
      THRU            PC01-X.

      MOVE            ZERO
      TO              TALLY-COUNTER

      INSPECT         AREA-B
      TALLYING        TALLY-COUNTER
      FOR ALL         "."

      IF              FULLSTOP
          NEXT SENTENCE
      ELSE            GO TO  P106-FIND-SELECT-END.


 *FILE STATUS MUST BE LAST SELECT LINE IF PRESENT
```

```
    MOVE            ZERO
    TO              TALLY-COUNTER
    INSPECT         AREA-B
    TALLYING        TALLY-COUNTER
    FOR ALL         "STATUS "

    IF              STATUS-CLAUSE
                    PERFORM PC10-INSERT-FILE-STATUS
                    THRU    PC10-X
                    GO TO   P104-FIND-SELECT
    ELSE   NEXT SENTENCE.

*SELECT CLAUSE DOES NOT CONTAIN FILE STATUS; WRITE OUT
*CURRENT SOURCE LINE WITHOUT FULLSTOP
    INSPECT         AREA-B
    REPLACING FIRST  "."
    BY              SPACE

    PERFORM         PC02-WRITE-COBLPROG
    THRU            PC02-X.

    PERFORM         PC10-INSERT-FILE-STATUS
    THRU            PC10-X.

    GO TO           PC104-FIND-SELECT.

  P106-FIND-WS.
*FIND WORKING STORAGE TO INSERT FILE STATUS ELEMENTARY ITEM

    PERFORM         PC01-READ-COBLPROG
    THRU            PC01-X.

    IF              WS-SECTION
       NEXT SENTENCE
    ELSE            GO TO  P106-FIND-WS.

    MOVE            "NEW"
    TO              WRITE-SWITCH

    MOVE            "COPY COBOL-FILE-STATUS"
    TO              NEW-AREA-B

    PERFORM         PC02-WRITE-COBLPROG
    THRU            PC02-X.

    MOVE            "*INSTALLATION STANDARD FILE STATUS ITEM"
```

```
           TO              NEW-INDICATOR-A-B

           PERFORM         PC02-WRITE-COBLPROG
           THRU            PC02-X.

           MOVE            SPACES
           TO              NEW-SOURCE-LINE

           PERFORM         PC02-WRITE-COBLPROG
           THRU            PC02-X.

           MOVE            "OLD"
           TO              WRITE-SWITCH

           MOVE            "COPY"
           TO              COPY-SWITCH
      *TURN AUTO COPY ON
           GO TO           P107-PROCEDURE-DIVISION.

       P107-PROCEDURE-DIVISION.

           PERFORM         PC01-READ-COBLPROG
           THRU            PC01-X.

           IF              PROCEDURE-DIVISION
                           MOVE    "FOUND"
                           TO      PROCEDURE-SWITCH
                           GO TO  P108-FIND-IO-VERB
           ELSE            GO TO  P107-PROCEDURE-DIVISION.

       P108-FIND-IO-VERB.

           PERFORM         PC01-READ-COBLPROG
           THRU            PC01-X.

           PERFORM         PC03-FIND-WORDS
           THRU            PC03-X.

           IF              IO-VERB
                           MOVE    "READ"
                           TO      COPY-SWITCH
      *TURN AUTO COPY OFF
                           GO TO  P109-FIND-PROC-FILE-STATUS
           ELSE            GO TO  P108-FIND-IO-VERB.

       P109-FIND-PROC-FILE-STATUS.
      *ASSUMES THAT FILE STATUS IF VERB IS NEXT STATEMENT IF
      *PRESENT; REPLACES IF WITH INSTALLATION FILE STATUS COPY
```

```
*IF IF VERB PRESENT; INSERTS INSTALLATION FILE STATUS COPY
*IF IF VERB NOT PRESENT

    PERFORM         PC10-READ-COBLPROG
    THRU            PC10-X.

    PERFORM         PC03-FIND-WORDS
    THRU            PC03-X.

    IF              VERB
       NEXT SENTENCE
    ELSE            GO TO  P109-FIND-PROC-FILE-STATUS.

    IF              IF-VERB
                    PERFORM   PC11-INSERT-COPY-FILE-STATUS
                    THRU    PC11-X
                    GO TO  P108-FIND-IO-VERB
    ELSE    NEXT SENTENCE.

*NEXT VERB IS NOT IF; PROGRAM DID NOT TEST FOR FILE STATUS
*INSERT BEFORE THIS VERB

    PERFORM         PC11-INSERT-COPY-FILE-STATUS
    THRU            PC11-X.

    PERFORM         PC02-WRITE-COBLPROG
    THRU            PC02-X.

    GO TO           P108-FIND-IO-VERB.

  PEOJ.

    CLOSE           COBOLIN
                    COBOLOUT.

    IF              ID-NOT-FOUND
                    DISPLAY "NO IDENTIFICATION DIVISION"
    ELSE
    IF              ENVIRONMENT-NOT-FOUND
                    DISPLAY "NO ENVIRONMENT DIVISION"
    ELSE NEXT SENTENCE.

    DISPLAY         "SUBFILES PROGRAM EOJ."

    STOP RUN.

    EJECT
```

```
    PC01-READ-COBOLIN.


    IF              DO-WRITE
*AUTO COPY OFF; WRITE OUT LAST READ SOURCE LINE BEFORE READ
                    PERFORM PC02-WRITE-COBOLOUT
                    THRU    PC02-X
    ELSE NEXT SENTENCE.


    READ            COBOLIN
    INTO            COBOL-LINE-WS
    AT END          GO TO PEOJ.
    IF              FILE-STATUS-OK
        NEXT SENTENCE
    ELSE            DISPLAY "RUN ABORTED - BAD FILE STATUS OF "
                        COBLPROG-FILE-STATUS
*ASSUMES OUTPUT TO PROGRAMMER'S TERMINAL
                    GO TO PEOJ.


    IF              DO-COPY
*AUTO COPY ON; DO IMMEDIATE WRITE; CANNOT INSERT NEW SOURCE
*LINE BEFORE SOURCE LINE JUST READ
                    PERFORM   PC02-WRITE-COBOLOUT
                    THRU    PC02-X
    IF              DO-READ
*AUTO COPY JUST TURNED OFF; MOVE WRITE TO SWITCH TO ENABLE
*WRITE BEFORE READ
                    MOVE    "WRIT"
                    TO      COPY-SWITCH
    ELSE NEXT SENTENCE.


*BYPASS NON STATEMENT LINE OR BLANK SOURCE LINE
    IF              NON-STATEMENT-LINE
    OR              BLANK-SOURCE-LINE
                    GO TO PCO1-READ-COBOLIN
    ELSE            GO TO PC01-X.


  PC01-X. EXIT.

  PABORT-PC01.
*RUNAWAY CODE ABEND

    DISPLAY         "RUN ABORTED - RUNAWAY CODE AT PC01"

    GO TO           PEOJ.

    EJECT
```

```
PC02-WRITE-COBOLOUT.

*WRITE-SWITCH USED TO DETERMINE FROM IDENTIFIER
     IF            OLD-SOURCE-LINE
                   WRITE   COBOL-LINE-OUT
                   FROM    COBOL-LINE-WS
     ELSE          WRITE   COBOL-LINE-OUT
                   FROM    NEW-SOURCE-LINE.
*NEW-SOURCE-LINE

     IF            FILE-STATUS-OK
                   GO TO  PC02-X
     ELSE          DISPLAY "RUN ABORTED - BAD FILE STATUS OF "
                            COBLPROG-FILE-STATUS
*ASSUMES OUTPUT TO PROGRAMMER'S TERMINAL
                   GO TO PEOJ.


   PC02-X. EXIT.

   PABORT-PC02.
*RUNAWAY CODE ABEND

     DISPLAY       "RUN ABORTED - RUNAWAY CODE AT PC02"

     GO TO         PEOJ.

     EJECT
```

```
   PC03-FIND-WORDS.

     MOVE          SPACES
     TO            B-WORDS
                   WORD-DELIMITERS

     SET           AREA-B-INDEX
                   UNSTRING-POINTER
     TO            1

     SEARCH        AREA-B-BYTES
     VARYING       UNSTRING-POINTER
*AREA-B-BYTES INDEXED BY AREA-B-INDEX; UNSTRING POINTER IS
*KEPT IN SYNC AND WILL POINT TO THE FIRST ALPHA CHARACTER
*IN AREA B
     AT END        DISPLAY "RUN ABORTED - NO ALPHA CHARACTER
  -               "FOUND AT SEQUENCE NUMBER "
                   SEQUENCE-NUMBER
```

```
                        GO TO PEOJ
 *CAN'T HAPPEN; IT MUST FIND AN ALPHA CHARACTER
       WHEN         ALPHA
          NEXT SENTENCE.
 *FIRST ALPHA CHARACTER OF FIRST WORD FOUND

       UNSTRING     AREA-B
       DELIMITED ALLSPACES OR "." OR "," OR ";"
 *.,; USED TO STRIP FROM WORD; FULL STOP NEEDED FOR SENTENCE
 *END
       INTO         WORD-1
       DELIMITER IN WORD-1-DELIMITER
       INTO         WORD-2
       DELIMITER IN WORD-2-DELIMITER
       INTO         WORD-3
       DELIMITER IN WORD-3-DELIMITER
       INTO         WORD-4
       DELIMITER IN WORD-4-DELIMITER
       INTO         WORD-5
       DELIMITER IN WORD-5-DELIMITER
       INTO         WORD-6
       DELIMITER IN WORD-6-DELIMITER
       INTO         WORD-7
       DELIMITER IN WORD-7-DELIMITER
       INTO         WORD-8
       DELIMITER IN WORD-8-DELIMITER
       WITH POINTER UNSTRING-POINTER
       ON OVERFLOW  DISPLAY "RUN ABORTED - TOO MANY WORDS IN
 -                  "SOURCE LINE AT SEQUENCE NUMBER "
                    SEQUENCE NUMBER
                    GO TO PEOJ.
 *OVERFLOW MEANS MORE THEN 8 WORDS IN AREA B - NOT ALLOWED
 *INCREASE RECEIVING WORDS IF REQUIRED

       GO TO              PC03-X.

  PCO3-X. EXIT.

  PABORT-PC03.
 *RUNAWAY CODE ABEND

       DISPLAY            "RUN ABORTED - RUNAWAY CODE AT PC03"

       GO TO              PEOJ.

       EJECT
```

```
 PC10-INSERT-FILE-STATUS.
*DEFAULT FILE STATUS DATA-NAME IS COBOL-FILE-STATUS


     MOVE               "NEW"
     TO                 "WRITE-SWITCH


     MOVE               "FILE STATUS IS COBOL-FILE-STATUS."
     TO                 NEW-AREA-B


     PERFORM            PC02-WRITE-COBLPROG
     THRU               PC02-X.


     MOVE               "*INSTALLATION FILE STATUS"
     TO                 NEW-INDICATOR-A-B


     PERFORM            PC02-WRITE-COBLPROG
     THRU               PC02-X.


     MOVE               SPACES
     TO                 NEW-SOURCE-LINE


     PERFORM            PC02-WRITE-COBLPROG
     THRU               PC02-X.


     MOVE               "OLD"
     TO                 "WRITE-SWITCH


     MOVE               "COPY"
     TO                 COPY-SWITCH
*TURN AUTO COPY ON

     GO TO              PC10-X.


 PC10-X.    EXIT.


 PABORT-PC10.
*RUNAWAY CODE ABEND


     DISPLAY            "RUN ABORTED - RUNAWAY CODE AT PC10"


     GO TO              PEOJ.


     EJECT
```

```
 PC11-INSERT-COPY-FILE-STATUS.
*INSERTS COPY FOR INSTALLATION FILE-STATUS ROUTINE
```

```
        MOVE              "NEW"
        TO                "WRITE-SWITCH

        MOVE               "COPY COBOL-FILE-STATUS-VETTER"
        TO                NEW-AREA-B

        PERFORM           PC02-WRITE-COBLPROG
        THRU              PC02-X.

        MOVE              "*INSTALLATION FILE STATUS VETTING S/R"
        TO                NEW-INDICATOR-A-B

        PERFORM           PC02-WRITE-COBLPROG
        THRU              PC02-X.

        MOVE              SPACES
        TO                NEW-SOURCE-LINE

        PERFORM           PC02-WRITE-COBLPROG
        THRU              PC02-X.

        MOVE              "OLD"
        TO                "WRITE-SWITCH

        MOVE              "COPY"
        TO                COPY-SWITCH
*TURN AUTO COPY ON

        GO TO             PC11-X.

  PC11-X.    EXIT.

  PABORT-PC11.
*RUNAWAY CODE ABEND

        DISPLAY           "RUN ABORTED - RUNAWAY CODE AT PC11"

        GO TO             PEOJ.

        EJECT
```

Appendix B
Glossary

This glossary is a combination of the ANSI-1974 and ANSI-1985 manuals. A $_{74}$ subscript means that definition is only in 1974 manual; $_{85}$ only in the 1985 manual.

INTRODUCTION

The terms are defined in accordance with their meaning in COBOL and may not have the same meaning for other languages.

These definitions are intended as reference. These definitions are brief and do not include detailed syntactical rules.

DEFINITIONS

Abbreviated Combined Relation Condition
The combined condition that results from the explicit omission of a common subject or a common subject and common relational operator in a consecutive sequence of relation conditions.

ACCESS MODE
The manner in which RECORDS are to be operated upon within a FILE.

Actual Decimal Point
The physical representation, using the decimal point CHARACTERS period (.) or COMMA (,), of the decimal point POSITION in a data item.

Alphabet-Name
A user-defined word, in the SPECIAL-NAMES paragraph of the ENVIRONMENT DIVISION, that assigns a name to a specific CHARACTER set and/or COLLATING SEQUENCE.

ALPHABETIC CHARACTER
A letter or a SPACE CHARACTER.

ALPHANUMERIC CHARACTER
Any CHARACTER in the computer's CHARACTER set.

ALTERNATE RECORD KEY
A KEY, other than the prime RECORD KEY, whose contents identify a RECORD within an INDEXED FILE.

Arithmetic Expression
An identifier of a NUMERIC elementary item, a NUMERIC literal, such identifiers and literals separated by arithmetic operators, two arithmetic expressions separated by an arithmetic operator, or an arithmetic expression enclosed in parentheses.

Arithmetic Operation$_{85}$
The process caused by the execution of an arithmetic statement, or the evaluation of an arithmetic expression, that results in a mathematically correct solution to the arguments presented.

Arithmetic Operator
A single CHARACTER or fixed two-character combination which belongs to the following set:

CHARACTER	*Meaning*
+	addition
-	subtraction
*	multiplication
/	division
**	exponentiation

Arithmetic Statement$_{85}$
A statement that causes an arithmetic operation to be executed. The arithmetic statements are the ADD, COMPUTE, DIVIDE, MULTIPLY, and SUBTRACT statements.

ASCENDING KEY
A KEY upon the VALUES of which data is ordered starting with the lowest VALUE of KEY up to the highest VALUE of KEY in accordance with the rules for comparing data items.

Assumed Decimal Point
A decimal point position which does not involve the existence of an actual CHARACTER in a data item. The assumed decimal point has logical meaning but no physical representation.

AT END Condition
A condition caused:

1. During the execution of a READ statement for a sequentially accessed FILE, when NO NEXT logical RECORD exists in the FILE, or when the NUMBER of significant digits in the RELATIVE RECORD NUMBER is larger than the SIZE of the RELATIVE KEY data item, or when an OPTIONAL INPUT FILE is NOT present.
2. During the execution of a RETURN statement, when NO NEXT logical RECORD exists for the associated SORT or MERGE FILE.
3. During the execution of a SEARCH statement, when the SEARCH operation terminates without satisfying the condition specified in any of the associated WHEN phrases.

BLOCK

A physical unit of data that is normally composed of one or more logical RECORDS. For mass storage FILEs, a BLOCK may contain a portion of a logical RECORD. The SIZE of a BLOCK has no direct relationship to the SIZE of the FILE within which the BLOCK is contained or to the SIZE of the logical record(s) that are either contained within the BLOCK or that overlap the BLOCK. The term is synonymous with physical RECORD.

Body GROUP

Generic name for a REPORT GROUP of TYPE DETAIL, CONTROL HEADING, or CONTROL FOOTING.

BOTTOM Margin$_{85}$

An empty area which follows the page body.

Called PROGRAM

A PROGRAM which is the object of a CALL statement combined at object time with the calling PROGRAM to produce a RUN UNIT.

Calling PROGRAM

A PROGRAM which executes a CALL to another PROGRAM.

Cd-Name

A user-defined word that names an MCS interface AREA described in a COMMUNICATION description entry within the COMMUNICATION SECTION of the DATA DIVISION.

CHARACTER

The basic indivisible unit of the language.

CHARACTER POSITION

A CHARACTER POSITION is the amount of physical storage required to store a single standard data format CHARACTER described as USAGE IS DISPLAY. Further characteristics of the physical storage are defined by the implementor.

Character-String

A sequence of contiguous CHARACTERS which form a COBOL word, a literal, a PICTURE character-string, or a comment-entry.

CLASS Condition

The proposition, for which a truth VALUE can be determined, that the content of an item is wholly ALPHABETIC, or is wholly NUMERIC, or consists exclusively of those CHARACTERS listed in the definition of a class-name.

Class-Name₈₅

A user-defined word defined in the SPECIAL-NAMES paragraph of the ENVIRON-MENT DIVISION that assigns a name to the proposition for which a truth value can be defined, that the content of a data item consists exclusively of those CHARACTERS listed in the definition of the class-name.

Clause

A clause is an ordered set of consecutive COBOL character-strings whose purpose is to specify an attribute of an entry.

COBOL CHARACTER Set

The complete COBOL CHARACTER set consists of the CHARACTERS listed below:

CHARACTER	Meaning
0,1,...,9	digit
A,B,...,Z	uppercase letter
a,b,...,z	lowercase letter
	SPACE
+	PLUS SIGN
-	minus SIGN (hyphen)
*	asterisk
/	slant (solidus)
=	EQUAL SIGN
$	CURRENCY SIGN (represented as @ in the International Reference Version of International Standard ISO 646-1973)
,	COMMA (decimal point)
;	semicolon
.	period (decimal point, full stop)
"	quotation mark
(	LEFT parenthesis
)	RIGHT parenthesis
>	GREATER THAN symbol
<	LESS THAN symbol
:	colon

Note 1: In the cases where an implementation does not provide all of the COBOL CHARACTER set to be graphically represented, substitute graphics may be specified by the implementor to replace the CHARACTERS not represented. The COBOL CHARACTER set graphics are a subset of American National Standard X3.4-1977, Code for Information Interchange. With the exception of "$", they are also a subset of the graphics defined for the International Reference Version of International Standard ISO 646-1973, 7-Bit Coded CHARACTER Set for Information Processing Interchange.

Note 2: When the computer CHARACTER set includes lowercase letters, they may be used in character-strings. Except when used in nonnumeric literals and some PICTURE symbols, each lowercase letter is equivalent to the corresponding uppercase letter.

COBOL Word

A character-string of not more than 30 CHARACTERS which forms a user-defined word, a system-name, or a reserved word.

COLLATING SEQUENCE

The SEQUENCE in which the CHARACTERS that are acceptable to a computer are ordered for purposes of sorting, merging, comparing, and for processing INDEXED FILEs sequentially.

COLUMN

A CHARACTER POSITION within a print LINE. The COLUMNs are numbered from 1, by 1, starting at the leftmost CHARACTER POSITION of the print LINE and extending to the rightmost POSITION of the print LINE.

Combined Condition

A condition that is the result of connecting two or more conditions with the "AND" or the "OR" logical operator.

Comment-Entry

An entry in the IDENTIFICATION DIVISION that may be any combination of CHARACTERS from the computer's CHARACTER set.

Comment Line

A SOURCE PROGRAM LINE represented by an asterisk (*) in the indicator area of the LINE and any CHARACTERS from the computer's CHARACTER set in area A and area B of that line. The comment LINE serves only for documentation in a PROGRAM. A special form of comment line represented by a slant (/) in the indicator area of the LINE and any CHARACTERS from the computer's CHARACTER set in area A and area B of that line causes PAGE ejection prior to printing the comment.

COMMON PROGRAM₈₅

A PROGRAM which, despite being directly contained within another PROGRAM, may be called from any PROGRAM directly or indirectly contained in that other PROGRAM.

COMMUNICATION Description Entry

An entry in the COMMUNICATION SECTION of the DATA DIVISION that is composed of the level indicator CD, followed by a cd-name, and then followed by a set of clauses as required. It describes the interface between the message CONTROL system (MCS) and the COBOL PROGRAM.

COMMUNICATION Device

A mechanism (hardware or hardware/software) capable of sending data to a QUEUE and/or receiving data from a QUEUE. This mechanism may be a computer or a peripheral device. One or more PROGRAMs containing COMMUNICATION desription entries and residing within the same computer define one or more of these mechanisms.

COMMUNICATION SECTION

The SECTION of the DATA DIVISION that describes the interface areas between the message CONTROL system (MCS) and the PROGRAM, composed of one or more COMMUNICATION description AREAS.

Compile Time

The time at which a COBOL SOURCE PROGRAM is translated, by a COBOL compiler, to a COBOL object PROGRAM.

Compiler Directing Statement

A statement, beginning with a compiler directing verb, that causes the compiler to take a specific action during compilation. The compiler directing statements are the COPY, ENTER, REPLACE, and USE statements.

Complex Condition

A condition in which one or more logical operators act upon one or more conditions. (See Negated Simple Condition, Combined Condition, Negated Combined Condition).

Computer-Name

A system-name that identifies the computer upon which the PROGRAM is to be compiled or run.

Condition

A STATUS of a PROGRAM at execution time for which a truth VALUE can be determined. Where the term "condition" (condition-1, condition-2, ...) appears in these language specifications in or in reference to "condition" (condition-1, condition-2, ...) of a general format, it is a conditional expression consisting of either a simple condition optionally parenthesized, or a combined condition consisting of the syntactically correct combination of simple conditions, logical operators, and parentheses, for which a truth VALUE can be determined.

Condition-Name

A user-defined word that assigns a name to a subset of VALUES that a conditional variable may assume; or a user-defined word assigned to a STATUS of an implementor-defined switch or device. When "condition-name" is used in the general formats, it represents a unique data item reference consisting of a syntactically correct combination of a condition-name, together with qualifiers and subscripts, as required for uniqueness of reference.

Condition-Name Condition

The proposition, for which a truth VALUE can be determined, that the VALUE of a conditional variable is a member of the set of VALUES attributed to a condition-name associated with the conditional variable.

Conditional Expression

A simple condition or a complex condition specified in an EVALUATE, IF, PERFORM, or SEARCH statement. (See Simple Condition and Complex Condition).

Conditional Phrase$_{85}$

A conditional phrase specifies the action to be taken upon determination of the truth VALUE of a condition resulting from the execution of a conditional statement.

Conditional Statement

A conditional statement specifies that the truth VALUE of a condition is to be determined and that the subsequent action of the object program is dependent on this truth VALUE.

Conditional Variable

A data item, one or more VALUES of which has a condition-name assigned to it.

CONFIGURATION SECTION

A SECTION of the ENVIRONMENT DIVISION that describes overall specifications of SOURCE and object PROGRAMs.

Connective$_{74}$

A reserved word that is used to:

1. associate a data-name, paragraph-name, condition-name, or text-name with its qualifier;
2. link two or more operands written in a series;
3. form conditions (logical connectives). (See Logical Operator).

Contiguous Items

Items that are described by consecutive entries in the DATA DIVISION, and that bear a definite hierarchical relationship to each other.

CONTROL Break

A change in the VALUE of a data item that is referenced in the CONTROL clause. More generally, a change in the VALUE of a data item that is used to CONTROL the hierarchical structure of a REPORT.

CONTROL Break Level

The relative position within a CONTROL hierarchy at which the most major CONTROL break occurred.

CONTROL Data Item

A data item, a change in whose contents may produce a CONTROL break.

CONTROL Data-Name

A data-name that appears in a CONTROL clause and refers to a CONTROL data item.

CONTROL FOOTING

A REPORT GROUP that is presented at the end of the CONTROL GROUP of which it is a member.

CONTROL GROUP

A set of body GROUPs that is presented for a given VALUE of a CONTROL data item or of FINAL. Each CONTROL GROUP may begin with a CONTROL HEADING, END with a CONTROL FOOTING, and contain DETAIL REPORT GROUPs.

CONTROL HEADING

A REPORT GROUP that is presented at the beginning of the CONTROL GROUP of which it is a member.

CONTROL Hierarchy

A designated SEQUENCE of REPORT subdivisions defined by the positional order of FINAL and the data-names within a CONTROL clause.

Counter

A data item used for storing NUMBERs or NUMBER representations in a manner that permits these NUMBERs to be increased or decreased by the VALUE of another NUMBER, or to be changed or reset to ZERO or to an arbitrary POSITIVE or NEGATIVE VALUE.

CURRENCY SIGN

The CHARACTER "$" of the COBOL CHARACTER set.

CURRENCY Symbol

The CHARACTER defined by the CURRENCY SIGN clause in the SPECIAL-NAMES paragraph. If NO CURRENCY SIGN clause is present in a COBOL SOURCE PROGRAM, the CURRENCY symbol is identical to the CURRENCY SIGN.

Current RECORD

In FILE processing, the RECORD which is available in the RECORD AREA associated with the FILE.

Current RECORD POINTER$_{74}$

A conceptual entity that is used in the selection of the NEXT RECORD.

Current Volume POINTER$_{85}$

A conceptual entity that points to the current volume of a SEQUENTIAL FILE.

Data Clause

A clause, appearing in a data description entry in the DATA DIVISION of a COBOL PROGRAM, that provides information describing a particular attribute of a data item.

Data Description Entry

An entry, in the DATA DIVISION of a COBOL PROGRAM, that is composed of a level-number followed by a data-name, if required, and then followed by a set of data clauses, as required.

Data Item

A unit of data (excluding literals) defined by the COBOL PROGRAM.

Data-Name

A user-defined word that names a data item described in a data description entry. When used in the general formats, "data-name" represents a word which must not be reference-modified, subscripted, or qualified unless specifically permitted by the rules of the format.

DEBUGGING LINE

A DEBUGGING LINE is any LINE with "D" in the indicator area of the LINE.

DEBUGGING SECTION

A DEBUGGING SECTION is a SECTION that contains a USE FOR DEBUGGING statement.

Declarative-Sentence

A compiler directing sentence consisting of a single USE statement terminated by the separator period.

DECLARATIVES

A set of one or more special purpose SECTIONs, written at the beginning of the PROCEDURE DIVISION, the first of which is preceded by the key word DECLARATIVES and the last of which is followed by the key WORDS END DECLARATIVES. A declarative is composed of a SECTION header, followed by a USE compiler directing sentence, followed by a set of zero, one, or more associated paragraphs.

De-Edit$_{85}$
> The logical removal of all editing CHARACTERS from a NUMERIC edited data item in order to determine that item's unedited NUMERIC VALUE.

DELIMITED Scope Statement$_{85}$
> Any statement which includes its explicit scope terminator.

DELIMITER
> A CHARACTER or a SEQUENCE of contiguous CHARACTERS that identify the end of a string of CHARACTERS and separates that string of CHARACTERS from the following string of CHARACTERS. A DELIMITER is not part of the string of CHARACTERS that it delimits.

DESCENDING KEY
> A KEY upon the VALUES of which data is ordered starting with the highest VALUE of KEY down to the lowest VALUE of KEY, in accordance with the rules for comparing data items.

DESTINATION
> The symbolic identification of the receiver of a transmission from a QUEUE.

Digit POSITION
> A digit POSITION is the amount of physical storage required to store a single digit. This amount may vary depending on the USAGE specified in the data description entry that defines the data item. If the data description entry specifies that USAGE IS DISPLAY, then a digit POSITION is synonymous with a CHARACTER POSITION. Further characteristics of the physical storage are defined by the implementor.

DIVISION
> A collection of zero, one, or more SECTIONS or paragraphs, called the DIVISION body, that are formed and combined in accordance with a specific set of rules. Each DIVISION consists of the DIVISION header and the related DIVISION body. There are four DIVISIONS in a COBOL PROGRAM: IDENTIFICATION, ENVIRONMENT, DATA, and PROCEDURE.

DIVISION header
> A combination of WORDS, followed by a separator period, that indicates the beginning of a DIVISION. The DIVISION headers in a COBOL PROGRAM are:

```
IDENTIFICATION DIVISION.
ENVIRONMENT DIVISION.
DATA DIVISION.
PROCEDURE DIVISION(USING {data-name-1} ... ).
```

DYNAMIC ACCESS

An ACCESS MODE in which specific logical RECORDS can be obtained from or placed into a mass storage file in a nonsequential manner and obtained from a FILE in a SEQUENTIAL manner during the scope of the same OPEN statement.

Editing CHARACTER

A single CHARACTER or a fixed two-character combination belonging to the following set:

CHARACTER	Meaning
B	SPACE
0	ZERO
+	PLUS
-	minus
CR	credit
DB	debit
Z	ZERO SUPPRESS
*	check protect
$	CURRENCY SIGN
,	COMMA (decimal point)
.	period (decimal point)
/	slant (solidus)

Elementary Item

A data item that is described as not being further logically subdivided.

End of PROCEDURE DIVISION

The physical position in a COBOL SOURCE PROGRAM after which no further PROCEDUREs appear.

END PROGRAM header[85]

A combination of WORDS, followed by a separator period, that indicates the END of a COBOL SOURCE PROGRAM. The END PROGRAM header is:

```
END PROGRAM program-name.
```

Entry

Any descriptive set of consecutive clauses terminated by a period and written in the IDENTIFICATION DIVISION, ENVIRONMENT DIVISION, or DATA DIVISION of a COBOL PROGRAM.

ENVIRONMENT Clause

A clause that appears as part of an ENVIRONMENT DIVISION entry.

Execution Time

> The time at which an object PROGRAM is executed. The term is synonymous with object time.

Explicit Scope Terminator$_{85}$

> A reserved word which terminates the scope of a particular PROCEDURE DIVISION statement.

Expression$_{85}$

> An arithmetic or conditional expression.

EXTEND MODE

> The state of a FILE after execution of an OPEN statement, with the EXTEND phrase specified for that FILE, and before the execution of a CLOSE statement without the REEL or UNIT phrase for that FILE.

EXTERNAL Data$_{85}$

> The data described in a program as EXTERNAL data items and EXTERNAL FILE connectors.

EXTERNAL Data Item$_{85}$

> A data item which is described as part of an EXTERNAL RECORD in one or more PROGRAMs of a RUN UNIT and which itself may be referenced from any PROGRAM in which it is described.

EXTERNAL Data RECORD$_{85}$

> A logical RECORD which is described in one or more PROGRAMS of a RUN UNIT and whose constituent data items may be referenced from any PROGRAM in which they are described.

EXTERNAL FILE Connector$_{85}$

> A FILE connector which is accessible to one or more object PROGRAMs in the RUN UNIT.

EXTERNAL Switch$_{85}$

> A hardware or software device, defined and named by the implementor, which is used to indicate that one of two alternate states exists.

Figurative Constant

> A compiler generated VALUE referenced through the use of certain reserved WORDS.

FILE

> A collection of logical RECORDS.

FILE Attribute Conflict Condition$_{85}$
An unsuccessful attempt has been made to execute an INPUT-OUTPUT operation on a FILE, and the FILE attributes, as specified for that FILE in the PROGRAM, do not match the fixed attributes for that FILE.

FILE Clause
A clause that appears as part of any of the following DATA DIVISION entries: FILE description entry (FD entry) and SORT-MERGE FILE description entry (SD entry.)

FILE Connector$_{85}$
A storage AREA which contains information about a FILE and is used as the linkage between a file-name and a physical FILE and between a file-name and its associated RECORD AREA.

FILE-CONTROL
The name of an ENVIRONMENT DIVISION paragraph in which the data FILEs for a given SOURCE PROGRAM are declared.

FILE CONTROL Entry$_{85}$
A SELECT clause and all its subordinate clauses which declare the relevant physical attributes of a FILE.

FILE Description Entry
An entry in the FILE SECTION of the DATA DIVISION that is composed of the level indicator FD, followed by a file-name, and then followed by a set of FILE clauses as required.

File-Name
A user-defined word that names a FILE connector described in a FILE description entry or a SORT-MERGE FILE description entry within the FILE SECTION of the DATA DIVISION.

FILE ORGANIZATION
The permanent logical FILE structure established at the time that a FILE is created.

FILE POSITION Indicator$_{85}$
A conceptual entity that contains the VALUE of the current KEY within the KEY of reference for an INDEXED FILE, or the RECORD NUMBER of the current RECORD for a SEQUENTIAL FILE, or the RELATIVE RECORD NUMBER of the current RECORD for a RELATIVE FILE, or indicates that NO NEXT logical RECORD exists, or that the NUMBER of significant digits in the RELATIVE RECORD NUMBER is larger than the SIZE of the RELATIVE KEY data item, or that an OPTIONAL INPUT FILE is not present, or that the AT END condition already exists, or that NO valid NEXT RECORD has been established.

FILE SECTION

The SECTION of the DATA DIVISION that contains FILE description entries and SORT-MERGE FILE description entries together with their associated RECORD descriptions.

Fixed FILE Attributes$_{85}$

Information about a FILE which is established when a FILE is created and cannot subsequently be changed during the existence of the FILE. These attributes include the ORGANIZATION of the FILE (SEQUENTIAL, RELATIVE, or INDEXED), the prime RECORD KEY, the ALTERNATIVE RECORD KEYs, the CODE SET, the minimum and maximum RECORD SIZE, the RECORD TYPE (fixed or variable), the COLLATING SEQUENCE of the KEYs for INDEXED FILEs, the blocking factor, the PADDING CHARACTER, and the RECORD DELIMITER.

Fixed LENGTH RECORD$_{85}$

A RECORD associated with a FILE whose FILE description or SORT-MERGE description entry requires that all RECORDS contain the same NUMBER of CHARACTER POSITIONs.

FOOTING AREA$_{85}$

The POSITION of the PAGE body adjacent to the BOTTOM margin.

Format

A specific arrangement of a set of data.

GLOBAL Name$_{85}$

A name which is declared in only one PROGRAM but which may be referenced from that PROGRAM and from any PROGRAM contained within that PROGRAM Condition-names, data-names, file-names, record-names, report-names, and some special registers may be GLOBAL names.

GROUP Item

A data item that is composed of subordinate data items.

High ORDER End

The leftmost CHARACTER of a string of CHARACTERS.

I-O-CONTROL

The name of an ENVIRONMENT DIVISION paragraph in which object PROGRAM requirements for rerun points, sharing of SAME AREAS by several data FILEs, and multiple FILE storage on a single INPUT-OUTPUT device are specified.

I-O-CONTROL Entry$_{85}$

An entry in the I-O-CONTROL paragraph of the ENVIRONMENT DIVISION which contains clauses which provide information required for the transmission and handling of data on named FILEs during the execution of a PROGRAM.

I-O-Mode

The state of a FILE after execution of an OPEN statement, with the I-O phrase specified, for that FILE and before the execution of a CLOSE statement without the REEL or UNIT phrase for that FILE.

I-O-Status$_{85}$

A conceptual entity which contains the two-character VALUE indicating the resulting STATUS of an INPUT-OUTPUT operation. This VALUE is made available to the PROGRAM through the use of the FILE STATUS clause in the FILE CONTROL entry for the FILE.

Identifier

A syntactically correct combination of a data-name, with its qualifiers, subscripts, and reference modifiers, as required for uniqueness of reference, that names a data item. The rules for "identifier" associated with the general formats may, however, specifically prohibit qualification, subscripting, or reference modification.

Imperative Statement

A statement either begins with an imperative verb and specifies an unconditional action to be taken or is a conditional statement that is delimited by its explicit scope terminator (DELIMITED scope statement). An imperative statement may consist of a SEQUENCE of imperative statements.

Implementor-Name

A system-name that refers to a particular feature available on that implementor's computing system.

Implicit Scope Terminator$_{85}$

A separator period which terminates the scope of any preceding unterminated statement, or a phrase of a statement which by its occurrence indicates the end of the scope of any statement contained within the preceding phrase.

INDEX

A computer storage area or register, the contents of which represent the identification of a particular element in a TABLE.

INDEX Data Item

A data item in which the VALUES associated with an index-name can be stored in a form specified by the implementor.

Index-Name

A user-defined word that names an INDEX associated with a specific TABLE.

INDEXED Data-Name$_{74}$

An identifier that is composed of a data-name, followed by one or more index-names enclosed in parentheses.

INDEXED FILE

A FILE with INDEXED organization.

INDEXED ORGANIZATION

The permanent logical FILE structure in which each RECORD is identified by the VALUE of one or more KEYs within that RECORD.

INITIAL PROGRAM₈₅

A PROGRAM that is placed into an INITIAL state every time the PROGRAM is called in a RUN UNIT.

INITIAL State₈₅

The state of a PROGRAM when it is first called in a RUN UNIT.

INPUT FILE

A FILE that is opened in the INPUT MODE.

INPUT MODE

The state of a FILE after execution of an OPEN statement, with the INPUT phrase specified, for that FILE and before the execution of a CLOSE statement without the REEL or UNIT phrase for that FILE.

INPUT-OUTPUT FILE

A FILE that is opened in the I-O MODE.

INPUT-OUTPUT SECTION

The SECTION of the ENVIRONMENT DIVISION that names the FILEs and the external media required by an object PROGRAM and which provides information required for transmission and handling of data during execution of the object PROGRAM.

INPUT-OUTPUT Statement₈₅

A statement that causes FILEs to be processed by performing operations upon individual RECORDS or upon the FILE as a UNIT. The INPUT-OUTPUT statements are: ACCEPT (with the identifier phrase), CLOSE, DELETE, DISABLE, DISPLAY, ENABLE, OPEN, PURGE, READ, RECEIVE, REWRITE, SEND, SET (with the TO ON or TO OFF phrase), START, and WRITE.

INPUT PROCEDURE

A set of statements, to which CONTROL is given during the execution of a SORT statement, for the purpose of controlling the release of specified RECORDS to be sorted.

Integer

A NUMERIC literal or a NUMERIC data item that does not include any digit POSITION to the right of the assumed decimal point. Where the term "integer" appears in general formats, integer must not be a NUMERIC data item, and must not be signed, nor ZERO unless explicitly allowed by the rules of that format.

Internal Data$_{85}$

The data described in a PROGRAM excluding all EXTERNAL data items and EXTERNAL FILE connectors. Items described in the LINKAGE SECTION of a PROGRAM are treated as internal data.

Internal Data Item$_{85}$

A data item which is described in one PROGRAM in a RUN UNIT. An internal data item may have a GLOBAL name.

Internal FILE Connector$_{85}$

A FILE connector which is accessible to only one object PROGRAM in the RUN UNIT.

Intra-Record Data Structure$_{85}$

The entire collection of groups and elementary data items from a logical RECORD which is defined by a contiguous subset of the data description entries which describe that RECORD. These data description entries include all entries whose level number is greater than the level-number of the first data description entry describing the intra-record data structure.

INVALID KEY Condition

A condition, at object time, caused when a specific VALUE of the KEY associated with an INDEXED or RELATIVE FILE is determined to be INVALID.

KEY

A data item which identifies the location of a RECORD, or a set of data items which serve to identify the ordering of data.

KEY of Reference

The KEY, either prime or ALTERNATE, currently being used to ACCESS RECORDS within an INDEXED FILE.

KEY Word

A reserved word whose presence is required when the format in which the word appears is used in a SOURCE PROGRAM.

Language-Name

A system-name that specifies a particular programming language.

Letter$_{85}$

A CHARACTER belonging to one of the following two sets: (1) uppercase letters: A, B, C, D, E, F, G, H, I, J, K, L, M, N, O, P, Q, R, S, T, U, V, W, X, Y, Z; (2) lowercase letters: a, b, c, d, e, f, g, h, i, j, k, l, m, n, o, p, q, r, s, t, u, v, w, x, y, z.

Level Indicator

Two ALPHABETIC CHARACTERS that identify a specific TYPE of FILE or a POSITION in a hierarchy. The level indicators in the DATA DIVISION are: CD, FD, RD, and SD.

Level-Number

A user-defined word, expressed as a one or two digit NUMBER, which indicates the hierarchical position of a data item or the special properties of a data description entry. Level-numbers in the range 1 through 49 indicate the position of a data item in the hierarchical structure of a logical RECORD. Level-numbers in the range 1 through 9 may be written either as a single digit or as a ZERO followed by a significant digit. Level-numbers 66, 77, and 88 identify special properties of a data description entry.

Library-Name

A user-defined word that names a COBOL library that is to be used by the compiler for a given SOURCE PROGRAM compilation.

Library Text

A sequence of text words, comment lines, the separator SPACE, or the separator pseudo-text delimiter in a COBOL library.

LINAGE-COUNTER$_{85}$

A special register whose VALUE points to the current POSITION within the PAGE body.

LINE

A division of a PAGE representing one row of horizontal CHARACTER POSITIONs. Each CHARACTER POSITION of a REPORT LINE is aligned vertically beneath the corresponding CHARACTER POSITION of the REPORT LINE above it. REPORT LINES are numbered from 1, by 1, starting at the TOP of the PAGE. The term is synonymous with REPORT LINE.

LINE NUMBER

An integer that denotes the vertical POSITION of a REPORT LINE on a PAGE.

LINKAGE SECTION

The SECTION in the DATA DIVISION of the called PROGRAM that describes data items available from the calling PROGRAM. These data items may be referred to by both the calling and called PROGRAM.

Literal

A character-string whose VALUE is implied by the ordered set of CHARACTERS comprising the string.

Logical Operator

One of the reserved words AND, OR, or NOT. In the formation of a condition, either AND, or OR, or both, can be used as logical connectives. NOT can be used for logical negation.

Logical PAGE$_{85}$

A conceptual entity consisting of the TOP margin, the PAGE body, and the BOTTOM margin.

Logical RECORD

The most inclusive data item. The level-number for a RECORD is 01. A RECORD may be either an elementary item or a GROUP item. The term is synonymous with RECORD.

Low ORDER End

The rightmost CHARACTER of a string of CHARACTERS.

Mass Storage

A storage medium in which data may be organized and maintained in both a SEQUENTIAL and nonsequential manner.

Mass Storage CONTROL System (MSCS)

An INPUT-OUTPUT CONTROL system that directs, or CONTROLs, the processing of mass storage FILEs.

Mass Storage FILE

A collection of RECORDS that is assigned to a mass storage medium.

MCS

MESSAGE CONTROL system; a COMMUNICATION CONTROL system that supports the processing of MESSAGEs.

MERGE FILE

A collection of RECORDS to be merged by a MERGE statement. The MERGE FILE is created and can be used only by the MERGE function.

MESSAGE

Data associated with an END OF MESSAGE indicator or an END OF GROUP indicator.

MESSAGE CONTROL System (MCS)

A COMMUNICATION CONTROL system that supports the processing of MESSAGEs.

MESSAGE COUNT

The COUNT of the NUMBER of complete MESSAGEs that exist in the designated QUEUE of MESSAGEs.

MESSAGE Indicators

EGI (END OF GROUP indicator), EMI (END OF MESSAGE indicator), and ESI (END OF SEGMENT indicator) are conceptual indications that serve to notify the MESSAGE CONTROL system that a specific condition exists (END OF GROUP, END OF MESSAGE, END OF SEGMENT).Within the hierarchy of EGI, EMI, and ESI, an EGI is conceptually equivalent to an ESI, EMI, and EGI. An EMI is conceptually equivalent to an ESI and EMI. Thus, a SEGMENT may be terminated by an ESI, EMI, or EGI. A MESSAGE may be terminated by an EMI or EGI.

MESSAGE SEGMENT

Data that forms a logical subdivision of a MESSAGE, normally associated with an END OF SEGMENT indicator. (See MESSAGE Indicators.)

Mnemonic-Name

A user-defined word that is associated in the ENVIRONMENT DIVISION with a specific implementor-name.

MSCS

Mass storage CONTROL system; an INPUT-OUTPUT CONTROL system that directs, or CONTROLs, the processing of mass storage FILEs.

NATIVE CHARACTER Set

The implementor-defined CHARACTER set associated with the computer specified in the OBJECT-COMPUTER paragraph.

NATIVE COLLATING SEQUENCE

The implementor-defined COLLATING SEQUENCE associated with the computer specified in the OBJECT-COMPUTER paragraph.

Negated Combined Condition

The "NOT" logical operator immediately followed by a parenthesized combined condition.

Negated Simple Condition

The "NOT" logical operator immediately followed by a simple condition.

NEXT Executable Sentence

The NEXT sentence to which CONTROL will be transferred after execution of the current statement is complete.

NEXT Executable Statement

The NEXT statement to which CONTROL will be transferred after execution of the current statement is complete.

NEXT RECORD
  The RECORD which logically follows the current RECORD of a FILE.

Noncontiguous Item
  Elementary data items, in the WORKING-STORAGE and LINKAGE SECTIONs, which bear no hierarchic relationship to other data items.

Nonnumeric Item
  A data item whose description permits its contents to be composed of any combination of CHARACTERS taken from the computer's CHARACTER set. Certain categories of nonnumeric items may be formed from more restricted CHARACTER sets.

Nonnumeric Literal
  A literal bounded by quotation marks. The string of CHARACTERS may include any CHARACTER in the computer's CHARACTER set.

NUMERIC CHARACTER
  A CHARACTER that belongs to the following set of digits: 0, 1, 2, 3, 4, 5, 6, 7, 8, 9.

NUMERIC Item
  A data item whose description restricts its contents to a VALUE represented by CHARACTERS chosen from the digits "0" through "9"; if signed, the item may also contain a "+", "-", or other representation of an operational SIGN.

NUMERIC Literal
  A literal composed of one or more NUMERIC CHARACTERS that may contain either a decimal point, or an algebraic SIGN, or both. The decimal point must not be the rightmost CHARACTER. The algebraic SIGN, if present, must be the leftmost CHARACTER.

OBJECT-COMPUTER
  The name of an ENVIRONMENT DIVISION paragraph in which the computer environment, within which the object PROGRAM is executed, is described.

Object Computer Entry$_{85}$
  An entry in the OBJECT-COMPUTER paragraph of the ENVIRONMENT DIVISION which contains clauses which describe the computer environment in which the object PROGRAM is to be executed.

Object of Entry
  A set of operands and reserved words, within a DATA DIVISION entry of a COBOL PROGRAM, that immediately follows the subject of the entry.

Object PROGRAM
  A set or group of executable machine language instructions and other material designed to interact with data to provide problem solutions. In this context, an object

PROGRAM is generally the machine language result of the operation of a COBOL compiler on a SOURCE PROGRAG. Where there is no danger of ambiguity, the word "PROGRAM" alone may be used in place of the phrase "object PROGRAM".

Object Time

The time at which an object PROGRAM is executed. The term is synonymous with execution time.

Obsolete Element[85]

A COBOL language element in Standard COBOL that is to be deleted from the next revision of Standard COBOL.

OPEN MODE

The state of a FILE after execution of an OPEN statement for that FILE and before the execution of a CLOSE statement without the REEL or UNIT phrase for that FILE. The particular OPEN MODE is specified in the OPEN statement as either INPUT, OUTPUT, I-O, or EXTEND.

Operand

Whereas the general definition of operand is "that component which is operated upon", for the purposes of this document, any lowercase word (or WORDS) that appears in a statement or entry format may be considered to be an operand and, as such, is an implied reference to the data indicated by the operand.

Operational SIGN

An algebraic SIGN, associated with a NUMERIC data item or a NUMERIC literal, to indicate whether its value is POSITIVE or NEGATIVE.

OPTIONAL FILE[85]

A FILE which is declared as being not necessarily present each time the object PROGRAM is executed. The object PROGRAM causes an interrogation for the presence or absence of the FILE.

OPTIONAL Word

A reserved word that is included in a specific format only to improve the readability of the language and whose presence is OPTIONAL to the user when the format in which the word appears is used in a SOURCE PROGRAM.

OUTPUT FILE

A FILE that is opened in either the OUTPUT MODE or EXTEND MODE.

OUTPUT MODE

The state of a FILE after execution of an OPEN statement, with the OUTPUT or EXTEND phrase specified, for that FILE and before the execution of a CLOSE statement without the REEL or UNIT phrase for that FILE.

OUTPUT PROCEDURE

A set of statements to which CONTROL is given during execution of a SORT statement after the SORT function is completed, or during execution of a MERGE statement after the MERGE function reaches a point at which it can SELECT the NEXT RECORD in merged order when requested.

Padding CHARACTER$_{85}$

An ALPHANUMERIC CHARACTER used to fill the unused CHARACTER POSITIONs in a physical RECORD.

PAGE

A vertical division of a REPORT representing a physical separation of REPORT data, the separation being based on internal reporting requirements and/or external characteristics of the reporting medium.

PAGE Body

That part of the logical PAGE in which LINEs can be written and/or spaced.

PAGE FOOTING

A REPORT GROUP that is presented at the END OF a REPORT PAGE as determined by the REPORT writer CONTROL system.

PAGE HEADING

A REPORT GROUP that is presented at the beginning of a REPORT PAGE and determined by the REPORT writer CONTROL system.

Paragraph

In the PROCEDURE DIVISION, a paragraph-name followed by a separator period and by zero, one, or more sentences. In the IDENTIFICATION and ENVIRONMENT DIVISIONs, a paragraph header followed by zero, one, or more entries.

Paragraph header

A reserved word, followed by the separator period, that indicates the beginning of a paragraph in the IDENTIFICATION and ENVIRONMENT DIVISIONs. The permissible paragraph headers in the IDENTIFICATION DIVISION are:

```
PROGRAM-ID.
AUTHOR.
INSTALLATION.
DATE-WRITTEN.
DATE-COMPILED.
SECURITY.
```

The permissible paragraph headers in the ENVIRONMENT DIVISION are:

```
SOURCE-COMPUTER.
OBJECT-COMPUTER.
SPECIAL-NAMES.
FILE-CONTROL.
I-O-CONTROL.
```

Paragraph-Name

A user-defined word that identifies and begins a paragraph in the PROCEDURE DIVISION.

Phrase

A phrase is an ordered set of one or more consecutive COBOL character-strings that form a portion of a COBOL procedural statement or of a COBOL clause.

Physical PAGE₈₅

A device-dependent concept defined by the implementor.

Physical RECORD

The term is synonymous with BLOCK.

Prime RECORD KEY

A KEY whose contents uniquely identify a RECORD within an INDEXED FILE.

Printable GROUP

A REPORT GROUP that contains at least one print LINE.

Printable Item

A data item, the extent and contents of which are specified by an elementary REPORT entry. This elementary REPORT entry contains a COLUMN NUMBER clause, a PICTURE clause, and a SOURCE, SUM, or VALUE clause.

PROCEDURE

A paragraph or group of logically successive paragraphs, or a SECTION or group of logically successive SECTIONs, within the PROCEDURE DIVISION.

PROCEDURE Branching Statement₈₅

A statement that causes the explicit transfer of CONTROL to a statement other than the next executable statement in the sequence in which the statements are written in the SOURCE PROGRAM. The PROCEDURE branching statements are: ALTER, CALL, EXIT, EXIT PROGRAM, GO TO, MERGE (with the OUTPUT PROCEDURE phrase), PERFORM and SORT (with the INPUT PROCEDURE or OUTPUT PROCEDURE phrase).

Procedure-Name

A user-defined word which is used to name a paragraph or SECTION in the

PROCEDURE DIVISION. It consists of a paragraph-name (which may be qualified), or a section-name.

PROGRAM Identification Entry[85]

An entry in the PROGRAM-ID paragraph of the IDENTIFICATION DIVISION which contains clauses that specify the program-name and assign selected PROGRAM attributes to the PROGRAM.

Program-Name

In the IDENTIFICATION DIVISION and the END PROGRAM header, a user-defined word that identifies a COBOL SOURCE PROGRAM.

Pseudo-Text

A SEQUENCE of TEXT WORDS, comment lines, or the separator SPACES in a SOURCE PROGRAM or COBOL library bounded by, but not including, pseudo-text DELIMITERs.

Pseudo-Text Delimiter

Two contiguous EQUAL SIGN (==) CHARACTERS used to delimit pseudo-text.

Punctuation CHARACTER

A CHARACTER that belongs to the following set:

CHARACTER	Meaning
,	COMMA
;	semicolon
:	colon
.	period (full stop)
"	quotation mark
(	LEFT parenthesis
)	RIGHT parenthesis
	SPACE
=	EQUAL SIGN

Qualified Data-Name

An identifier that is composed of a data-name followed by one or more sets of either of the connectives OF and IN followed by a data-name qualifier.

Qualifier

1. A data-name or a name associated with a level indicator which is used in a reference either together with another data name which is a name of an item that is subordinate to the qualifier or together with a condition-name.
2. A section-name which is used in a reference together with a paragraph-name specified in that SECTION.

3.   A library-name which is used in a reference together with a text-name associated with that library.

QUEUE

A logical collection of MESSAGEs awaiting transmission or processing.

QUEUE Name

A symbolic name that indicates to the MESSAGE CONTROL system the logical path by which a MESSAGE or a portion of a completed MESSAGE may be accessible in a QUEUE.

RANDOM ACCESS

An ACCESS MODE in which the program-specified VALUE of a KEY data item identifies the logical RECORD that is obtained from, deleted from or placed into a RELATIVE or INDEXED FILE.

RECORD

The most inclusive data item. The level-number for a RECORD is 01. A RECORD may be either an elementary item or a group item.The term is synonymous with logical RECORD.

RECORD AREA

A storage AREA allocated for the purpose of processing the RECORD described in a RECORD description entry in the FILE SECTION of the DATA DIVISION. In the FILE SECTION, the current NUMBER of CHARACTER POSITIONs in the RECORD AREA is determined by the explicit or implicit RECORD clause.

RECORD Description

The total set of data description entries associated with a particular RECORD. The term is synonymous with RECORD description entry.

RECORD Description Entry

The total set of data description entries associated with a particular RECORD. The term is synonymous with RECORD description.

RECORD KEY

A KEY, whose contents identify a RECORD within an INDEXED FILE. Within an INDEXED FILE, a RECORD KEY is either the prime RECORD KEY or an ALTERNATE RECORD KEY.

Record-Name

A user-defined word that names a RECORD described in a RECORD description entry in the DATA DIVISION of a COBOL PROGRAM.

RECORD NUMBER[85]

The ordinal NUMBER of a RECORD in the FILE whose ORGANIZATION IS SEQUENTIAL.

REEL[85]

A discrete portion of a storage medium, the dimensions of which are determined by each implementor, that contains part of a FILE, all of a FILE, or any NUMBER of FILEs. The term is synonymous with UNIT and volume.

Reference Format

A format that provides a standard method for describing COBOL SOURCE PROGRAMs.

Reference Modifier[85]

The leftmost-character-position and LENGTH used to establish and reference a data item.

Relation

The term is synonymous with relational operator.

Relation CHARACTER

A CHARACTER that belongs to the following set:

CHARACTER	Meaning
>	GREATER THAN
<	LESS THAN
=	EQUAL TO

Relation Condition

The proposition, for which a truth VALUE can be determined, that the value of an arithmetic expression, or data item, nonnumeric literal, or index-name has a specific relationship to the VALUE of another arithmetic expression, data item, nonnumeric literal, or index-name.

Relational Operator

A reserved word, a relation CHARACTER, a group of consecutive reserved WORDS, or a group of consecutive reserved WORDS and relation CHARACTERS used in the construction of a relation condition. The permissible operators and their meaning are:

Relational Operator	Meaning
`IS [NOT] GREATER THAN` `IS [NOT] >`	GREATER THAN OR NOT GREATER THAN
`IS [NOT] LESS THAN` `IS [NOT] <`	LESS THAN OR NOT LESS THAN
`IS [NOT] EQUAL TO` `IS [NOT] =`	EQUAL TO OR NOT EQUAL TO

```
IS GREATER THAN OR EQUAL TO    GREATER THAN OR EQUAL TO
IS >=

IS LESS THAN OR EQUAL TO       LESS THAN OR EQUAL TO
IS <=
```

RELATIVE FILE
A FILE with RELATIVE ORGANIZATION.

RELATIVE KEY
A KEY whose contents identify a logical RECORD in a RELATIVE FILE.

RELATIVE ORGANIZATION
The permanent logical FILE structure in which each RECORD is uniquely identified by an integer VALUE GREATER THAN ZERO, which specifies the record's logical ordinal POSITION in the FILE.

RELATIVE RECORD NUMBER[85]
The ordinal NUMBER of a RECORD in a FILE whose ORGANIZATION IS RELATIVE. This NUMBER is treated as a NUMERIC literal which is an integer.

REPORT Clause
A clause, in the REPORT SECTION of the DATA DIVISION, that appears in a REPORT description entry or a REPORT GROUP description entry.

REPORT Description Entry
An entry in the REPORT SECTION of the DATA DIVISION that is composed of the level indicator RD, followed by the report-name, followed by a set of REPORT clauses as required.

REPORT FILE
An OUTPUT FILE whose FILE description entry contains a REPORT clause. The contents of a REPORT FILE consist of RECORDS that are written under CONTROL of the REPORT writer CONTROL system.

REPORT FOOTING
A REPORT GROUP that is presented only at the END OF a REPORT.

REPORT GROUP
In the REPORT SECTION of the DATA DIVISION, an 01 level-number entry and its subordinate entries.

REPORT GROUP Description Entry
An entry in the REPORT SECTION of the DATA DIVISION that is composed of the level-number 01, an OPTIONAL data-name, a TYPE clause, and an OPTIONAL set of REPORT clauses.

REPORT HEADING
>A REPORT GROUP that is presented only at the beginning of a REPORT.

REPORT LINE
>A division of a PAGE representing one row of horizontal CHARACTER POSITIONs. Each CHARACTER POSITION of a REPORT LINE is aligned vertically beneath the corresponding CHARACTER POSITION of the REPORT LINE above it. REPORT LINEs are numbered from 1, by 1, starting at the TOP OF the PAGE.

Report-Name
>A user-defined word that names a REPORT described in a REPORT description entry within the REPORT SECTION of the DATA DIVISION.

REPORT SECTION
>The SECTION of the DATA DIVISION that contains zero, one, or more REPORT description entries and their associated REPORT GROUP description entries.

REPORT Writer CONTROL System (RWCS)
>An object time CONTROL system, provided by the implementor, that accomplishes the construction of REPORTs.

REPORT Writer Logical RECORD
>A RECORD that consists of the REPORT writer print LINE and associated CONTROL information necessary for its selection and vertical positioning.

Reserved Word
>A COBOL word specified in the list of WORDS which may be used in a COBOL SOURCE PROGRAM, but which must not appear in the PROGRAM as user-defined words or system-names.

Resource$_{85}$
>A facility or service, controlled by the operating system, that can be used by an executing PROGRAM.

Resultant Identifier$_{85}$
>A user-defined data item that is to contain the result of an arithmetic operation.

Routine-Name
>A user-defined word that identifies a PROCEDURE written in a language other than COBOL.

RUN UNIT
>One or more object PROGRAMS which interact with one another and which function, at object time, as an entity to provide problem solutions.

RWCS

REPORT writer CONTROL system; an object time CONTROL system, provided by the implementor, that accomplishes the construction of REPORTs.

SECTION

A set of zero, one, or more paragraphs or entries, called a SECTION body, the first of which is preceded by a SECTION header. Each SECTION consists of the SECTION header and the related SECTION body.

SECTION header

A combination of WORDS followed by a separator period that indicates the beginning of a SECTION in the ENVIRONMENT. DATA. and PROCEDURE DIVISION. In the ENVIRONMENT and DATA DIVISIONs, a SECTION header is composed of reserved WORDS followed by a separator period. The permissible SECTION headers in the ENVIRONMENT DIVISION are:

```
CONFIGURATION SECTION.
INPUT-OUTPUT SECTION.
```

The permissible SECTION headers in the DATA DIVISION are:

```
FILE SECTION.
WORKING-STORAGE SECTION.
LINKAGE SECTION.
COMMUNICATION SECTION.
REPORT SECTION.
```

In the PROCEDURE DIVISION, a SECTION header is composed of a section-name, followed by the reserved word SECTION, followed by a segment-number (OPTIONAL), followed by a separator period.

Section-Name

A user-defined word which names a SECTION in the PROCEDURE DIVISION.

Segment-Number

A user-defined word which classifies SECTIONs in the PROCEDURE DIVISION for purposes of segmentation. Segment-numbers may contain only the CHARACTERS "0", "1", ..., "9". A segment-number may be expressed either as a one or two digit NUMBER.

Sentence

A sequence of one or more statements, the last of which is terminated by a separator period.

Separately Compiled PROGRAM$_{85}$
A PROGRAM which, together with its contained PROGRAMs, is compiled separately from all other PROGRAMs.

Separator
A CHARACTER or two contiguous CHARACTERS used to delimit character-strings.

SEQUENTIAL ACCESS
An ACCESS MODE in which logical RECORDS are obtained from or placed into a FILE in a consecutive predecessor-to-successor logical RECORD SEQUENCE determined by the ORDER of RECORDS in the FILE.

SEQUENTIAL FILE
A FILE with SEQUENTIAL ORGANIZATION.

SEQUENTIAL ORGANIZATION
The permanent logical FILE structure in which a RECORD is identified by a predecessor-successor relationship established when the RECORD is placed into the FILE.

SIGN Condition
The proposition, for which a truth VALUE can be determined, that the algebraic VALUE of a data item or an arithmetic expression is either LESS THAN, GREATER THAN, OR EQUAL TO ZERO.

Simple Condition
Any single condition chosen from the set:

> relation condition
> CLASS condition
> condition-name condition
> switch-status condition
> SIGN condition
> (simple-condition)

SORT FILE
A collection of RECORDS to be sorted by a SORT statement. The SORT FILE is created and can be used by the SORT function only.

SORT-MERGE FILE Description Entry
An entry in the FILE SECTION of the DATA DIVISION that is composed of the level indicator SD, followed by a file-name, and then followed by a set of FILE clauses as required.

SOURCE

The symbolic identification of the originator of a transmission to a QUEUE.

SOURCE-COMPUTER

The name of an ENVIRONMENT DIVISION paragraph in which the computer environment, within which the SOURCE PROGRAM is compiled, is described.

SOURCE Computer Entry[85]

An entry in the SOURCE-COMPUTER paragraph of the ENVIRONMENT DIVISION which contains clauses which describe the computer environment in which the SOURCE PROGRAM is to be compiled.

SOURCE Item

An identifier designated by a SOURCE clause that provides the VALUE of a printable item.

SOURCE PROGRAM

Although it is recognized that a SOURCE PROGRAM may be represented by other forms and symbols, in this document it always refers to a syntactically correct set of COBOL statements. A COBOL SOURCE PROGRAM commences with the IDENTIFICATION DIVISION; a COPY statement; or a REPLACE statement. A COBOL SOURCE PROGRAM is terminated by the END PROGRAM header, if specified, or by the absence of additional source PROGRAM lines.

Special CHARACTER

A CHARACTER that belongs to the following set:

CHARACTER	Meaning
+	PLUS SIGN
-	minus SIGN
*	asterisk
/	slant (solidus)
=	EQUAL SIGN
$	CURRENCY SIGN
,	COMMA (decimal point)
;	semicolon
.	period (decimal point, full stop)
"	quotation mark
(	LEFT parenthesis
)	RIGHT parenthesis
>	GREATER THAN symbol
<	LESS THAN symbol
:	colon

Special-Character Word

A reserved word which is an arithmetic operator or a relation CHARACTER.

SPECIAL-NAMES

The name of an ENVIRONMENT DIVISION paragraph in which implementor-names are related to user specified mnemonic-names.

Special Names Entry$_{85}$

An entry in the SPECIAL-NAMES paragraph of the ENVIRONMENT DIVISION which provides means for specifying the CURRENCY SIGN; choosing the decimal point; specifying symbolic CHARACTERS; relating implementor-names to user-specified mnemonic-names; relating alphabet-names to CHARACTER sets or COLLATING SEQUENCEs; and relating class-names to sets of CHARACTERS.

Special Registers

Compiler-generated storage areas whose primary use is to store information produced in conjunction with the use of specific COBOL features.

Standard Data Format

The concept used in describing data in a COBOL DATA DIVISION under which the characteristics or properties of the data are expressed in a form oriented to the appearance of the data on a printed PAGE of infinite LENGTH and breadth, rather than a form oriented to the manner in which the data is stored internally in the computer, or on a particular medium.

Statement

A syntactically valid combination of WORDS, literals, and separators, beginning with a verb, written in a COBOL SOURCE PROGRAM.

Sub-Queue

A logical hierarchical division of a QUEUE.

Subject of Entry

An operand or reserved word that appears immediately following the level indicator or the level-number in a DATA DIVISION entry.

Subprogram

A PROGRAM which is the object of a CALL statement combined at object time with the calling PROGRAM to produce a RUN UNIT. The term is synonymous with called PROGRAM.

Subscript

An occurrence NUMBER represented by either an integer, a data-name optionally followed by an integer with the operator + or -, or an index-name optionally followed by an integer with the operator + or -, which identifies a particular element in a TABLE.

Subscripted Data-Name

An identifier that is composed of a data-name followed by one or more subscripts enclosed in parentheses.

SUM Counter

A signed NUMERIC data item established by a SUM clause in the REPORT SECTION of the DATA DIVISION. The SUM counter is used by the REPORT Writer CONTROL System to contain the result of designated summing operations that take place during production of a REPORT.

Switch-Status Condition

The proposition, for which a truth VALUE can be determined, that an implementor-defined switch, capable of being set to an "on" or "off" STATUS, has been set to a specific STATUS.

Symbolic-Character[85]

A user-defined word that specifies a user-defined figurative constant.

System-Name

A COBOL word which is used to communicate with the operating environment.

TABLE

A set of logically consecutive items of data that are defined in the DATA DIVISION of a COBOL PROGRAM by means of the OCCURS clause.

TABLE Element

A data item that belongs to the set of repeated items comprising a TABLE.

TERMINAL

The originator of a transmission to a QUEUE, or the receiver of a transmission from a QUEUE.

Text-Name

A user-defined word which identifies library text.

Text-Word

Any CHARACTER or a SEQUENCE of contiguous CHARACTERS between margin A and margin R in a COBOL library, SOURCE PROGRAM, or in pseudo-text which is:

1. A separator, except for: SPACE; a pseudo-text DELIMITER; and the opening and closing DELIMITERs for nonnumeric literals. The RIGHT parenthesis and LEFT parenthesis CHARACTERS, regardless of context within the

library, SOURCE PROGRAM, or pseudo-text, are always considered TEXT
WORDS.

2. A literal including, in the case of nonnumeric literals, the opening quotation mark
    and the closing quotation mark which bound the literal.

3. Any other sequence of contiguous COBOL CHARACTERS except comment
    lines and the word "COPY", bounded by separators, which is neither a separator
    nor a literal.

TOP Margin$_{85}$

An empty area which precedes the PAGE body.

Truth VALUE

The representation of the result of the evaluation of a condition in terms of one of two
VALUES: TRUE, FALSE.

Unary Operator

A PLUS (+) or a minus (-) sign, which precedes a variable or a LEFT parenthesis in an
arithmetic expression and which has the effect of multiplying the expression by +1 or
-1 respectively.

UNIT

A discrete portion of a storage medium, the dimensions of which are determined by
each implementor, that contains part of a FILE, all of a FILE, or any NUMBER of
FILEs. The term is synonymous with REEL and Volume.

Unsuccessful Execution$_{85}$

The attempted execution of a statement that does not result in the execution of all
the operations specified by that statement. The unsuccessful execution of a statement
does not affect any data referenced by that statement, but may affect STATUS
indicators.

User-Defined Word

A COBOL word that must be supplied by the user to satisfy the format of a clause or
statement.

Variable

A data item whose value may be changed by execution of the object PROGRAM. A
variable used in an arithmetic-expression must be a NUMERIC elementary item.

Variable LENGTH RECORD$_{85}$

A RECORD associated with a FILE whose FILE description or SORT-MERGE
description entry permits RECORDS to contain a varying number of CHARACTER
POSITIONs.

Variable Occurrence Data Item$_{85}$

A variable occurrence data item is a TABLE element which is repeated a variable number of TIMES. Such an item must contain an OCCURS DEPENDING ON clause in its data description entry, or be subordinate to such an item.

Verb

A word that expresses an action to be taken by a COBOL compiler or object PROGRAM.

Volume$_{85}$

A discrete portion of a storage medium, the dimensions of which are determined by each implementor, that contains part of a FILE, all of a FILE, or any NUMBER of FILEs. The term is synonymous with REEL and UNIT.

Word

A character-string of not more than 30 CHARACTERS which forms a user-defined word, a system-name, or a reserved word.

WORKING-STORAGE SECTION

The SECTION of the DATA DIVISION that describes working storage data items, composed either of noncontiguous items or working storage RECORDS or of both.

77-Level-Description-Entry

A data description entry that describes a noncontiguous data item with the level-number 77.

Appendix C
Annotated COBOL
reserved word list

Any word with a $_{74}$ subscript is an obsolete word in $COBOL_{85}$ and should be eliminated from existing programs. The word will become unreserved in the next revision to COBOL and will be rejected.

Any word with an $_{On}$ subscript is an obsolete word in $COBOL_{85}$ in some usages; $_n$ is the footnote that describes the obsolete usages. These usages should also be eliminated from existing programs since that usage will also become unsupported in the next revision to COBOL.

Any word with a ^{pn} superscript is a $COBOL_{74}$ word that ANSI has identified as potentially executing incorrectly in $COBOL_{85}$; ^{n} is the footnote that describes the potential problem. Existing use of these words in $COBOL_{74}$ programs should be reviewed and corrected if their usage would cause problems in $COBOL_{85}$.

Any word with a ^{cd} superscript is only used in the $COBOL_{85}$ optional COMMUNICA-TION module; a conforming $COBOL_{85}$ compiler does **not** have to support and its function should be transferred to other software for future portability.

Any word with a ^{rw} superscript is only used in the $COBOL_{85}$ optional REPORT WRITER module; a conforming $COBOL_{85}$ compiler does **not** to have support and its function should be transferred to other software for future portability.

Any word with $_{85}$ subscript is a new reserved word for $COBOL_{85}$. Usage of these words in $COBOL_{74}$ programs should be eliminated to prevent $COBOL_{85}$ syntax problems.

ACCEPT	ACCESS	ADD
ADVANCING	AFTER	$ALL_{O1,2}{}^{p14}$
$ALPHABET_{85}{}^{p21}$	ALPHABETIC	$ALPHABETIC\text{-}LOWER_{85}$
$ALPHABETIC\text{-}UPPER_{85}$	$ALPHANUMERIC_{85}$	$ALPHANUMERIC\text{-}EDITED_{85}$
$ALSO_{85}$	$ALTER_{74}$	ALTERNATE
AND^{p25}	ANY_{85}	ARE_{O8}
AREA	AREAS	ASCENDING
$ASSIGN^{p2}$	AT	$AUTHOR_{74}$
BEFORE	$BINARY_{85}$	BLANK
BLOCK	BOTTOM	BY

311

CALL [p13]   CANCEL[p26]   CD[cd]

CF [rw]   CH[rw]   CHARACTER

CHARACTERS[O3,10]   CLASS[85]   CLOCK-UNITS[74]

CLOSE   COBOL   CODE[rw]

CODE-SET [p6]   COLLATING[O3,10]   COLUMN[rw]

COMMA   COMMON[85]   COMMUNICATION [cd]

COMP   COMPUTATIONAL   COMPUTE

CONFIGURATION   CONTAINS   CONTENT[85]

CONTINUE[85]   CONTROL[rw]   CONTROLS[rw]

CONVERTING[85]   COPY   CORR

CORRESPONDING   COUNT   CURRENCY[p22]

DATA[O5]   DATE   DATE-COMPILED[74]

DATE-WRITTEN[74]   DAY   DAY-OF-WEEK[85]

DE[rw]   DEBUG-CONTENTS[74]   DEBUG-ITEM[74]

DEBUG-LINE[74]   DEBUG-NAME[74]   DEBUG-SUB-1[74]

DEBUG-SUB-2[74]   DEBUG-SUB-3[74]   DEBUGGING[74]

DECIMAL-POINT   DECLARATIVES[O2]   DELETE

DELIMITED   DELIMITER   DEPENDING

DESCENDING   DESTINATION[cd]   DETAIL[rw]

DISABLE[cd]   DISPLAY   DIVIDE

DIVISION   DOWN   DUPLICATES

DYNAMIC

EGI[cd]   ELSE   EMI[cd]

ENABLE[cd]   END[O2]   END-ADD[85]

END-CALL[85]   END-COMPUTE[85]   END-DELETE[85]

END-DIVIDE[85]   END-EVALUATE[85]   END-IF[85]

END-MULTIPLY[85]   END-OF-PAGE[p23]   END-PERFORM[85]

END-READ[85]   END-RECEIVE[85]   END-RETURN[85]

END-REWRITE[85]   END-SEARCH[85]   END-START[85]

END-STRING[85]   END-SUBTRACT[85]   END-UNSTRING[85]

END-WRITE[85]   ENTER[74]   ENVIRONMENT

EOP   EQUAL   ERROR

ESI[cd]   EVALUATE[85]   EVERY[O4]

EXCEPTION   EXIT   EXTEND[p16]

EXTERNAL[85]

FALSE[85]   FD   FILE[O9]

FILE-CONTROL	FILLER$_{O2}$[p8]	FINAL[rw]
FIRST	FOOTING[rw]	FOR$_{O2}$
FROM		
GENERATE[rw]	GIVING	GLOBAL$_{85}$
GO	GREATER	GROUP[rw]
HEADING[rw]	HIGH-VALUE	HIGH-VALUES
I-O	I-O-CONTROL[p5]	IDENTIFICATION
IF	IN	INDEX
INDEXED	INDICATE	INITIAL
INITIALIZED$_{85}$	INITIATE[rw]	INPUT
INPUT-OUTPUT	INSPECT[p28]	INSTALLATION
INTO[p29]	INVALID	IS$_{O3,6,8,10}$
JUST	JUSTIFIED	
KEY$_{O7}$		
LABEL$_{O8}$	LAST[rw]	LEADING
LEFT	LENGTH[cd]	LESS
LIMIT[rw]	LIMITS[rw]	LINAGE[p7]
LINAGE-COUNTER	LINE	LINE-COUNTER[rw]
LINES	LINKAGE	LOCK
LOW-VALUE	LOW-VALUES	
MEMORY$_{O3,10}$	MERGE[p15]	MESSAGE[cd]
MODE$_{74}$	MODULES$_{O3,10}$	MOVE
MULTIPLE$_{O9}$	MULTIPLY	
NATIVE	NEGATIVE	NEXT
NO	NOT	NUMBER[rw]
NUMERIC	NUMERIC-EDITED$_{85}$	
OBJECT-COMPUTER$_{O10}$	OCCURS[p9]	OF$_{O6}$
OFF	OMITTED$_{O8}$	ON$_{O2,4}$
OPEN	OPTIONAL[p3]	OR[p25]
ORDER$_{85}$	ORGANIZATION[p4]	OTHER$_{85}$
OUTPUT	OVERFLOW	

PACKED-DECIMAL[85]   PADDING[85]   PAGE
PAGE-COUNTER[rw]   PERFORM[p17]   PF[rw]
PH[rw]   PIC   PICTURE
PLUS[rw]   POINTER   POSITION
POSITIVE   PRINTING   PROCEDURE
PROCEDURES[O2]   PROCEED   PROGRAM[O3,10]
PROGRAM-ID   PURGE[cd]

QUEUE[cd]   QUOTE   QUOTES

RANDOM   RD[rw]   READ
RECEIVE[cd]   RECORD[O8]   RECORDS[O4,5,8]
REDEFINES[p10]   REEL[O4]   REFERENCE[85]
REFERENCES[O2]   RELATIVE   RELEASE
REMAINDER[p27]   REMOVAL   RENAMES
REPLACE[85]   REPLACING   REPORT[rw]
REPORTING[rw]   REPORTS[rw]   RERUN[74]
RESERVE   RESET[rw]   RETURN[p18]
REVERSED[74]   REWIND   REWRITE[p19]
RF[rw]   RH[rw]   RIGHT
ROUNDED   RUN

SAME   SD   SEARCH
SECTION[O2,10]   SECURITY   SEGMENT[74]
SEGMENT-LIMIT[74]   SELECT   SEND[cd]
SENTENCE   SEPARATE   SEQUENCE[O3,10]
SEQUENTIAL   SET   SIGN[p11]
SIZE[O3,10]   SORT[p15]   SORT-MERGE
SOURCE[rw]   SOURCE-COMPUTER   SPACE
SPACES   SPECIAL-NAMES   STANDARD[O8]
STANDARD-1   STANDARD-2[85]   START
STATUS[cd]   STOP   STRING[p20,30]
SUB-QUEUE-1[cd]   SUB-QUEUE-2[cd]   SUB-QUEUE-3[cd]
SUBTRACT   SUM[rw]   SUPPRESS[rw]
SYMBOLIC   SYNC   SYNCHRONIZED

TABLE   TALLYING   TAPE[O9]
TERMINAL[cd]   TERMINATE[cd]   TEST[85]
TEXT   THAN   THEN[85]

THROUGH$_{85}$	THRU	TIME
TIMES	TO	TOP
TRAILING	TRUE$_{85}$	TYPE^{rw}
UNIT$_{O4}$	UNSTRING^{p30}	UNTIL
UP	UPON	USAGE
USE$_{O2}$	USING^{p24}	
VALUE$_{O6}$^{p12}	VALUES	VARYING
WHEN$_{O7}$	WITH$_{O2}$	WORDS$_{O3,10}$
WORKING-STORAGE	WRITE	
ZERO^{p1}	ZEROES	ZEROS
+	-	*
/	**	>
<	=	>=$_{85}$
<=$_{85}$		

There are also some new COBOL$_{85}$ rules pertaining to the punctuation marks:

1. colon (:) is used in reference modification

2. COMMA (,) and semicolon (;) and space ( ) are interchangeable

3. period (.) and COMMA (,) can be last CHARACTER in a PIC clause

Other COBOL$_{85}$ language modifications:

1. nonnumeric literal can be up to 160 CHARACTERS in LENGTH

2. there can be fifty [50] levels of qualification

3. a TABLE can have seven [7] dimensions

4. relative subscripting is allowed

5. subscripts and indexes can be intermixed

6. DATA can be referenced by specifying a leftmost CHARACTER and LENGTH

7. SEQUENCE field can contain any CHARACTER

8. DATA DIVISION word following level indicator, 01, or 77 can start in A area

9. END PROGRAM can be followed by the IDENTIFICATION DIVISION of another COBOL PROGRAM

10. PROGRAMs can be nested

11. the ENVIRONMENT, DATA, and PROCEDURE DIVISION are optional

12. a MOVE of NUMERIC-EDITED data item to NUMERIC data item causes de-editing

13. P in PIC clause has new limitations

14. exponentiation results have been redefined

15. new I-O STATUS VALUES have been added

OBSOLETE FOOTNOTES

1. when used as a figurative constant literal associated with a NUMERIC or NUMERIC-EDITED item with a LENGTH > 1

2. when used in DEBUG module

3. when used in MEMORY SIZE clause

4. when used in RERUN clause

5. when used in data RECORDS clause

6. when used in VALUE OF clause

7. when used in COMMUNICATION module

8. when used in LABEL RECORD and LABEL RECORDS clauses

9. when used in MULTIPLE FILE TAPE clause

10. when used in SEGMENTATION module

PROBLEM FOOTNOTES

1. ZERO is allowed in arithmetic expressions

2. nonnumeric literal allowed in ASSIGN clause

3. OPTIONAL can be used with RELATIVE and INDEXED FILE which are OPEN in the INPUT, I-O, or EXTEND MODE

4. ORGANIZATION is OPTIONAL in the FILE control entry

5. clause order is immaterial

6. CODE-SET can be specified for any SEQUENTIAL FILE ORGANIZATION

7. data-names can be qualified; a FILE cannot be OPEN in the EXTEND MODE

8. FILLER is OPTIONAL

9. OCCURS can have a ZERO VALUE

10. REDEFINES item may have a smaller SIZE than the redefined item

11. multiple SIGN clauses can be specified; SIGN allowed in REPORT GROUP

12. VALUE allowed in OCCURS clause

13. parameter can be subscripted and/or referenced modified

14. ALL allowed in DISPLAY statement; LENGTH may be defined as the literal LENGTH

15. multiple file-names allowed; FILE can be variable LENGTH and be RELATIVE or INDEXED; explicit transfers of control allowed outside of INPUT-OUTPUT procedures

16. EXTEND can be used with RELATIVE or INDEXED FILE

17. PERFORM can be in-line; six [6] AFTER phrases must be allowed; the ORDER of initialization of multiple VARYING identifiers is specified; the order of execution for evaluating subscripts is specified

18. variable LENGTH RECORDS allowed

19. different LENGTH RECORDS can replace a RECORD within a RELATIVE or INDEXED FILE

20. identifier in INTO phrase can be a GROUP item

21. ALPHABET must precede the alphabet-name clause of the SPECIAL-NAMES paragraph

22. figurative constant cannot be specified in the CURRENCY SIGN clause

23. END-OF-PAGE condition does not exist if a FOOTING phrase is not specified; cannot be specified with ADVANCING PAGE in a single WRITE statement

24. USING DATA item cannot be redefined

25. AND/OR ORDER of execution has been redefined for conditional expressions

26. CANCEL CLOSE ALL OPEN FILEs

27. subscripts for the REMAINDER phrase are evaluated after the quotient is stored

28. INSPECT subscript evaluation has been specified

29. INTO phrase of READ statement has new rules

30. subscripting rules are specified

Caveat: THE ANSI X3.23-1985 [ISO 1989-1985] COBOL MANUAL CONTAINS MANY OTHER CHANGES THAT HAVE **NOT** BEEN SPECIFIED IN THIS ANNOTATION; PLEASE REFER TO THIS MANUAL FOR COMPLETE DESCRIPTION.

Appendix D
Care vendors

Australian Office

Headquarters

ADPAC Computing Languages
340 Brannan, Suite 501
San Francisco, CA 94107

Analyst Workbench Consulting
24 Jalan Carey 1A/71-G
46000 Petaling Jaya
Selangor, West Malaysia

IBM

Your local represenative

Executive Computing
Cuneo House, Suite 8
35 Alexandra Street
Hunters Hill NSW 2110

Language Technology
27 Congress Street
Salem, MA 01970
USA

Waterfield Company
270 Pacific Highway
Crows Nest NSW 2065

VIASOFT
3033 North 44th Street
Phoenix AR 85018
USA

PANSOPHIC
120 Pacific Highway
St Leonards NSW 2065

XA Systems
983 University Avenue
Los Gatos, CA 95030
USA

Index